SENSATIONAL
FASHIONS & CRAFTS

Editorial Director   Arthur Hettich
Editor   Nora O'Leary   •   Art Director   Joseph Taveroni
Special Books Editor   Marie T. Walsh
Managing Editor   Susan Kiely Tierney
Associate Editors   Sandra Stern, Karen Laurence, Ceri E. Hadda
Art Associates   Walter Schwartz, Dana Nordhausen
Assistant Editor   Raeanne B. Hytone   •   Copy   Marjorie Magidson
Workroom   Barbara King   •   Assistant to the Editor   Anita Counsman
Production Manager   Kathy Maurer Reilly

Created by Family Circle Great Ideas Magazine and published 1979 by Arno Press, Inc., a subsidiary of The New York Times Company. Copyright © by The Family Circle, Inc. All rights reserved. Protected under Berne and other international copyright conventions. Title and Trademark FAMILY CIRCLE registered U. S. Patent and Trademark Office, Canada, Great Britain, Australia, New Zealand, Japan and other countries. Marca Registrada. This volume may not be reproduced in whole or in part in any form without written permission from the publisher. Printed in U.S.A. Library of Congress Catalog Card Number/78-68629 ISBN 0-405-12052-4

A New York Times Company Publication

DESIGNED BY SARA GUTIERREZ USING PATERNAYAN PERSIAN YARNS.

CONTENTS

THE PILLOW BRIGADE

Raggedy Ann, move
over! This trio of mustachioed
gents is waiting to be
loved by little children. Barbara
Marsten's pillow dolls
sport whimsical costumes
on rectangular bodies.

The engineer proudly shows his
trainman's stripes and
the soldier is at ease in his dress
uniform. Dan'l Boone, in
"buckskin" jacket and frontier
cap will protect the wary
from bears—and bad dreams.
Great make-ahead Christmas
gifts. See page 90.

PHOTOGRAPHY RENÉ VELEZ

BASIC NEEDLEPOINT

You'll be able to create and execute your own beautiful needlepoint designs, once you've learned a few stitches. The continental, cross and half cross stitches shown below are the most basic, and after you've mastered these, be adventuresome and try the more complicated stitches. These basic stitches all slant diagonally across one intersection of the canvas mesh, and are easy to learn with a little practice.

IMPORTANT: If you're left handed, reverse all the hand directions we give you, or practice stitches in front of a mirror.

CONTINENTAL STITCH: One of the most durable stitches, it's great for articles which will see a lot of wear and tear. You can use this stitch on either single or double mesh canvas with equally good results, but because of the distortion caused by the stitches you'll **always** have to block your finished canvas.

HOW TO WORK: Bring your needle up at A; work from right to left, put needle down at B; up again at C; down at D. Continue across row in this manner. At the end of the row, put your needle down at H; turn canvas around, bring needle up at A, and continue back across row as before (1). It's important to turn the canvas so your needle will always be in a **slanted** position when making stitches (1). Your needle is parallel to the canvas mesh only when you start a new row (2).

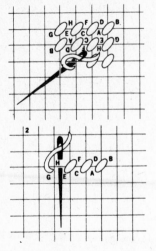

HALF CROSS STITCH: This is a good stitch to use when the article you're making **will not** receive heavy wear (wall hangings, pillows, etc.). It requires less yarn than the continental stitch, but you'll get better results if you work this stitch on the firmer-weave, double thread (penelope) canvas. (Many experts believe the half cross should **only** be worked on penelope.)

HOW TO WORK: Working from left to right, bring needle up at A and down at B; up at C; then down at D; continue in this manner across row. At the end of the row, put needle down at F, turn canvas; bring up at A, and continue back across row as before.

CROSS STITCH: Good for lettering because the finished stitch forms a square; also this stitch should be used when you want additional texture to your canvas.

HOW TO WORK: Start by making a row of half cross stitches; then go back across the same row, slanting stitches in the opposite direction. Or, if you prefer, work individual stitches. No matter how

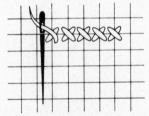

the stitches are worked, **they must all cross in the same direction.**

NEEDLES: Always use blunt-tip "tapestry" needles since they'll never split the mesh threads. The needles come in an array of sizes, so you'll easily find a needle to fit your canvas and threads.

TRANSFERRING A DESIGN: It's easier than you think to transfer a design to canvas. First, cut the canvas about three inches larger on each side than your planned design. Then fold it in half vertically down the center, then horizontally. Unfold canvas and lightly mark the crease lines with a pencil. Fold and mark the design in the same way as you did the canvas. Now tape the design, unfolded, to a window; place and tape canvas over the design, matching centers, and vertical and horizontal lines. Using a **water-proof** marking pen, **starting from the center and working outward,** carefully trace the pattern onto canvas. If you make a mistake, paint over it with white acrylic paint. Remove pattern and canvas from window. Bind canvas edges with masking tape so they will not ravel. Leave canvas as is, or color in design with **waterproof** paints or nylon felt-tip markers.

TO BLOCK NEEDLEPOINT: Cover a table or any other flat board with a piece of brown paper, or old sheet, larger than

your canvas; tack it down flat. With a pencil, mark the size of the canvas on the paper or sheet, making sure all corners are square. Soak canvas in cold water. Note: If you wish to wash needlepoint before hanging, use one of the cold water soaps, or a very mild detergent in cool water. Do not wring; rinse thoroughly to remove all soap. Pull or stretch the canvas **worked side up** until it conforms to the penciled outline. **Using rust proof tacks or nails** (if you aren't sure, ask your hardware dealer), tack down the four corners, ½" outside design edge making sure the corners are at **right angles,** and match the outline you've drawn on the paper or sheet. Then, in the center of each side, nail down four more tacks. Continue around all four sides, until tacks are about ¼" apart. **Let dry thoroughly** — (approximately 48 hours). Remove canvas from board. If you're not going to immediately mount your canvas, roll it around any cardboard tube, with the worked side out. (This will keep stitches from crushing against each other).

STRAIGHT OR UPRIGHT GOBELIN: Worked on single- or double-thread canvas. It is one of the oldest of canvas stitches used to imitate the woven Gobelin tapestries, giving a very effective texture.

HOW TO WORK: Stitches are worked vertically over 2 threads of the canvas. If the yarn does not entirely cover the canvas, lay a strand over the row as a padding and work stitches over.

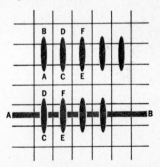

BASKET WEAVE: Used mainly for backgrounds and filling shapes, can be worked on single- or double-thread canvas. It does not pull the canvas out of shape, looks smooth. Hard wearing with a firm back which looks woven.

HOW TO WORK: Work on the diagonal with the needle horizontal as rows

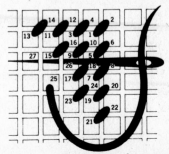

(Continued on page 7.)

BIG, BOLD, BRIGHT

Color is all around us and we've chosen the brightest for these two sweaters. Crayon-colored boatneck is knitted in one flat piece, and ties at the sides and sleeves. Lion Brand yarn. Inset: Rainbow shades zig-zag across sleeves and body of pullover. Pattern produces scalloped effect at hem. Designed by Karen Stern. Brunswick yarn. Instructions, page 91.

(Continued from page 5.)
go up from right to left, then vertical as they go down from left to right.

BARGELLO: This stitch looks as complicated as it is beautiful, but actually, it's just a simple up-and-down stitch covering four or more meshes of the canvas (1). There are no hard and fast rules to creating with this stitch. The flame stitch is the most common pattern used, and is particularly effective when worked in one or more coordinating colors; or several tones of a single color (2).

HOW TO WORK: Is an *upright Gobelin* usually worked in a zigzag or geometric pattern. The basic stitch is worked over 4 threads of canvas and

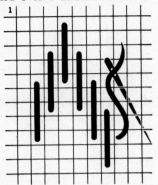

under 2, rising and falling. It's best to start a bargello pattern by lightly penciling in one row of the design you want to make; work that row; then the rest of the pattern should easily fall into place. Bargello looks best worked on a single-thread (mono) canvas.

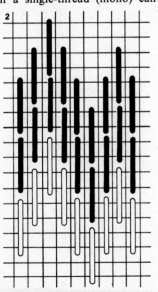

SCOTCH STITCH: The basic stitch is done in squares of 3 meshes, but it can be increased to 4, 5, or 6 meshes.
HOW TO WORK: Starting at the upper left 1, bring needle to front, then over to 2. Bring needle up at 3 and over to 4. Continue, following diagram below to 10. Give canvas a quarter turn to the right. Bring needle up at 11 and over to 12. Continue until double squares are completed.

TENT STITCH: This is basically a slant stitch that gives more backing to the canvas for a firmer finished piece with a more interesting texture on the front.
HOW TO WORK: Starting at the right of canvas (A), bring needle to front. Working from right to left, bring needle down diagonally to row below. Continue until row is completed. Give

canvas a half turn. Insert needle 1 row above and bring down diagonally to the left on the next row. Give canvas a half turn at the beginning of each row (B).

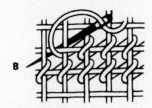

SATIN STITCH: This stitch is the most basic and simplest needlepoint stitch. It can be worked vertically or horizontally over 2, 3, 4, 5 or 6 meshes.
HOW TO WORK: Bring needle up at 1 and over to 2, then down and up at 3. Continue for required number of rows.

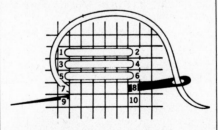

FRENCH KNOT: This stitch is never used as a background stitch, but rather as a stitch to put over the background to add more pattern or texture. The easiest way to learn to make a good French knot is to have the cloth stretched taut as possible in a hoop or on a frame. And be sure to use good, heavy yarns.
HOW TO WORK: Bring the needle out at A. Swing your yarn to the left of A, circle it down from left to right and hold it flat on the cloth with your left thumb at a place about an inch to the left of A. With your right hand, hold the needle by the eye and slide the point downward "under the bridge",

without picking up background. Now think of a clock: Your needle should be pointing to 6 o'clock. Still holding the needle by the eye, turn the point of the needle clockwise, over the yarn held by your left thumb, until it points to 12 o'clock. Continue to hold the yarn down with your left thumb. Insert the point of the needle very close to A but not in the same hole. Now gently pull the yarn with your left thumb and index finger to snug it around the needle. Push the needle straight down with your right hand and pull through gently. If you want bigger knots, use two or three yarns at the same time; try several shades of the same color in your needle for an interesting effect.

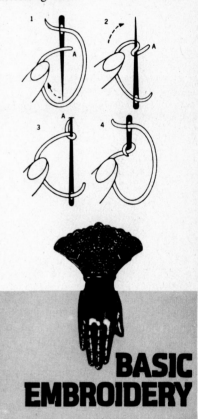

BASIC EMBROIDERY

Embroidery has no rigid rules, and it's great fun to invent your own stitches to create a very personal design. The beginner, though, may be confused by what stitch to use where, so we show a selection of basic stitches: directions on how to do them, and suggestions for the way we think they'll work best. Master these stitches, then experiment on your own!

CHAIN STITCH: This is one of the most satisfying ways to follow an outline or to fill in a shape. It also can be worked on canvas. Bring the needle up at A, form a loop by holding thread down with thumb. Put the needle down in A and bring up B (1). Repeat, always inserting needle exactly where the thread came out, inside the last loop you've worked.

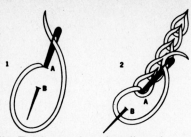

(2). For leaves, broad outlines, houses, flower stems and backgrounds.

BACK STITCH: Bring thread up at A, go down at B, and come up again at C;

repeat pattern, making sure you go back into the same hole as the previous stitch. Keep stitches uniform. Good for outlining, lines and foundation.

COUCHING: Place thread(s) along sewing line; tack down at even intervals wirh small stitches. Use for outlining, and to secure very long satin stitches.

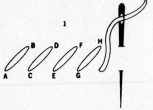

CROSS STITCH: Start at lower left corner (left-handed people start at right); work left to right (right to left); making diagonal stitches to end of row

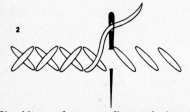

(1); then work back over these stitches

(2). Always keep needle vertical and go into the same holes of the first row of diagonal stitches. Stitches may be worked separately, but all should cross in the same direction. Best used for background, borderwork and filling.

FRENCH KNOT: Bring needle up, wrap around needle once or twice (1);

hold taut: then insert needle as close as possible to where thread emerged (2). The size of the knot is determined by the number and size of the threads you use, and how many times you wrap them around the needle. For eyes, seeds, and in clusters to fill spaces.

SATIN STITCH: Bring needle up at one edge of area to be covered (A); in-

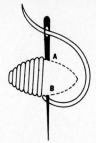

sert at opposite edge (B), keeping stitches together to form a smooth banding.

HERRINGBONE: Bring needle up; make diagonal stitch, keeping thread under needle. Draw thread through;

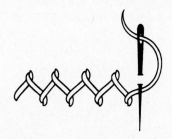

work needle as shown to pick up a vertical stitch; continue pattern. This stitch may be worked close together or far apart.

LAZY DAISY: Bring needle up through fabric, leaving a small loop, then go back and insert needle as close as possible to where thread emerged first; come out at center of loop; go back over loop to anchor it. To make next loop, pass needle beneath work;

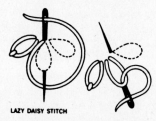

LAZY DAISY STITCH

begin next loop as shown. Several loops around a center point make lovely flowers, leaves or clusters.

BUTTONHOLE OR BLANKET STITCH: The only difference is that *buttonhole stitches* are closer together. Work from left to right. Come out at A. Hold the yarn down with your left thumb, insert the needle at B. Come out at C, just above and close to A, drawing the needle out over the yarn coming from A to form a loop. In at D, out at E.

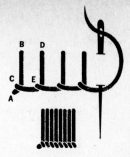

CLOSED BUTTONHOLE STITCH: Made up of 2 *buttonhole stitches* worked from the same hole, the first one from right to left, the second from left to right, making little triangles.

FLY STITCH: Bring the needle out at A. Hold the yarn down with the left thumb, looping it towards the right. Insert at B, coming out at C, below, half-way between A and B. The yarn is looped under the point of the needle from left to right. Pull it through over the loop. Anchor down by inserting at D with a small or long stitch.

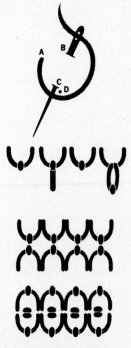

RUNNING STITCH: Run the needle in and out at regular intervals.

FEATHER STITCH: It is really a *blanket stitch* with the stitches slanting instead of at right angles. Work from the top down, towards you.

(Continued on page 11.)

KIDS CAN CROCHET!

Childhood is a learning time, and an early introduction to crocheting teaches skills that can last a lifetime.

STEP ONE: With fingers, cross yarn to form loop near end.

STEP TWO: Hold loop in place; push long end of yarn through loop. First chain made.

STEP THREE: Pull short end of yarn; loop is knotted. Repeat Step Two, pulling completed chain to knot each loop. Build on chain until desired length. Shape into a finished project by coiling or joining row on row. Join together by weaving in and out of loops with yarn needle and thin yarn of a contrasting color.

CROCHETING with great enthusiasm, Katie, Andrea, and Jenny spend a busy afternoon learning an exciting new craft.

FINISHED!
Working with Bucilla's "Colossal" yarn yields fast results. Pot holder, doll blanket and purse are shown, but kids can make pillows, colorful belts, table mats, and much more!

PHOTOGRAPHER: RON COLBY

TWO BY TWO

Pair a romantic sweater with a skirt in a compatible fabric—and each will benefit. Our choices of pink and lavender are enhanced by the tapestry-like fabric of ankle-length dirndl skirts, Vogue 9812. Sweater colors are picked up in patterned fabric. It's the perfect partnership for casual evenings at any time of year! Instructions, page 92.

CROCHET this pullover with drawstrings at neck and waist. Designed by Anni Hayum. Coats & Clark yarn. Peasant styling looks great with fabric by Roth Imports.

KNIT a cardigan for at-home entertaining. Wear it against bare skin for evening, with a blouse for day. Designed by Miriam Greenfield. Unger yarn. Stylecrest fabric.

(Continued from page 8.)

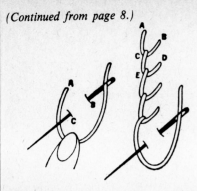

OUTLINE: Come out at A. Holding the thread down with your left thumb, insert the needle at B. Come out at C, halfway between AB. Over to D, still with the thread down, out at B, over to E and out at D. When the yarn is kept *above* the line, it is called an *outline stitch*. When the yarn is kept *down*, the stitch is called a *stem* or *crewel*.

STEM OR OUTLINE STITCH

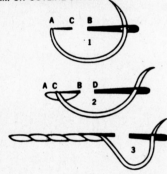

HOW TO CROCHET

Directions for right-handed and left-handed crocheters

Most crochet stitches are started from a base of chain stitches. However, our stitches are started from a row of single crochet stitches which gives body to the sample swatches and makes practice work easier. When making a specific item, follow stitch directions as given.

Holding the crochet hook properly (*see* FIG. 1), start by practicing the slip

FIG. 1 HOLDING THE HOOK

knot (*see* FIG. 2) and base chain (*see* FIG. 3).

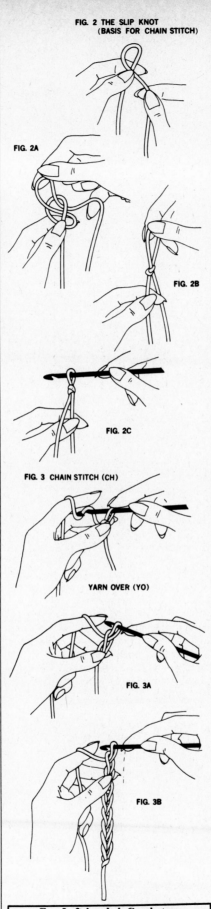

FIG. 2 THE SLIP KNOT
(BASIS FOR CHAIN STITCH)

FIG. 2A

FIG. 2B

FIG. 2C

FIG. 3 CHAIN STITCH (CH)

YARN OVER (YO)

FIG. 3A

FIG. 3B

For Left-handed Crocheters
FIGS. 1 to 3 for right-handed crocheters and are repeated in FIGS. 1 Left to 3 Left for left-handed crocheters.

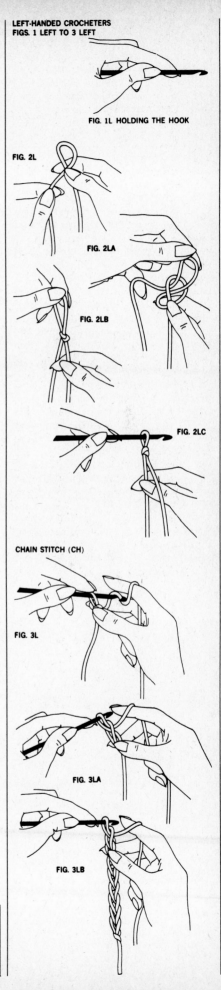

LEFT-HANDED CROCHETERS
FIGS. 1 LEFT TO 3 LEFT

FIG. 1L HOLDING THE HOOK

FIG. 2L

FIG. 2LA

FIG. 2LB

FIG. 2LC

CHAIN STITCH (CH)

FIG. 3L

FIG. 3LA

FIG. 3LB

Chain Stitch (ch): Follow the Steps in FIG. 3. As you make the chain stitch loops, the yarn should slide easily between your index and middle fingers. Make about 15 loops. If they are all the same size, you have maintained even tension. If uneven, rip them out by pulling on the long end of the yarn. Practice making chains and ripping out until you have a perfect chain.

Single Crochet (sc): Follow the Steps in FIG. 4. To practice, make a 20 loop chain (this means 20 loops in addition to the slip knot). Turn the chain, as shown, and insert the hook in the second chain from the hook (*see arrow*) to make the first sc stitch. Yarn over (yo); for second stitch see next arrow. Repeat to end of chain. Because you started in the second chain from the hook, you end up with only 19 sc. To add the 20th stitch, chain one (called a turning chain) and pull the yarn through. Now turn your work around (the "back" is now facing you) and start the second row of sc in the first stitch of the previous row (at the arrow). Make sure your hook goes under both of the strands at the top of the stitch. Don't forget to make a ch 1 turning chain at the end before turning your work. Keep practicing until your rows are perfect.

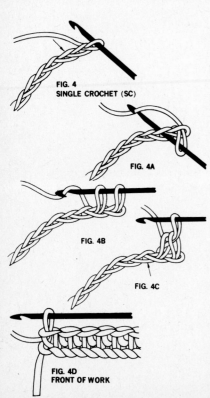

FIG. 4
SINGLE CROCHET (SC)

FIG. 4A

FIG. 4B

FIG. 4C

FIG. 4D
FRONT OF WORK

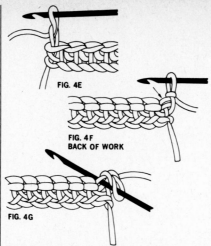

FIG. 4E

FIG. 4F
BACK OF WORK

FIG. 4G

Ending Off: Follow Steps in FIG. 5. To finish off your crochet, cut off all but 6″ of yarn and end off as shown. (To "break off and fasten," follow the same procedure.)

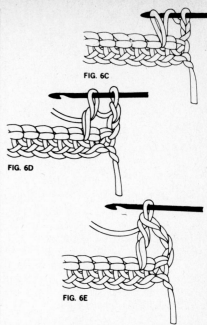

FIG. 5

ENDING OFF

FIG. 5A

Double Crochet (dc): Follow the Steps in FIG. 6. To practice, ch 20, then make a row of 20 sc. Now, instead of a ch 1, you will make a ch 3. Turn your work, yo and insert the hook in the second stitch of the previous row (*at the arrow*), going under both strands at the top of the stitch. Pull the yarn through. You now have three loops on the hook. Yo and pull through the first two, then yo and pull through the remaining two — one double crochet (dc) made. Continue across row, making a dc in each stitch

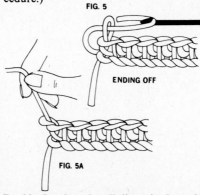

FIG. 6
DOUBLE CROCHET (DC)

FIG. 6A

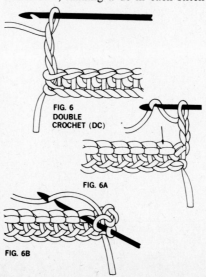

FIG. 6B

(st) across. Dc in the top of the turning chain (*see arrow in* FIG. 7). Ch 3. Turn work. Dc in second stitch in the previous row and continue as before.

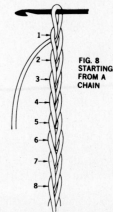

FIG. 6C

FIG. 6D

FIG. 6E

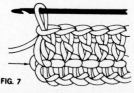

FIG. 7

Note: You may also start a row of dc on a base chain (omitting the sc row). In this case, insert hook in fourth chain from hook, instead of second (*see* FIG. 8).

1
2
3
4
5
6
7
8

FIG. 8
STARTING FROM A CHAIN

Slip Stitch (sl st): Follow Steps in FIG. 11. This is a utility stitch you will use for joining, shaping and ending off. After you chain and turn, *do not yo.* Just insert the hook into the *first* stitch of the previous row (*see* FIG. 8), and pull the yarn through the stitch then right through the loop on the hook — sl st made.

FIG. 11
SLIP STITCH (SL ST)

(Continued on page 15.)

THE WONDERS OF WEAVING

When a weaver, novice or not, faces an empty weaving board, a world of experimentation is at her fingertips. Try our simple projects, with your own variations!

These two clutch bags (and woven pillow, page 43.) were worked on simple board (left) with yarns of various widths, textures, and colors, from a special weaving collection by Bucilla. Bright clutch was fringed by leaving ends of yarn on outside. Earth-tone bag, with tassel at one end, looks great with autumn tweeds. Both closed with Velcro® fasteners. Add your personal touches by weaving ribbons, metallic yarns, or strips of fabric through the yarn. Board is small enough to hold on lap, but big enough to accommodate a limitless imagination! See instructions, page 93.

PHOTOGRAPHER: RENÉ VELEZ

Any mommy would be proud to display this never-wilt flower. Tiles make super birthday gifts.

The love in a child's drawing cannot be measured, but it can be preserved. With crayons and ceramic tiles, Andrea and Casey Rosen have created endearing gifts and greetings that will last long after childhood has been outgrown. The steps are simple. Draw on unglazed white tiles with Crayola® regular or fabric crayons. Paint over drawing with Liquitex polymer gloss to seal tile. Bake in 350° oven for thirty minutes. A great rainy day, any day activity—and Mom and Grandma will treasure the results! To order tiles, see page 127.

TILES SAY LOVE YOU

A drawing of a sailing ship can become a small table top, a tray, or a cheese board.

An eagle in a forest comes to rest on a little easel. Kids' art, like children, is truly unique.

PHOTOGRAPHER: RON COLBY

A tiger in a jungle decorates a hot plate. Grown-up imaginations will be challenged to think of new uses for kids' tiles.

14

(Continued from page 12.)

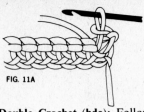

FIG. 11A

Half Double Crochet (hdc): Follow the Steps in FIG. 12. To practice, make a chain and a row of sc. Ch 2 and turn; yo. Insert hook in second stitch, as shown; yo and pull through to make three loops on hook. Yo and pull the yarn through *all* three loops at the same time — hdc made. This stitch is used primarily as a transitional stitch from an sc to a dc. Try it and see — starting with sc's then an hdc and then dc's.

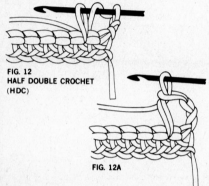

FIG. 12
HALF DOUBLE CROCHET
(HDC)

FIG. 12A

The Techniques of Crocheting: Now that you have practiced and made sample squares of all the basic stitches, you are ready to learn about adding and subtracting stitches to change the length of a row whenever it's called for. This is achieved by increasing (inc) and decreasing (dec).

To increase (inc) — Just make two stitches in the same stitch in the previous row (*see arrow in* FIG. 13). The technique is the same for any kind of stitch.

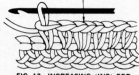

FIG. 13 INCREASING (INC) FOR
SINGLE CROCHET

To decrease (dec) for single crochet (sc) — Yo and pull the yarn through two stitches to make three loops on hook (*see Steps in* FIG. 14). Pull yarn through all loops at once — dec made. Continue in regular stitches.

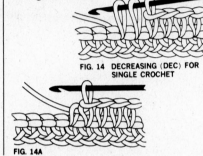

FIG. 14 DECREASING (DEC) FOR
SINGLE CROCHET

FIG. 14A

To decrease for double crochet — In a dc row make the next stitch and stop when you have two loops on the hook. Now yo and make a dc in the next stitch. At the point where you have three loops on the hook, pull yarn through all loops at the same time. Finish the row with regular dc.

Abbreviations for Crochet: The box that follows is a crochet abbreviations listing, with definitions of the terms given. To help you become accustomed to them, we have repeated these abbreviations throughout our stitch instructions.

CROCHET ABBREVIATIONS

beg — begin, beginning; **ch** — chain; **dc** — double crochet; **dec** — decrease, **dtr** — double treble crochet; **hdc** — half double crochet; **in(s) or "** — inch(es); **inc** — increase; **oz(s)** — ounce(s) **pat** — pattern; **pc** — picot; **rem** — remaining; **rnd** — round; **rpt** — repeat; **sc** — single crochet; **skn(s)** — skein(s) **sk** — skip; **sl st** — slip stitch; **sp** — space; **st(s)** — stitch(es); **tog** — together; **tr** — triple crochet; **work even** — continue without further increase of decrease; **yo** — yarn over; ***** — repeat whatever follows * as many times as indicated; **( )** — do what is in parentheses as many times as indicated.

HOW TO KNIT

KNITTING ABBREVIATIONS AND SYMBOLS

Knitting directions are always written in standard abbreviations. They look mysterious at first, but you'll soon know them. **beg** — beginning; **bet** — between; **bl** — block; **ch** — chain; **CC** — contrasting color; **dec(s)** — decrease(s); **dp** — double-pointed; **" or in(s)** — inch(es); **incl** — inclusive; **inc(s)** — increase(s); **k** — knit; **lp(s)** — loop(s); **MC** — main color; **oz(s)** — ounce(s); **psso** — pass slipped stitch over last stitch worked; **pat(s)** — pattern(s); **p** — purl; **rem** — remaining; **rpt** — repeat; **rnd(s)** — round(s); **sc** — single crochet; **sk** — skip; **sl** — slip; **sl st** — slip stitch; **sp(s)** — space(s); **st(s)** — stitch(es); **st st** — stockinette stitch; **tog** — together; **yo** — yarn over; **pc** — popcorn st.

* (asterisk) — directions immediately following * are to be repeated the specified number of times indicated, in addition to the first time — i.e., "repeat from * 3 times more means 4 times in all.

( ) parentheses — directions should be worked as often as specified — i.e., (k 1, k 2 tog, k 3) 5 times, means to work what is in ( ) 5 times in all.

THE BASIC STITCHES

Get out your needles and yarn and slowly read your way through this special section — practicing the basic stitches illustrated here as you go along. Once you know them you're ready to start knitting.

CASTING ON: This puts the first row of stitches on the needle. Measure off about two yards of yarn, (or about an inch for each stitch you are going to cast on). Make a slip knot at this point by making a medium size loop of yarn; then pull another small loop through it. Place the slip knot on one needle and pull one end gently to tighten (FIG. 1).

Fig. 1

• Hold needle in right hand. Hold both strands of yarn in the palm of your left hand securely but not rigidly. Slide your left thumb and forefinger between the two strands and spread these two fingers out so that you have formed a triangle of yarn. Your left thumb should hold the free end of yarn and your forefinger the yarn from the ball, while the needle in your right hand securely holds the first stitch (FIG. 2).

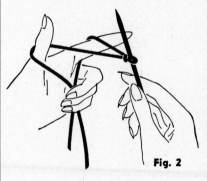

Fig. 2

You are now is position to cast on. See KNITTING ABBREVIATIONS AND SYMBOLS box at the left, this page, for explanation of asterisk (*).

• * Bring the needle in your right hand toward you; slip the tip of the needle under the front strand of the loop on left thumb (FIG. 3).

(Continued on page 17.)

ROCK-A-BYE BABY GIFTS

Welcome newborn babies with gifts from the heart—those with a handmade touch. Our ideas should prompt baby's first smile!

CRADLE CRAFTS: For the pre-shoe set, knitted Mary Jane booties by Zelda Dana. Crocheted collar dresses up Carter's sacque. Anni Hayum for Coats & Clark. Embroidered "bébé" tells who's who! Add rick rack to tiny tinted shirt. Two Cannon facecloths make dress or bib. See page 94.

(Continued from page 15.)

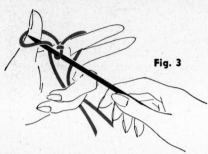

Fig. 3

• Now, with the needle, catch the strand of yarn that is on your left forefinger (FIG. 4).

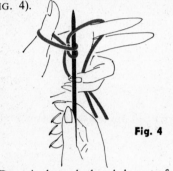

Fig. 4

• Draw it through thumb loop to form a stitch on needle (FIG. 5).

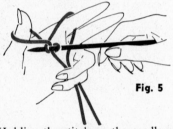

Fig. 5

• Holding the stitch on the needle with the right index finger, slip loop off left thumb (FIG. 6). Tighten up the stitch on the needle by pulling the freed strand back with left thumb, bringing the yarn back into position for casting on more stitches (FIG. 2 again).

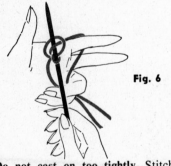

Fig. 6

• **Do not cast on too tightly.** Stitches should slide easily on the needle. Repeat from * until you have cast on the number of stitches specified in your instructions.
KNIT STITCH: (k): Hold needle with cast-on stitches in left hand (FIG. 7).

Fig. 7

• Pick up the other needle in your right hand. With yarn from ball in **back** of the work, insert the tip of right-hand needle from **left to right** through front loop of first stitch on left-hand needle (FIG. 8).

Fig. 8

• Holding both needles in this position with left hand, wrap the yarn over your little finger, under your two middle fingers and over the forefingers of your right hand. Hold the yarn firmly, but loosely enough so that it will slide through your fingers as you knit. Return right-hand needle to right hand.
• With right forefinger, pass the yarn under (from right to left) and then over (from left to right) the tip of the right-hand needle, forming a loop on needle (FIG. 9).

Fig. 9

• Now draw this loop through the stitch on left-hand needle (FIG. 10).

Fig. 10

• Slip original stitch off the left-hand needle, leaving new stitch on right-hand needle (FIG. 11).

Fig. 11

Keep stitches loose enough so that you can slide them along the needles, but firm enough so they do not slide when you don't want them to. Continue until you have knitted all the stitches from the left-hand needle onto the right-hand needle.
• To start the next row, pass needle with stitches on it to the left hand, reversing it, so that it now becomes the left-hand needle.
PURL STITCH: (p): Purling is the reverse of knitting. Again, keep the stitches loose enough to slide, but firm enough to work with. To purl, hold the needle with the stitches in your left hand, with the yarn in **front** of your work. Insert the tip of the right-hand needle from **right to left** through the front loop of the first stitch on left-hand needle (FIG. 12).

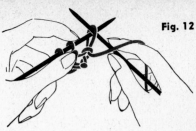

Fig. 12

• With your right hand holding the yarn in the same manner as to knit, but in **front** of the needles, pass the yarn over the tip of right-hand needle, then under it, forming loop on needle (FIG. 13).

Fig. 13

• Holding the yarn firmly, so that it won't slip off, draw this loop through the stitch on left-hand needle (FIG. 14).

Fig. 14

• Slip original stitch off the left-hand needle, leaving new stitch on the right-hand needle (FIG. 15).

Fig. 15

SLIP STITCH (sl st): Insert the tip of the right-hand needle into the next stitch on left-hand needle, as if to purl, unless otherwise directed. Slip this stitch off the left-hand needle onto the right, **without working it** (FIG. 16.)

Fig. 16

BINDING OFF: This makes a finished edge and locks the stitches securely in place. Knit (or purl) two stitches. Then, with the tip of the left-hand needle, lift the first of these two stitches over the second stitch and drop it off the tip of the right-hand needle (FIG. 17).

Fig. 17

One stitch remains on the right-hand needle and one stitch has been bound off. * Knit (or purl) the next stitch; lift the first stitch over the last stitch and off the tip of the needle. Again, one stitch remains on the right-hand needle and another stitch had been bound off. Repeat from * until the required number of stitches has been bound off.

• Remember that you work **two** stitches to bind off one stitch. If, for example, the directions read, "k 6, bind off the next 4 sts, k 6 . . ." you must knit six stitches, then knit **two more** stitches before starting to bind off. Bind off four times. After the four stitches have been bound off, count the last stitch remaining on the right-hand needle as the first stitch of the next six stitches. When binding off, always knit the knitted stitches and purl the purled stitches.

• Be careful not to bind off too tightly or too loosely. The tension should be the same as the rest of the knitting.

• To end off the last stitch on the bound-off edge, if you are ending this piece of work here, cut yarn leaving a six-inch end; pass the cut end through the remaining loop on the right-hand needle and pull snugly (FIG. 18).

Fig. 18

SHAPING TECHNIQUES

Now that you know the basics, all that's left to learn are a few techniques which will help shape whatever it is you are making.

Increasing (inc): This means adding stitches in a given area to shape your work. There are several ways to increase.

1. To increase by knitting twice into the same stitch: Knit the stitch in the usual way through the front loop (FIG. 19), but

Fig. 19

before dropping the stitch from the left-hand needle, knit **another** stitch on the same loop by placing the needle into the **back** of the stitch (FIG. 20).

Fig. 20

Slip the original stitch off your left-hand needle. You have made two stitches from one stitch.

2. To increase by knitting between

stitches: Insert tip of the right-hand needle under the strand of yarn **between** the stitch you've just worked and the following stitch; slip it onto tip of the left-hand needle (FIG. 21).

Fig. 21

Now knit into the back of this new loop (FIG. 22).

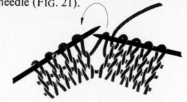

Fig. 22

3. To increase by "yarn-over" (yo): Pass the yarn over the right-hand needle after finishing one stitch and before starting the next stitch, **making an extra stitch (arrow in Fig. 23).** If you are knitting, bring the yarn under the needle to the back. **If you are purling,** wind the yarn around the needle once. On the next row, work all yarn-overs as stitches.

Fig. 23

Decreasing: (dec): This means reducing the number of stitches in a given area to shape your work. Two methods for decreasing are:

1. To decrease by knitting (FIG. 24 or **purling** (FIG . 25) **two stitches together:**

Fig. 24

Fig. 25

Insert right-hand needle through the loops of two stitches on left-hand needle at the same time; complete stitch. This is written k 2 tog, or p 2 tog.

• If you work through the **front** loops of the stitches in the usual way, your decreasing stitch will slant to the right. If you work through the **back** loops of the stitches, your decreasing stitch will slant to the left.

2. Slip 1 stitch, knit 1 and psso: Insert

right-hand needle through the stitch on the left-hand needle, but instead of working it, just slip it off onto the right-hand needle (go back to FIG. 16). Work the next stitch in the usual way. With the tip of the left-hand needle, lift the slipped stitch over the last stitch worked and off the tip of the right-hand needle (FIG. 26).

Fig. 26

Your decreasing stitch will slant to the left. This is written sl 1, k 1, psso.

Pass Slipped Stitch Over (psso): Slip one stitch from the left-hand needle to the right-hand needle and, being careful to keep it in position, work the next stitch. Then, with the tip of the left-hand needle, lift the slipped stitch over the last stitch and off the tip of the needle (Fig. 26).

ATTACHING YARN When you end one ball of yarn or wish to change colors: Begin at the start of row and tie new yarn with previous yarn, making a secure joining. Continue to knit or purl.

HOW TO ENLARGE AND REDUCE DESIGNS
METHOD 1

If the design is not already marked off in squares, make a tracing of it. Then mark the tracing off in squares; for a small design, make squares ¼"; for larger designs, use ½", 1" or 2" squares. Decide the size of your reduction or enlargement; on another sheet of tracing paper; mark off the same number of squares that are on the design or original tracing. Remember that to make your design six times larger than the original design, each new square must be six times larger than the original. Carefully copy the outline from your original tracing to the new one, square by square. Use dressmaker's carbon and a tracing wheel to transfer the design.

METHOD 2

First, take the original design and make a tracing. Then determine the finished size you want and draw another outline. To accurately proportion the new design, first draw diagonal lines through both outlines. Second, draw one horizontal and one vertical line at the center where the two diagonal lines meet. In each quarter of the original design and outline, complete the other diagonal lines; then divide the quarters with horizontal and vertical lines where the diagonals intersect. Follow Method 1 to copy design from original. There are several shortcuts you can take: 1. A wire screen, placed over the original,

(Continued on page 90.)

WE HAVE GREAT IDEAS!

Experience the thrill of creativity. Our pages are spilling over with dozens of tempting, innovative ideas to challenge the mind and delight the eye! We offer a year full of knitting, crocheting, sewing, and crafts. Be a part of the excitement!

LAYERING DELUXE Make sense out of your wardrobe! This is the stunning result of color-keyed layering—our way. Your way, the possibilities are endless! For step-by-step mixing and matching, see next pages.

Our monochromatic wardrobe should put an end to all "what-shall-I-wear" worries! Start with old-fashioned undies by Vassarette, tinted with Rit Dyes. Add a wallpaper-print ruffled skirt (Butterick 6065) and stop there. Or, add a reverse-print blouse (Butterick 5569) with scalloped detail. More? Top shirt and skirt with double-crocheted T-sweater. Designed by Joan Vass. Unger yarn. Pull on a gored skirt with mitered stripes by Willi Smith (Butterick 6260). Floral underskirt is now a petticoat! Put a bow at the neck and take a breather. Going out? Willi Smith's unlined, boxy blazer and striped vest (Butterick 6260) fit over layers with room to spare. Sweater-matching crocheted hat is last, but not least. Ready? Set? Go! Striped and solid fabrics, Arthur Zeiler. Floral fabrics, Ameritex. Shoes, Joan and David for Foreign Affairs. Danskin sweater-tights. La Bagagerie bag. For dye recipe, and instructions for hat and sweater, turn to page 94. Backviews, page 25.

ETHNIC INFLUENCES

Guatemala has been pinpointed on the fashion map by those who crave bold, primitive sweaters. This page: Jeanne Bayer used graphic stripes to structure this rugged sweater and matching scarf. It is knitted in the garter of hand-spun, natural dyed Vermont yarns. Pouch belt by Elegant. Opposite: A rustic jacket is abbreviated to vest-like proportions for the last word in layering. Kathy Sorkin's crocheted design is a triumph in color scheming. Yarn is by Reynolds. For all of these sweater how-to's, turn to page 77.

Ethnic influences continue to change our fashion outlook. A tapestry skirt by Karen Laurence will keep you knitting into the wee small hours, enthralled by the colorful ethnic plot. Note the primitive vitality of both the colors and pattern. You can crochet a pair of neck pouches with the leftover Lion Brand yarn. Accessories: Sash, La Tienda. For how-to's, turn to page 79.

PATTERN BACKVIEWS

All yardage for Size 10 unless specified. Please note special instructions where specified. (Prices are in U.S. Currency.)

BUTTERICK 5887—page 39. Misses' Skirt. $1.50. Misses' waist sizes 24"-30". Waist 25" requires 3⅛ yds. of 33" fabric.

BUTTERICK 5931—page 38. Misses' Dirndl Skirt. Misses' sizes 8-16. $2. Requires 2⅝ yds. 33" fabric.

BUTTERICK 6065—pages 20-21. Misses' Skirt (petticoat). Misses' sizes 8-16. 99¢. Requires 2¼ yds. of 45" fabric.

BUTTERICK 6217—page 68. Misses' Jacket. Misses' sizes 8-18. 99¢. Requires 2⅜ yds. of 45" fabric.

BUTTERICK 5569—pages 20-21. Misses' Blouse. Misses' sizes 8-18. $1.50. Requires 2⅛ yds. of 45" fabric. We added machine scallop embroidery to collar, cuffs & front tabs.

BUTTERICK 6260—pages 20-21. Misses' Unlined Jacket, Lined Vest and Skirt. Misses' sizes 8-16. $2.00. Jacket requires 1¾ yds.; vest requires ¾ yd. and skirt 2⅝ yds. all of 60/62" fabric.

VOGUE 9812—page 10. Misses' Skirt. Misses waist sizes 24"-30". $3.00. Waist 25" requires 2¼ yds. of 45" fabric.

VOGUE 9887—pages 62-63. Misses' Jacket & Skirt. Misses' sizes 8-16. $4.50. Jacket requires 1⅝ yds. and skirt 1¾ yds. both of 60" fabric.

FOLKWEAR 112—page 72. Japanese Field Clothing sized for Men & Women. $4.50. Women's Hippari requires 2¼ yds. of 45" fabric. Women's Field Pants require 2¼ yds. of 45" fabric.

FOLKWEAR 113—page 73. Japanese Kimono sized for Men & Women. $4.00. Average man's (5'8") requires 4¾ yds. of 45" fabric. Average woman's (5'4") requires 4⅝ yds. of 45" fabric. Each kimono was cut from a Queen-sized flat sheet. For bordered sheets, remove border and open it flat to use for sleeves. Add a shoulder seam to Kimono.

TO ORDER FOLKWEAR PATTERNS: Send check or money order (add 75¢ for postage & handling per order) to: FOLKWEAR, P. O. Box 98, Forestville, California 95436. (California residents, add 6% Sales Tax.)

McCALL'S 5931—page 51. Misses' Dress. Misses' sizes 6-16. $2.25. Requires 2⅝ yds. of 54" fabric.

McCALL'S 5761—page 50. Misses' Dress. Misses' sizes Petite, Small, Medium and Large. $1.75. Small requires 2¾ yds. of 54" fabric.

McCALL'S 6003—page 41. Misses' Skirt. Misses' sizes 8-20. $2.00. Size 18 requires 4¼ yds. of 45" fabric.

McCALL'S 6159—page 69. Misses' vest. Misses' size 8-20. $2.00. Ours was cut from two 31" square scarves. Add a center back seam to match scarf borders at side seams.

McCALL'S 5670—page 69. Misses' Unlined Jacket & Vest. Misses' sizes 6-16. $1.75. Jacket requires 1½ yds. and vest 1¼ yds. both of 45" fabric. (**Note:** Peter Pan fabric is also available as reversible fabric, pre-quilted in a diamond pattern.)

5887   5931   6065   6217

5569   6260

9812   9887   5931   5761

6003   6159   5670

(Continued on page 114.)

Left: Variegated bands provide the color and garter stitch ribbing brings texture to this knitted pullover. Matching brimmed hat will ward off the wind. Designed by Bea Field. Columbia-Minerva and Lion Brand yarns. Left and below: The rugged feel of bulky Donegal tweed yarn, worked in horizontal ribs, makes this a heavyweight champ among sweaters. Ribbed turtleneck, cuffs and hem guard against cold. Tahki yarn. By Marianne Ake. Hat, scarf and pants by Evan Picone.

THE SWEATERS FOR ALL OUTDOORS!

These are the great ones! Big sweaters so richly textured, they meet the weather head on. Sweaters so strong in design, we can proudly call them classics. Our knits and crochets will tackle the cold while you make a spirited fashion statement! Instructions, page 95.

HALE AND HEARTY: You love the outdoors—show it by wearing your hearts on knitted crewneck sweater and amusing legwarmers. Matching hat has rolled brim for extra warmth. Reynolds yarn. All instructions, page 96.

ONE wonderful sweater! Chain-stitched loops give a deep pile texture to crochet. Coats & Clark yarn. Designed by Anni Hayum.

TWO stitches—the garter on convertible collar, hem, cuffs, and popcorn on the body and sleeves make great knitting. Tahki yarn.

THREE reasons for making this cardigan: raglan sleeves, clever mix of variegated and solid yarns, and matching hat! Plymouth.

FOUR shades of green in a lovely variegated yarn make a special knitted pullover. Designed by Andre Rubin. Unger yarn.

SLEEVE STORY: Patterned
sleeves make this white sweater a stand-out.
Popcorn motifs and garter-stitched rows
work their way up the sleeves, making an
interesting contrast to easy-knit
stockinette body. Open collar shows off
under layers. Reynolds yarn.
See page 99.

PHOTOGRAPHY: JOHN STEMBER · ROSANNA TURTLENECKS

WARM-UP!
With popcorn
motifs on yoke and
collar, and
garter-stitch details on
sleeves and hem,
this sweater is winter
white at its best.
Bernat yarn. Brighten
with scarf and
hat. See page 100.

A

Is there a spot in your home that needs brightening? Try one of our colorful

accent rugs. We show six different techniques, all fun to do. Instructions, page 101.

RUG OPTIONS

A Anemones, opposite, echo the colors of a simple-to-make rug of coiled yarn cords. Jack Bodi used an inexpensive gadget and American Thread's Dawn Sayelle to make coils, then sewed them together. The whole family can help!

B House Blessing, above, is Lib Callaway's adaptation of an early American hooked rug. To create the richiy-colored cornucopia of fruit, strips of wool fabric are pulled through a burlap backing. The result is breathtaking!

C South-of-the Border embroidery in Paternayan rug yarn borders a heavy cotton rectangle. Jumbo tassel fringe finishes the ends. It's a quick project to make for any room in the house.

C

D Vivid colors of Reynolds' precut acrylic yarn are intensified by alternating them with squares of white. Jack Bodi made this latch-hooked beauty 33"x44"; you could adapt it to other sizes.

D

E Dramatic bargello rug is an exercise in stitchery. Mira Silverstein used three different bargello patterns for the six geometric squares; navy bands are worked in brick stitch.

F Two techniques are combined in this 30" circular rug. A Shillcraft latch-hook kit is used for the center; wool braids form the border. The zodiac theme makes it a great birthday gift idea.

E

F

SCULPTURAL CROCHET

A super trio of sweaters and caps to make in the twinkling of an eye. Style goes sporting in these rugged, but womanly, pullover tops with caps to match. Here are one, two, three choices for the crocheter who relishes bulky yarn and bold stitches. Designer Linda Blood has taken the sculptural approach to her craft, fashioning great basic shapes in both long- and short-sleeved styles with accents of texture. The yarn, in creamy natural colors and mellow, heathery shades, is from Bernat. For our easy-to-follow crochet instructions, turn to page 81.

PAIRED UP

Special sweaters are paired with skirts made-to-match in hand-loomed fabrics. See page 105.

GREEN yarns, in two leafy tones, lead to the striped effect in this knitted cardigan. Designed by Marianne Ake. Matching fabric binds sweater and completes the set with A-line skirt, Butterick 5931. Yarn and fabric from Pinecroft.

PINK,
the color of
heather, is an
irresistible choice
for this ribbed turtle-
neck. Designed
by Marianne Ake.
Skirt with
inverted center
pleat, But-
terick 5887,
and loosely-
knotted tie.
See page
105.

HOW TO LOOK GREAT
IF YOU'RE SIZE 18

Dodie O'Keefe readily admits to being size 18. And, why not? She wears her carefully chosen clothes with utmost confidence and great flair.

Her philosophy is simplicity. She likes clothes with clean, easy lines in quality fabrics . . . nothing gimmicky or fussy. She puts emphasis on fit and proportion. Dodie has established a style of her own with her great collection of oversized jewelry, her keen sense of color and her ability to whip up an original outfit over-night. Dodie's wardrobe

revolves around a Halston cape stole (McCall's 5829). The deep plum wool by Zeiler is a good basic color that mixes well with her other clothes. The super A-line jumper to match (Simplicity 8547) can be worn with blouses, a turtleneck or even over a dress. We show it over a mauve Apsco matte jersey blouse with a cowl neck (Simplicity 8162).

Ingenuity turned an Indian bedspread into a bordered skirt and stole that she wears with a black sweater. Skirt, McCall's 6003. A shirtdress in a rust polyester crepe is a perfect background for Dodie's collection of long gold chains. McCall's 5762. Ferragamo sandals. Dodie is partial to caftans and this colorful striped Indian cotton one is bound with foldover braid. Her fabulous Mexican necklace, picked up in her travels, is a becoming proportion. Caftan instructions, page 107. Dodie's beautiful hand crocheted sweater, designed by Bruce Woods in Tahki yarn, has a cardigan neckline and patch pockets. The longer length is a perfect proportion for large figures. Pants and tunic, McCall's 5917.

Striking snowflake motif and deep blue crocheted edging are the eye-catchers on an oatmeal-colored knitted pillow by Zelda Dana. Bucilla craft yarns.

Floral Liberty of London wool challis is ideal for outline quilting. Rust velvet ribbon and ecru lace edging complete the pillow's romantic look.

PILLOW VARIATIONS
Four designs and techniques to challenge your skills.

Weave your own textural magic! This lively, loopy pillow was worked on a simple weaving board with a variety of intriguing yarns. Bucilla craft yarns.

Created in the 1930's by Gudrun Johnson, this is a distinguished example of Art Deco needlepoint. Re-create it for the 1970's! DMC cotton.

Alone or together, our pillows add a note of originality to any room. Grouped as shown, they provide an interesting interplay of color and texture. Turn to page 107.

BIG NEWS IN SMALL SWEATERS

Among the big shapes in fashion, these small sweaters hold their own. Worn with blouses and pants or skirts, theirs is a total, dress-like look.

Go to work a new way! Free of the bulk of bigger sweaters, these four are perfect office wear. Opposite, upper left: Knitted waist-length sweater gets its tweed look from variegated yarn. V-neck and short sleeves show off blouse. Designed by Gabrielle Spelman. Bucilla yarn. Lower left: Lacy edging on neck and sleeves lends a feminine touch to knitted pullover. Designed by Ann Kling. Coats & Clark. Above left: The cardigan you've dreamed about, knitted from alpaca yarn by Plymouth. Above, right: Linda Blood's crocheted cardigan has pockets and a shawl collar. Scott's yarn.
See page 109.

GINGHAM CHECKS
are naturals for do-it-yourself projects . . . they provide guidelines for cutting and quilting. Lunch al fresco, above, with a ruffled quilted cloth and reversible casserole cover. Left, a hand-painted hurricane shade and a centerpiece of mix-and-match napkins. How-to's, page 111.

PHOTOGRAPHY: LEOMBRUNO-BODI

TURNING THE TABLES
Down with drab dinners and humdrum luncheons!
Our great ideas turn tables into visual delights.

SIGN IN PLEASE... Have each guest at the dinner party add a signature to the tablecloth! Later, embroider each name ... ours was done in satin stitch on Nelco Xonic 2000 machine.

**If you like to sew, crochet, appliqué or embroider...
or even if you only have time to cut and fold...you'll be
inspired by our do-it-yourself table settings. Yes, you
can create a new environment! Our easy-to-follow
instructions begin on page 111.**

ORIENT EXPRESS
sets up in an instant because
the tablecloth is cut from a
printed Wamsutta sheet. Pick
one to fit your table.

Keep it informal with paper
accessories and origami water
lily napkins. For fun, tie
flower-decorated place cards
on back of chairs!

48

CLASSIC CROCHET sets an elegant mood. Floral-motif cloth, rectangular mat are crocheted of DMC cotton. Edge napkins with narrow lace trim.

PATCHWORK calico cloth and matching napkins are at home in a city apartment or a country setting. Crochet bread basket and hot mat of Lily's jute.

WAKE UP someone you love with breakfast in bed on this "Bon Jour" place setting. Tea cozy house and flowered napkin are appliquéd; braided cotton place mat picks up cheery colors of china.

TABLE SETTING BY RUSS NORRIS OF CALDWELL ALEXANDER, WESTHAMPTON, NEW YORK. FOR ACCESSORY DETAILS, SEE P. 127.

SHAWLS LOVE CHALLIS!

The best way to accessorize challis—is with more challis! These dresses are enhanced by shawls made from squares of running yardage.

FLORAL PRINT challis is made into long sleeved dress with drawstring neck and deep ruffle at hem. Matching shawl takes this dress through the seasons. Dress McCall's 5761. Fabric Stylecrest

BORDER PRINT challis was made for this easy-sew dress, and vice-versa. With matching shawl, dress is a celebration of color! Wear shawl over shoulders, over head. Dress, McCall's 5931, has elasticized neck and sleeves. Stylecrest fabric.

DRESSES LOVE CHALLIS!

Sing the praises of challis! It is soft, it comes in seasonless prints, and it looks great in these easy-to-sew dresses!

TWO-PIECE dress is just right for the softness of challis. Top has simple neck, drawstring waist, and dolman sleeves. Tucks add detail at skirt waist. Dress, Simplicity 8571. Fabric, Liberty of London.

VICTORIAN
pullover dress has lace-trimmed collar, full sleeves, and dropped waistline, with side pockets. Old-fashioned floral print challis adds to the "innocent" look. Dress, Simplicity 8673. Fabric, Stylecrest.

ABOUT FACE!

The unpredictable wrap-around coat has two great fashion faces. Above: A foxy fur makes no bones about being fake. It reverses to a Landau highland plaid, bound with braid from William N. Ginsberg. The hooded coat is Butterick 4538, designed by Kenzo. The bag, Butterick 4530, is finished with a plaid needlepoint flap, following our instructions (page 84). Opposite: Simplicity coat pattern 6633 is made of make-believe chinchilla, joined and trimmed with hand crochet. Its other face is grey flannel by Pendleton Woolen Mills. Both fur fabrics from Collins & Aikman. See our easy crochet instructions on page 84.

HEIDI AND HER FRIENDS

In her storybook world, Heidi picked wildflowers in embroidered clothes like these. Now, little kids can play at peasantry in Jane Pappidas' crocheted designs. See page **114.**

Left: Red suspender skirt has a heart-shaped bib full of embroidered flowers. Green edging on hem and bib is a bright contrast. Right: Tyrolean shorts in green have mushroom motif on bib and red blanket stitching on cuffs and straps.

This tiny peasant looks right at home in black crocheted jacket with white lace trim. Embroidered flowers brighten front and sleeves. Her border-print skirt is made from one challis scarf.

Very special storybook designs to crochet... with love. See page 114.

Upper left: Multi-colored embroidered flowers cover the bib of a black suspender dress. White lace trim circles the hem. Matching Tyrolean cap ties under the chin. Lower left: One-piece jumper has a bright green camisole top (with floral embroidery) and black skirt. Right: White ribbed-look jacket is a child's sampler of colorful embroidery stitches. She pairs it with a dirndl skirt trimmed with rick rack. All clothes crocheted from Lion Brand yarn. All turtlenecks and tights, Danskin.

PHOTOGRAPHY, THESE PAGES: ELYSE LEWIN

IT'S
FUN TO
KNIT
FOR
CHILDREN

Status on the playground is a hand-knit sweater, made at home by Mom or Gran. Right: He strikes a casual pose in a rough-and-ready fisherman's pullover by Ann Cicale. Yarn is by Coats & Clark. Center: The middy sweater captures another generation of young hearts. By Monna Weinman of Spinnerin yarn. Left: Two irresistible Irish knits are made in perfect miniature. The dress and cap are by Monna Weinman for Bernat. Marga Bremer designed the zip-front jacket, hat and scarf for Bucilla. For how-to's, turn to page 85.

VERY VISIBLE VESTS

These are vests with a difference! Bigger shapes and larger armholes allow them to be outer layers, worn over coats or blazers. See page 120.

BLAZER PLUS: When it is too cool for just a jacket, add this super vest (opposite). Seed stitch on upper half and lower edge contrasts with stockinette body. Jaunty tassels are an original touch. Autumnal colors are ideal for wearing over blazer and skirt, Vogue 9887. Rosanna cowl. Bernat yarn.

BOLERO VEST (upper right) is an interesting combination of garter and stockinette stitches. Aztec-inspired pattern is a novel use of curly yarn on knitting worsted base. Great with full-length coat. Coats & Clark yarns.

CAP SLEEVES and Indian motifs highlight this 3/4 length vest. Heavy texture of yarn adds extra warmth, and magenta-on-natural pattern lends spark to your outdoor appearance. Knitted-in pockets hold cold hands! Stanley Berrocco yarn. All vests designed by Zelda Dana.

Simple dresses come alive when sewn in elegant panné velvet. Our one and two-piece dresses light up the night in paint-the-town colors!

FASHION FIREWORKS

JADE GREEN panné velvet catches the light and gives this button-front pullover and gathered skirt a special sparkle. Simplicity 8651. All panné fabric imported by Hamilton Adams.

TOMATO RED catches the chef's eye! Big dress has drawstring neckline and easy-sew elasticized waist. Kimono sleeves and blouson make this a perfect dinner dress. Simplicity 8588.

ROYAL BLUE V-neck pullover dress deserves a medal! (All three dresses do; note our accessories!) Basic sweatshirt styling finds new sophistication with choice of fabric. Simplicity 8676.

GREAT VARIATIONS!
This page: Grey cowl neck, short sleeves and blouson make this an over-and-under sweater—over another cowl neck, under our knitted vest. Unger yarn. Opposite: Zesty cranberry pullover with plain neckline and long sleeves. Wear it with vest and string tie. Melrose yarn. Inset: The collar is deep, the length is long, the look is yours! Spinnerin.

It is a knitter's prerogative to change her mind, but switching patterns midstitch may lead to unfinished sweaters. We've remedied the situation: one basic pattern that offers your choice of sleeve length, collar or plain neckline, blouson effect or none. Yarns can vary, too. Vive le difference! See page 123.

THREE FROM ONE

THE QUILTING CRAZE

Everyone knows that quilting *looks* great—now getting there is half the fun! Choose fabric best suited to outline or cartridge quilting— or work with scarves!

SHAWL COLLAR blazer, Butterick 6217, is bound in contrasting color. Follow elements of traditional crewel-design print for outline quilting. Ameritex fabric.

SEE BACK VIEWS, PAGE 25

THE NEW IDEA

here is that vest is made from two print scarves, 31″ square. Border is ideal for outline quilting; diamond quilting criss-crosses the center. Pierre Deux scarves. Vest, an outer layer, is McCall's 6159.

CARTRIDGE QUILTING

is easily accomplished by following the stripes in fabric. Jacket and vest, McCall's 5670, are made from Peter Pan stripes and prints and bound with solid fabric. Each is backed with coordinating fabric for double face quilting. A complete guide for all quilting is on page 128.

PHOTOGRAPHER: JIM DORRANCE   POLYESTER QUILT BATTING BY FAIRFIELD PROCESSING.

Wait...don't throw that sweater away yet! Old favorites or unsuccessful purchases can get a new lease on life with easy alterations or fabric trim.

The blouson pullover above, for instance, was once a man's turtleneck with a burn hole. Ingenious use of the ribbing produces neck binding and pockets.

A loose mohair knit had stretched out of shape, but profits from fabric draw-strings and soft neck bow (left). Worn elbows didn't stop this crew-neck pullover. It's now a bolero (right), trimmed in challis fabric to match a skirt. Another idea for worn elbows… turn a sweater inside out and re-cut to make a tank top (left). A man we know never liked this patterned turtle-neck, but inside out and lined with Sherpa® fabric (right), it makes a great jacket! For how-to's, turn to page 124.

JAPANESE FOLKWEAR
Ethnic designs sewn from Folkwear Patterns. See page 25.

**FIELD
CLOTHES**
Think of the
possibilities! Mix
terra-cotta prints or
indigo Dutch wax cottons to personalize
traditional wrap jacket and calf-length pants.
International Printworks.

**CLASSIC
KIMONOS**
Floral sheets
are perfect for the
timeless styling of kimonos. A myriad
of patterns to choose from, plentiful yardage,
and bold borders to form dramatic sleeves.
Wamsutta sheets.

FOLKWEAR #113   PHOTOGRAPHY: LEOMBRUNO-BODI

Mohair is no fashion softie! It is worldly-wise—with as much savvy as you wish to give it. These three mohair designs stress natural shapes, big looks that mean comfort as well as sophistication. **For instructions, turn to page 125.**

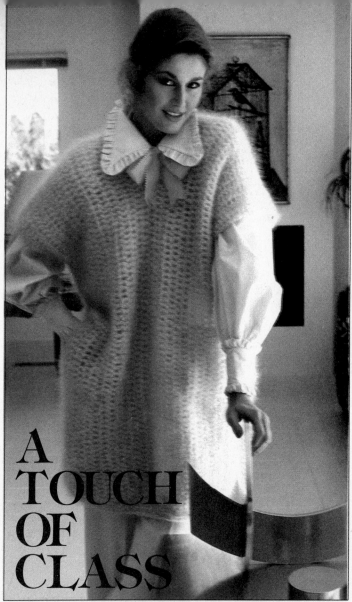

A TOUCH OF CLASS

THE TUNIC
The V-neck pullover has grown up! Made in any length, this crocheted tunic has a firm hold on fashion. Easy shaping makes it a best bet for layering over big-collared blouses and pants. Side seam pockets are a bonus. Designed by Bruce Woods. Bernat yarn.

THE WRAP
This knitted wrap sweater sets exciting standards for oversized shaping. Exaggerated sleeves are the super feature here, but even the blocks of blue and beige mohair seem to know no bounds! Plymouth yarn.

THE PONCHO
Wear-as-you-will poncho is a challenge to the imagination! It starts as a knitted rectangle with side slits; add a big collar, and sleeves. To fit your mood or the moment, the collar becomes a hood. Belt the poncho—and voila!—an evening look. Casual enough for day, it turns dramatic for night. Bernat.

SUPER SHAPES!

TAKE A GIANT step toward innovative fashion with these big shapes. Oversized blouson has bountiful sleeves, side ties, and a collar to cowl or wear turtlenecked. Designed by Greta Corins. Stanley Berroco yarn. Inset: The vest of the moment—large and loose. Crocheted in lush shades of green. Designed by Bruce Woods. Yarns, Threadbare Unlimited and Tahki. See page 125.

RUSTIC JACKET

(page 22)

Directions are given for size Small (8-10). Changes for sizes Medium (12-14) and Large (16-18) are in parentheses.

MATERIALS: Reynolds Lopi: 2(3,4) skns Dk. Grey (A); 1(2,2) skns of Lt. Grey (B), 1 skn each of White (C), Lt. Green (D), Lt. Blue (E), Salmon (F); crochet hook, Size J OR ANY SIZE HOOK WHICH WILL OBTAIN THE STITCH GAUGE BELOW; 4 buttons.

GAUGE: 8 sts = 3″.

MEASUREMENTS:

Sizes:	Small (8-10)	Medium (12-14)	Large (16-18)
Bust:	32″	36″	39½″
Width across back at underarms:	16″	18″	19½″
Width across each front at underarm (including band):	8½″	9½″	11″

DIRECTIONS: Start at neck edge with A, ch 41(41,47). **Row 1:** Dc in 5th ch from hook, dc in each of next 11 (11,13) ch, *ch 1, dc in each of next 12 (12,14) ch; rpt from * once more; ch 1, dc in last st — 38 (38,44) dc, counting ch at beg of row as 1 dc. Ch 3, turn. **Row 2:** *In next ch-1 sp make dc, ch 1 and dc; dc in each of next 12 (12,14) dc; rpt from * 2 more times; in turning ch sp make dc, ch 1 and 2 dc. Ch 3, turn. **Row 3:** Sk first dc, dc in next dc, *in next ch-1 sp make dc, ch 1 and dc; dc in each dc to next ch-1 sp; rpt from * 2 more times; in next sp make dc, ch 1 and dc; dc in next dc, dc in top of ch-3 — 54 (54,60) dc. Always count ch-3 as 1 dc. Ch 3, turn. **Row 4:** Sk first dc, *dc in each dc to next ch-1 sp, in ch-1 sp make dc, ch 1 and dc; rpt from * 3 more times; dc in each rem dc, dc in top of ch-3 — 8 dc increased. Ch 3, turn. Rpt last row 4 (5,5) more times — 94 (102,108) dc. Break off and fasten; attach C, ch 1, turn.

YOKE PATTERN — Row 1: With C, (sc in each dc to ch-1 sp, in sp make sc, ch 1 and sc) 4 times; sc in each rem dc and in top of ch-3. Ch 3, turn. **Row 2:** Place B strand along top edge of last row, with C, working over B, sk first sc, dc in next sc; *holding back on hook last loop of dc, dc in next sc, drop C, pick up B and draw a B loop through the 2 loops on hook — **color change made**; with B, working over C, holding back on hook last loop of dc, dc in next sc, drop B, pick up C and draw a loop through the 2 loops on hook — **another color change made**; (always make color change in this manner), with C, working over B, dc in each of next 3 sc, changing to B in last dc; with B dc in next sc, changing to C, with C, working over B dc in next 1(2,2) sc, *in ch-1 sp make dc, ch 1 and dc; dc in next 1(2,1) dc, changing to B; now, carrying color not in use inside sts and always changing color in last dc of each color group, make (B dc in next sc, C

dc in each of 3 sc) 6(6,7) times; B dc in next sc, with C dc in each of next 2 (3,2) sc; rpt from * 2 more times; in next sp with C make dc, ch 1 and dc; dc in next 1(2,2) sc, (B dc in next sc, C dc in next 3 sts) twice. With B ch 2 then with C ch 1 more st, turn. **Row 3:** Sk first dc, *with C dc in next dc, changing to B; working as before make 3 B dc and 1 C dc across to within next ch-1 sp, ending with B dc in 0 (1,1) st before ch-1 sp, with B make dc, ch 1 and dc in next ch-1 sp; with C dc in next 1(2,1) dc; rpt from * 3 more times, but end last rpt with B dc, ch 1 and dc in last ch-1 sp; with B dc in 0 (1,1) dc; complete row in 1 C and 3 B dc pat, end with B dc in top of ch-3. Break off C. With B ch 1, turn. **Row 4:** With B, rpt Row 1 of Yoke Pat — 126 (134,140) sc. Break off and fasten; attach A and ch 1, turn. **Row 5:** With A, *2 sc in first sc — inc made;* make sc in each sc and sc ch 1 and sc in each ch-1 sp across to within last sc, 2 sc in last sc. Break off and fasten; attach C and ch 1, turn. With C, rpt last row 1(2,3) times — 146 (164,180) sts in last row. Ch 3, turn. **Next Row:** With C, working over B, sk first st, dc in next 1(3,4) sts, changing to B in last dc; with B dc in next 6 sts, with C dc in next 2 sts, with B dc in 6 sts, with C dc in next 0 (1,2) dc, *in ch-1 sp with C make dc, ch 1 and dc; with C dc in next 0 (2,0) sts, (B dc in 6 sts, C dc in 2 sts) 4 (4,5) times; B dc in 6 sts, C dc in 0 (2,0) sts; rpt from * 2 more times; in next ch-1 sp with C make dc, ch 1 and dc; with C dc in next 0 (1,2) dc, B dc in 6 sts, C dc in 2 sts, B dc in 6 sts, C dc in last 2 (4,5) sts, changing to B in last st. Break off C. With B ch 3 turn. **Next Row:** Sk first dc, *working over A, with B dc in each dc to within center 2 sts of next 6-dc B group; with A dc in next 2 dc; rpt from * across all sts **at the same time** with B make dc, ch 1 and dc in each ch-1 sp, end with B dc in each rem dc, dc in top of ch-3 — 162 (180,196) sts. Break off A. Attach C and ch 3, turn.

TO DIVIDE SECTIONS — BODY — Row 1: With C, working over B, for Front work sk first dc, dc in next 1(3,4) dc, B dc in next 6 dc, C dc in 2 dc, B dc in 6 dc, with C, dc in each rem dc to next ch-1 sp; *holding back on hook last loop of each dc, make dc in next sp, sk next 42(46,50) dc for Sleeve, dc in next ch-1 sp, yarn over hook, draw through all 3 loops on hook — **joint dc made at**

underarm; with C dc in next 2 (4,2) dc, work in 6 B and 2 C pat across to next ch-1 sp for Back, end with C dc in each rem dc to sp, make joint dc over next 2 ch-1 sps, skipping 42 (46,50) dc in between for other Sleeve; for other Front work over rem sts to correspond with first Front — 80 (90,98) sts. Break off B. With C ch 1, turn. **Row 2:** With C, sc in each st across, increasing 1(3,3) sc evenly spaced across — 81 (93,101) sts. Break off and fasten; attach A, ch 1, turn. **Row 3:** With A, sc in each st across. Break off and fasten; attach B, ch 1, turn. **Row 4:** With B, sc in each st across. Ch 3, turn. **Rows 5 and 6:** Follow Chart 1 of Body. With C ch 1, turn. **Row 7:** With C sc in each st across. Break off and fasten; attach A, ch 3, turn. Break off and attach colors as needed; work as follows: Turn at end of each row. **Row 8:** With A, sk first st, dc in each rem st across. **Row 9:** With E sc in each st across. Attach A and ch 2, turn. **Row 10:** With A, sk first st, h dc in each st across. **Row 11:** With D, sc in each st across — 81(93,101) sc. With A, ch 2, turn. **Row 12:** Rpt Row 10. **Row 13:** Rpt. Row 9. **Row 14:** Rpt Row 8. **Row 15:** Rpt Row 7. **Rows 16,17 and 18:** Follow Chart 2 of Body. **Row 19:** Rpt Row 7. **Rows 20 and 21:** Rpt Row 8 twice. **Row 22:** With A, sc in each st across. Do not join.

Edging (right side): From same side as last row, with A sc evenly along front, back of neck and other front edges. Break off and fasten. Turn.

Collar — Row 1: Attach A to sc preceding beg of Yoke pat, working along neck edge, sc in each of next 3 sc, h dc in next 3 sc, dc in each st across to within 6 sts before beg of Yoke pat on other side, h dc in next 3 sts, sc in next 3 sts. Break off and fasten. Turn. **Row 2:** Sk first 8 sts on last row, attach A to next st, sc in same st and in next 2 sts, h dc in next 3 sts, dc in each st to within last 14 sts of previous row, h dc in next 3 sts, sc in next 3 sts; do not work over rem sts. Break off and fasten. Turn. **Rows 3 and 4:** Rpt last row. Turn. **Row 5:** Attach F to sc in line with top of Row 3 of Yoke pat, sc in same st, sc in each st, ending in corresponding sc on opposite edge. Break off and attach colors as needed. Turn at end of each row. **Row 6:** Sk first sc on last row, attach D to next sc, sc in same sc, h dc in each st across to within last 2 sc of previous row, sc in next sc.

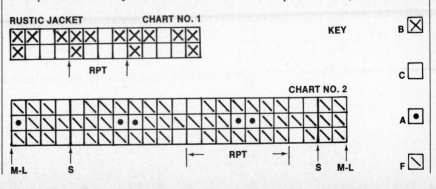

RUSTIC JACKET   CHART NO. 1

RPT

KEY

B ⊠

C ☐

CHART NO. 2

RPT

M-L   S   S   M-L

A ⊡

F ◩

ELEGANT

Plumed birds and filagreed pine boughs are
the center of attention on this luxurious embroidered tablecloth.
Elizabeth Steidel created the wreath design using
just two basic stitches and a subtle, satiny mingling of greens.
Directions are on page 89.

Row 7: Sk first st on last row, attach A to next st, sc in same st, h dc in next 2 sts; increasing 5 dc evenly spaced across center back of neck, dc in each st to within last 4 sts, h dc in next 2 sts, sc in next st.

Front and Collar Band — Row 1: Attach C to first sc of edging at lower corner of right front edge, ch 3, dc in each st along entire right front, collar and left front edge, down to end of edging. With B ch 2, turn. **Row 2:** With B, h dc in each dc across, inc 5 sts evenly spaced along back of neck, end with h dc in top of ch-3. With A, ch 2, turn. With pins, mark the position of 4 buttonholes evenly spaced along right front edge, having first pin ½" above lower edge and last pin ½" below beg of Collar. **Row 3:** *With A h dc in each st to next pin, ch 3, sk 3 sts for buttonhole; rpt from * 3 more times; h dc in each rem st across. Attach C, ch 2, turn. **Row 4:** With C, h dc in each st (including ch sts) across. Break off and fasten.

FINISHING: Pin jacket to measurements on a padded surface; cover with a damp cloth and allow to dry; do not press. Sew on buttons.

BULKY-KNIT WRAP CARDIGAN AND SCARF

(page 23)

Directions are given for size Small (8-10). Changes for sizes Medium (12-14) and Large (16-18) are in parentheses.
MATERIALS: Vermont 100% Virgin Wool, 3 Ply (1 lb. cone): 2(4,4) cones Natural (A) or 3-ply wool yarn of your choice; Reynolds Lopi yarn: 1(1,2) skns Dark Green (B); Stanley Berroco Yarn: 4(5,6) ozs Dark Brown (C); knitting needles, 1 pair each of No.10 and No.13 OR ANY SIZE NEEDLES WHICH WILL OBTAIN THE STITCH GAUGE BELOW.
GAUGE: Garter St on No.13 needles — 3 sts = 1"; 10 rows = 2".
Note: For Cardigan, use 2 strands of A held together throughout; wind single cone into 2 equal balls. Use a single strand of B and C throughout. Entire cardigan (except cuffs) is worked in garter st (k each row).

MEASUREMENTS:

	Small	Medium	Large
Sizes:	(8-10)	(12-14)	(16-18)
Bust: (cardigan overlapped):	33"	36"	40"
Width across back at underarms:	16½"	18"	20"
Width across each front at underarm (excluding band):	10¼"	11"	12"
Width across sleeve at upper arm:	12½"	13"	14"

Scarf measures approximately 10" X 44".

DIRECTIONS — CARDIGAN —
BACK: Start at lower edge with 2 strands of A held tog and with No.13 needles, cast on 50 (54,60) sts. Work in garter st (k each row) for 4 rows for hem. Mark first row for right side. Break off A, attach a single strand of C. With C, work 6 rows in garter st. Break off C; attach double strand of A. With A, continue in garter st until length is about 18" from first row of C.
Armhole Shaping: Continuing in garter st throughout, bind off 4 sts at beg of next 2 rows. Dec one st at each end every other row 4(5,6) times — 34(36,40) sts. Work 2 rows even. Break off A; attach single strand of C, always change color in this manner. Working even in garter st, work 4 rows C; 2 rows A; change to a single strand of B and with B, work even in garter st until length from first row of armhole shaping is 6½(7¼,8)".
Shoulder Shaping: With B, bind off 4 sts at beg of next 4 rows; then 3(4,5) sts at beg of following 2 rows. Bind off rem 12(12,14) sts.
LEFT FRONT: Start at lower edge with A and No.13 needles, cast on 32(34,36) sts. Mark first row for right side. Work same as for Back to underarm, end on wrong side.
Armhole Shaping: Continuing in garter st throughout, bind off 4 sts at beg of next row. Dec one st at same edge every other row 4 (5,6) times — 24 (25,26) sts. Work 2 rows even. Change to C.
Neck Shaping: With C, continuing in garter st, dec one st at neck edge (opposite armhole shaping) in each of next 4 rows. Continue to dec one st at neck edge on every row, work 2 rows A; then with B, continue to dec at neck edge every row until 11(12,13) sts rem. Work even over rem sts until armhole is same length as on Back, end at armhole edge.
Shoulder Shaping — Row 1: Bind off 4 sts, k across. **Row 2:** K across. Rpt last 2 rows once. Bind off rem 3 (4,5) sts.
RIGHT FRONT: Work to correspond with Left Front, reversing shaping.
SLEEVES: Start at cuff edge with 2 strands of A held tog and No.10 needles, cast on 28(30,32) sts. Work in k 1, p 1 ribbing for 3". Change to single strand of C and No.13 needles. **Next Row (right side):** *K in front and back of first st — inc made; *k 2, inc in next st, rpt from * across, end with k 0 (2,1) — 38(40,43) sts. K 5 rows. Continuing even in garter st throughout work Stripes as follows: With A work 20 rows, with B work 20 rows; with A work 4 rows; with B work 8 rows; with C work until length is about 17(17½,18)" from beg, end on wrong side. Change to B.
Top Shaping: With B, bind off 4 sts at beg of next 2 rows. Work 1 row even; dec one st at each end of following row. With A, dec one st at each end every 3rd row twice. With C, dec one st at each end every 3rd row until 18(18,19) sts rem. Bind off 2 sts at beg of next 4 rows. Bind off rem sts.
FINISHING: Pin pieces to meas-

urements on a padded surface; cover with a damp cloth and allow to dry; do not press. Sew shoulder, side and sleeve seams. Sew in sleeves. Turn first 4 rows at lower edge to wrong side for hem and stitch in place.
Front and Back-of-Neck Band: With a single strand of B and No.10 needles, cast on 6 sts. Work in garter st until band (when slightly stretched) fits along left front, back of neck and right front edges. Bind off. Sew band in place.
SCARF: With single strand of C and No.10 needles, cast on 36 sts. Entire scarf is worked in garter st (k each row). Work 12 rows with C. Mark first row for right side. Change to a **single** strand of A and work 6 rows. Change to B and work 14 rows. Change to single strand of A and work until length is about 38" from beg, end on wrong side. Now work 14 rows B, 6 rows A and 12 rows C. Bind off. Steam very lightly.

TAPESTRY SKIRT

(page 24)

The skirt can be adjusted to fit all sizes.
MATERIALS: Lion Brand, Sayelle* (100% Dupont Orlon Acrylic, 4 oz skns), 4 Ply Knitting Worsted type: 1 skn each of #153 Black (A), #99 Eggshell (B), #134 Brick (C), #106 Lt. Blue (D), #141 Dusty Pink (E), #130 Emerald (F), #142 Tapestry (G), #155 Sandstone (H), #133 Tile (I), #172 Dark Grass (J), #125 Taupe (K); knitting needles, No.10½ OR ANY SIZE NEEDLES WHICH WILL OBTAIN THE STITCH GAUGE BELOW; 1 skirt zipper, 8"

TAPESTRY SKIRT

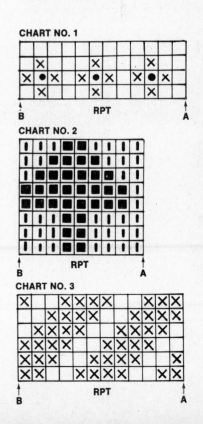

CHART NO. 1

CHART NO. 2

CHART NO. 3

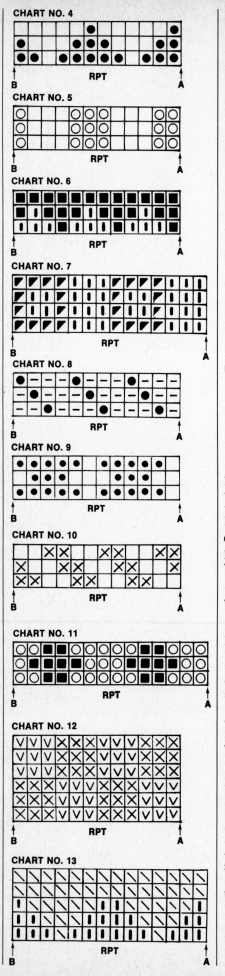

CHART NO. 4

CHART NO. 5

CHART NO. 6

CHART NO. 7

CHART NO. 8

CHART NO. 9

CHART NO. 10

CHART NO. 11

CHART NO. 12

CHART NO. 13

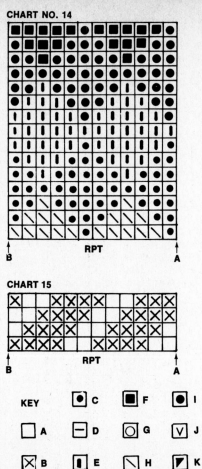

CHART NO. 14

CHART 15

KEY

⊡ C	■ F	⊡ I
□ A	⊟ D	⊚ G	⊻ J
⊠ B	❚ E	◺ H	◩ K

long; 1 yard white grosgrain ribbon 1½" wide; 3 yards black grosgrain ribbon, 1" wide; 1 yard tape; piece of taffeta (or any lining material) for pockets.

GAUGE: 4 sts = 1"; 9 rows = 2".

MEASUREMENTS:

Width across each skirt panel	21"	21"
Width across skirt at lower edge	63"	63"

Note: When changing colors always pick up new color from under dropped color to prevent making holes in work; carry colors not in use loosely along wrong side. Entire dress is worked in st st (k 1 row, p 1 row). In following Charts, for each **right-side row** (k row), work from A to B and rpt A to B across; for each **wrong-side row** (p row), work rpt from B to A across. Cut and attach colors as needed. Darn in all ends on wrong side when knitting has been completed. Skirt is worked in 3 identical panels.

Directions — Skirt Panel (Make 3): Start at lower edge with A, cast on 84 sts for all sizes. **Rows 1 through 4:** With A, work 4 rows in st st (k 1 row, p 1 row). **Rows 5 through 8:** Continuing in st st throughout, follow Chart 1 as directed. **Rows 9 through 13:** With D only work 2 rows; with E only work 3 rows. **Row 14:** With E, p 3; then rpt B to A on Row 1 of Chart 2 across. **Row 15:** Rpt A to B on Row 2 of Chart 2 across to within last 3 sts, k 3 E. **Rows 16 through 21:** Working same

as for last 2 rows, follow Chart 2 from row 3 to top. **Rows 22 through 26:** Work 3 rows E, 2 rows C. **Rows 27 through 32:** Follow Chart 3. **Rows 33, 34 and 35:** Work 2 rows G, 1 row H. **Rows 36, 37 and 38:** Follow Chart 4. **Rows 39, 40 and 41:** Work 1 row H, 2 rows G. **Rows 42, 43 and 44:** Follow Chart 5. **Rows 45 through 53:** Work 1 row C, 6 rows J, 2 rows D. **Rows 54, 55 and 56:** Follow Chart 6. **Rows 57 through 61:** Work 1 row B, 2 rows J, 2 rows E. **Rows 62 through 65:** Follow Chart 7. **Rows 66-67:** Work 2 rows E. **Rows 68, 69 and 70:** Follow Chart 8. **Rows 71 through 76:** Work 2 rows A, 4 rows C. **Rows 77 through 81:** Follow Chart 9; then work 2 rows C. **Rows 82, 83 and 84:** Follow Chart 10. **Rows 85 through 94:** Work 3 rows G; follow Chart 11; then work 4 rows G. **Rows 95 through 103:** Work 3 rows I; then follow Chart 12. **Rows 104 through 108:** Follow Chart 13. **Rows 109 through 114:** Work 1 row K; 2 rows A; 1 row K; 2 rows H. **Rows 115 through 129:** Follow Chart 14. **Rows 130 thorugh 133:** Work 2 rows F; 2 rows G. **Rows 134 through 137:** Follow Chart 15. Bind off using colors as established on last row.

FINISHING: To block, pin pieces to measurements on a padded surface; cover with a damp cloth and allow to dry; do not press. Join skirt panels as follows: Leaving 8" opening at top for zipper, sew center back seam, matching rows. Mark 6" opening for pocket at each side of front (3rd) panel, 4½" below top edge. Leaving opening for pockets free, sew front panel to other 2 panels, matching rows. Gather top edge of skirt to desired waist measurement (about 1" more than actual body waist size). Cut the 1½" ribbon 1" longer than top of skirt, turn back ½" at each end and sew to wrong side at top of skirt. Stitch narrow grosgrain ribbon to wrong side of lower edge of skirt, for hem. Face edges of entire back opening with tape; sew in zipper. For each pocket, cut a 6 x 8½" piece of taffeta, fold in half matching the 6" edges and stitch up sides; insert in pocket opening, turn back ¼" around raw edge; stitch in place.

NECK POUCHES

(page 24)

Directions are given for Crocheted Pouch to measure 3¼" in diameter; for Knitted Pouch to measure 3½" square.

MATERIALS: Coats & Clark's Red Heart "Wintuk" Sock & Sweater Yarn, 3 Ply (2 oz. skn). *For Crocheted Pouch:* 1 oz. each of #403 Lt. Oxford (A), #327 Camel (B), #111 Eggshell (C), #12 Black (D); corchet hook, Size E OR ANY SIZE HOOK WHICH WILL OBTAIN THE STITCH GAUGE BELOW. *For Knitted Pouch:* 1 oz. each of #858 Navy (A), #905 Red (B), #686 Paddy Green (C), #251 Vibrant Orange (D); knitting needles, 1 pair No. 1 OR ANY SIZE NEEDLES WHICH WILL OB-

TAIN THE STITCH GAUGE BELOW; crochet hook, Size E.

GAUGE: Crochet — 7 sc = 1″; 6 rnds = 1″. Knit — 8 sts = 1″; 9 rows = 1″.

DIRECTIONS — CROCHETED POUCH — BACK: Start at center with A, ch 4. Join with sl st to form ring. **Rnd 1:** Ch 1, 6 sc in ring. Do not join rnds; mark end of each rnd. **Rnd 2:** 2 sc in each sc around — 12 sc. **Rnd 3:** (Sc in next sc, 2 sc in next sc) 6 times — 18 sc. Break off A; attach B to last sc made. **Rnd 4:** With B, (sc in each of next 2 sc, 2 sc in next sc) 6 times — 24 sc. **Rnd 5:** (2 sc in next sc, sc in each of next 3 sc) 6 times — 30 sc. Break off B; attach C to last sc made. **Rnd 6:** Place strand of D along top of last rnd, * with C, working over D, sc in each of next 2 sc, *draw up a loop in next sc, drop C, pick up D and draw a loop through the 2 loops on hook* — **color change made**; with D, working over C, make 2 sc in next sc, *draw up a D loop in next sc, drop D, draw a C loop through the 2 loops on hook* — **another change of color made**; rpt from * around; do not change color at end of rnd — 36 sc. **Rnd 7:** With D sc in first sc, changing to C, * with C, working over D, sc in next 3 sc, changing to D in last sc; with D, working over C, sc in next 3 sc, changing to C in last sc; rpt from * around, end last rpt with D sc in last 2 sc. Break off C. **Rnd 8:** With D only, sc in each sc, increasing 6 sc evenly spaced around — 42 sc. **Rnd 9:** Sc in each sc around. Sl st in next sc. Break off and fasten.

FRONT: Work same as Back.

FINISHING: Hold front over back, wrong sides together; leaving 1½″ opening, sew pieces tog. With front facing, using D, work 1 row of sc along seam; then sc evenly around opening. Join with sl st to first sc on top opening. Break off and fasten.

Cord: With 2 strands of C held together, make a loop on hook and ch 1; using 2 strands of D held together * with D ch 1, drop D, pick up C from under other strand and ch 1, drop C, pick up D from under C strand; rpt from * until length is 31″ or desired length. Break off both colors and fasten. Sew cord to pouch.

Tassel: Cut 4 strands of C (or any color), each 5″ long. Hold strands together and fold in half to form a loop. Insert hook in center st at lower edge and draw loop through; draw loose ends through loop on hook and pull tightly to form a knot. Make a tassel in same way at each side.

KNITTED POUCH — Note: Pat is worked in st st (k 1 row, p 1 row). When changing color, always twist color not in use around the other once to prevent making holes in work. Carry color not in use loosely along wrong side. To following chart, follow Row 1 and all k rows (right-side rows) from right to left and 2nd and all p rows from left to right. Starting at top edge of front with A, cast on 26 sts. Follow Chart as directed from Row 1 to top. Bind off.

FINISHING: Fold knitted piece in half, matching short edges. Sew side seams. With C and crochet hook, working through both thickenesses, crochet 1 row of sc along each side seam. Crochet 1 row of sc along entire top edge. Join with sl st to first sc. Break off and fasten.

Cord: Cut 4 strands of B, each 65″ long. Hold strands evenly and twist tightly together; fold in half and allow to twist again. Knot each end. Sew ends of cord inside corners of top opening.

Pompon (Make 2): Cut 2 cardboard circles, each 1″ in diameter. Cut a hole ½″ in diameter in center of each circle. Cut a 3-yard length each of C and D. Place circles together and wind C yarn around the double circle, drawing yarn through center opening and over edge until center hole is half filled; then wind D yarn in same way until center hole is filled. Cut yarn around outer edge, between circles. Slip a double strand between cardboard circles and tie securely around strands. Remove cardboard; trim evenly. Sew pompon to each corner at lower edge of pouch. Pouches can be worn around neck, or tied to belts.

NECK POUCH

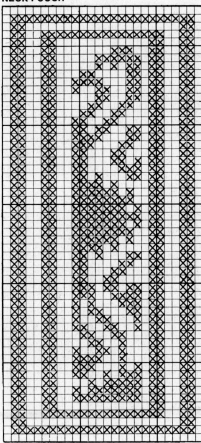

☐ A   ⊠ B

CROCHETED CABLE-STITCH PULLOVER AND HAT

(page 36)

Directions are given for Small (8-10) Size. Changes for Medium (12-14) and Large (16-18) are in parentheses. Hat will fit all sizes.

MATERIALS: Bernat Danish Bulky: 11(12,13) balls of #8042 Barley; crochet hook, Bernat Aero Size P OR ANY SIZE HOOK WHICH WILL OBTAIN THE STITCH GAUGE BELOW.

GAUGE: 2 sc = 1″; 10 rows = 4″.

MEASUREMENTS:

Size:	Small (8-10)	Medium (12-14)	Large (16-18)
Bust:	32″	36″	40″
Width across back or front at underarms:	16″	18″	20″
Width across sleeve at lower edge:	14″	15″	16″

DIRECTIONS — PULLOVER — BACK — Foundation Row: Start at lower edge, ch 34(38,42) to measure 17(19,21)″. Sc in 2nd ch from hook and in each rem ch — 33(37,41) sc. Ch 1, turn. **Row 1 (right side):** Sc in each sc across. Ch 1, turn. **Row 2:** Rpt Row 1. Ch 1, turn. **Row 3:** Sc in each of first 2 sc, *yarn twice around hook, working in front of last 2 rows, insert hook (from right to left) under post of 3rd sc on 3rd row below, yarn over hook and draw loop through, (yarn over hook, draw through 2 loops) 3 times* — **raised tr made;** *sk next free sc on last row (covered by raised tr), sc in next sc on last row, sk next free sc on 3rd row below, raised tr around next sc as before;* rpt from * across, end with sc in each of last 2 sc on last row — 15(17,19) raised tr. Ch 1, turn. **Row 4:** Sc in each st across. Ch 1, turn. **Row 5:** Sc in each of first 2 sc, *working in front of last row, make raised tr around post of raised tr directly below next sc, sk next sc on last row (covered by raised tr), sc in next sc;* rpt from * across, end last rpt with sc in each of last 2 sc. Ch 1, turn. **Row 8 and all wrong-side Rows:** Rpt Row 4. Hereafter directions are given for right-side rows only. **Row 9:** Sc in first 2(4,4) sc, *raised tr around tr directly below next sc, make raised tr around sc directly below next sc on 3rd row below, sk next 2 sc on last row (covered by 2 raised tr), sc in next sc on last row, raised tr around sc in line with next sc on 3rd row below, raised tr around next tr below, sk 2 sc (covered by raised tr), sc in each of next 7(7,9) sts on last row;* rpt from * once more; raised tr around tr below, raised tr around sc in line with next sc on 3rd row below, sk 2 sc covered by 2 raised tr, sc in next sc on last row, raised tr around sc in line with next sc on 3rd row below, raised tr around next tr below, sk 2 sc on last row, sc in each of last 2(4,4) sc on last row. There are 6 groups of 2 raised tr each. **Row 11:** Sc in each of first 2(4,4) sc, *sk first raised tr of 2-raised tr group below, make raised tr around 2nd tr, then make raised tr around skipped tr* — **cable made,** sk 2 sc (covered by raised tr cable), sc in next sc on last row, make cable over next tr group same as before; sk 2 sc (covered by cable just made), sc in each of next 7(7,9) sts on last row; rpt from * across but, end last rpt with sc in each of last 2(4,4) sc — 6 cables. Ch 1, turn. **Row 13:** Sc in first 1(3,3) sc, raised tr around each of 2 tr of first cable, sk next 2 free sc (covered by raised tr) on last row, sc in each of next 3 sc on last row, raised tr around each of next 2 tr below, sk 2 sc on last row, *sc in each of 5(5,7) sc, raised tr around each of next 2 tr, sk 2 sc on last row, sc in each of next 3 sc, raised tr around each of next 2 tr, sk 2 sc on last row; rpt from * once more; sc in last 1(3,3) sc. Ch 1, turn. **Row 15:** Making cable over each 2-tr goup, work same as for Row 13. **Row 17:** Sc in first 2(4,4) sc, *raised tr around each of 2-tr below, sk 2 sc on last row, sc in next sc, raised tr around each of next 2 tr, sk 2 sc on last row, sc in next 7(7,9) sc; rpt from * across, but, end last rpt with sc in last 2(4,4) sc. Ch 1, turn. **Row 18:** Rpt Row 4. Ch 1, turn. Last 8 rows (Rows 11 through 18) form cable pat. **Rows 19 through 26:** Rpt Rows 11 through 18. Ch 1, turn. **Row 27:** Rpt Row 11. Ch 1, turn. **Row 29:** Sc in first 1(3,3) sc, raised tr around each of 2 tr of first cable, sk next 2 sc (covered by raised tr) on last row, sc in each of next 3 sc, raised tr around each of next 2 tr, sk 2 sc on last row, sc in next 6(6,8) sc, raised tr around each of next 2 tr, sk 2 sc on last row, sc in next sc, raised tr around each of next 2 tr, sk 2 sc on last row, sc in next 6(6,8) sc, raised tr around each of next 2 tr, sk 2 sc on last row, sc in next 3 sc, raised tr around each of next 2 tr, sk 2 sc on last row, sc in last 1(3,3) sc. Ch 1, turn. **Row 31:** Sc in first 1(3,3) sc, cable over 2 tr below, sk 2 sc on last row, sc in each of next 3 sc, cable over next 2 tr, sk 2 sc on last row, sc in next 2 sc; now, making raised tr around either sc or raised tr below make (raised tr around st directly below next sc on 2nd row below, sk next sc covered by tr on last row, sc in next sc) 7(7,9) times; sc in next sc, cable over next 2 tr below, sk 2 sc on last row, sc in each of next 3 sc, cable over next 2 tr, sc in last 1(3,3) sc. Ch 1, turn. **Row 33:** Sc in first 2(4,4) sc, raised tr around each of next 2 tr below, sk 2 sc on last row, sc in next sc, raised tr around each of next 2 tr, sk 2 sc on last row, sc in each of next 3 sc, (raised tr around tr below, sk 1 sc on last row, sc in next sc) 7(7,9) times; keeping continuity of cable pat, complete row. Ch 1, turn. **Row 35:** Sc in first 2(4,4) sc, cable over 2 tr below, sk 2 sc on last row, sc in next sc, cable over next 2 tr, sk 2 sc on last row, sc in next 2 sc, (raised tr around next tr, sk 1 sc on last row, sc in next sc) 7(7,9) times; complete row in cable pat. Ch 1, turn. **Row 36:** Rpt Row 4. **Neck Shaping: Row 1:** Work in cable pat over first 10(12,12) sts; do not work over rem sts. Ch 1, turn. Keeping continuity of pat, work even over these sts until total length is about 17(17¾,18½)″ from beg, end at neck edge. Ch 1, turn.

Shoulder Shaping: Sc in each of first 5(6,6) sts, sl st in next st. Break off and fasten. Sk center 13(13,17) sts on last row made before neck shaping; attach yarn to next st, sc in same st, work to correspond with opposite side.
FRONT: Work Front of sweater same as Back.
SLEEVES: Start at outer edge, ch 32(34,36). Work same as Back until Row 8 has been completed. Ch 1, turn. **Row 9:** Rpt Row 8. Break off and fasten.
FINISHING: To block, pin pieces to measurements on a padded surface; cover with a damp cloth and allow to dry; do not press. Leaving top 7(7½,8)″ open for armholes, sew side seams; sew shoulder and sleeve seams. Sew top edge of sleeves to armholes, adjusting to fit. With right side facing, work 1 row of sl sts along entire neck edge, easing in edge slightly. Break off and fasten.
HAT — Cable Band: Row 1: Start at center back seam, ch 10. Sc in 2nd ch from hook and in each rem ch — 9 sc. Ch 1, turn. **Row 2:** Sc in each st across. Ch 1, turn. **Row 3 (right side):** Sc in each of first 2 sc, working raised tr same as on Back, sk first 2 sc on 2nd row below, raised tr around each of 2 sc, sk next 2 sc on last row (covered by raised tr), sc in next sc, sk next free sc on 2nd row below, raised tr around each of next 2 sc, sk 2 sc on last row, sc in each of last 2 sc. Ch 1, turn. **Row 4 and all wrongside Rows:** Sc in each st across. Ch 1, turn. **Row 5:** Sc in each of first 2 sc, make cable (same as on Back) over first 2 tr below, sc in center sc, cable over next 2 tr, sc in each of last 2 sc on last row. Ch 1, turn. **Row 7:** Sc in first sc, raised tr around each of first 2 tr, sc in each of center 3 sc on last row, raised tr around each of next 2 tr, sc in last sc. Ch 1, turn. **Row 9:** Sc in first sc, cable over first 2 tr, sc in center 3 sc, cable over next 2 tr, sc in last sc. Ch 1, turn. **Row 11:** Sc in each of first 2 sc, raised tr around first 2 tr below, sc in center sc on last row, raised tr around each of next 2 tr, sc in each of last 2 sc on last row. Ch 1, turn. Rpt Rows 4 through 11 until there are 53 rows in all. Break off and fasten. Sew short edges together.
Crown: Rnd 1: With right side facing, working along ends of rows on one long edge of band, attach yarn to end of first row, *sc in end of each of next 3 rows, *draw up a loop in end of each of next 2 rows, yarn over hook, draw through all 3 loops on hook — dec made:* rpt from * around, end last rpt with sc in end of each of last 2 rows. Do not join rnds; mark end of each rnd — 42 sts. **Rnd 2:** Sc in each sc around. **Rnd 3:** *Sc in each of next 5 sc, dec over next 2 sc; rpt from * around — 6 decs made. **Rnd 3:** Sc in each sc around. **Rnd 4:** Decreasing 6 sc evenly spaced, sc in each sc around. Rpt last 2 rnds until 6 sc rem. Leaving a 12″ length, break off and fasten. Using end of yarn, sew sts of last rnd tog.

CROCHETED MULTI-COLOR PULLOVER AND HAT

(page 37)
Directions are given for Small (8-10) Size. Changes for Medium (12-14) and Large (16-18) Sizes are in parentheses. Hat will fit all sizes.
MATERIALS: Bernat Danish Bulky: **For Pullover:** 2(2,3) balls each of #8042 Barley (A), #8041 Birch White (B), #8064 Ice Blue (C), #8081 Winter Moss (D), #8055 Copper Frost (E); 1 (1,2) ball each of #8003 Sun Gold (F), #8093 Flagstone (G), #8029 Redwood (H); **For Hat:** 2 balls A, 1 ball each of B,C,D,E,F,G and H; crochet hook, Bernat Aero Size P ANY SIZE HOOK WHICH WILL OBTAIN THE STITCH GAUGE BELOW.
GAUGE: 2 sc = 1″; 5 sc rows = 2″.
MEASUREMENTS:

Sizes:	Small (8-10)	Medium (12-14)	Large (16-18)
Bust:	33″	37″	41″
Width across back or front (below underarm shaping)	16½″	18½″	20½″
Width across sleeve at upper arm:	13″	14″	15″

Note 1: Back and Front sections are basically the same, except for the design. Use the Rainbow or the Flower design for either back or front, as you wish.
DIRECTIONS — PULLOVER — RAINBOW SIDE: Start at lower edge with H, ch 34(38,42) to measure 17(18½, 20½)″. **Row 1 (wrong side):** Sc in 2nd ch from hook and in each ch across — 33 (37,41) sc. Break off and fasten; attach E and ch 1, turn. **Row 2:** With E sc in each sc across. Ch 1, turn. **Row 3:** Sc in

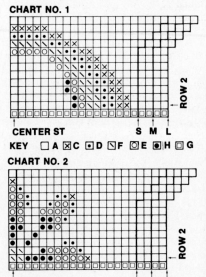

CROCHETED MULTI COLOR PULLOVER

CHART NO. 1

ROW 2

CENTER ST   S M L
KEY □A ☒C ⊡D ⊠F ⊙E ●H ⊡G

CHART NO. 2

ROW 2

CENTER ST   S M L

each st across. Ch 1, turn. **Row 4:** Sc in first sc, *yarn twice around hook, working in front of last row, insert hook (from right to left) under post of sc directly below next sc on 2nd row below, yarn over and draw

loop through, (yarn over, draw through 2 loops) 3 times — **raised tr made**; sk next sc on last row (covered by raised tr just made), sc in next sc; rpt from * across — 16 (18,20) raised tr. Ch 1, turn. **Row 5:** Sc in each st across. Break off and fasten; attach D and ch 1, turn. **Row 6:** Working raised tr around post of tr below, work same as Row 4. Ch 1, turn. **Row 7:** Sc in each st across. Ch 1, turn. Last 2 rows (Rows 6 and 7) form rib pat. **Rows 8 and 9:** Rpt Rows 6 and 7. Break off and fasten; attach C, ch 1, turn. **Rows 10 through 13:** With C, rpt Rows 6 and 7. Break off and fasten; attach B. **Rows 14, 15 and 16:** With B, rpt Rows 6,7 and 6. Break off and fasten; attach G, ch 1, turn. **Rainbow Design — Row 1:** With G, sc in each st across. Break off and fasten; attach A and ch 1, turn. **Note 2:** Design is worked in sc's. Charts show half of design; to follow Chart, start at line on right-hand side indicating size being made, and follow row across to center st inclusive; to complete row, omit center st and follow same row back in reverse order to starting line. To change color, draw up a loop in next sc, drop color being used, pick up next color and draw a loop through the 2 loops on hook; always change color in last sc of each color group. Carry A across inside sts; drop all other colors to wrong side of work; use a separate strand of each color for each side of design.
Starting with Row 2 on Chart, follow Chart 1 as directed to end of Row 9. Now, continuing to follow Chart 1 for design, inc one st at each end of next 4 rows as indicated on Chart, for underarm shaping (to inc, make 2 sc in same st). Break off all colors and fasten. Turn. **Center Ribbed Section—Row 1:** With right side facing, sk first 13 (15,16) sc; attach A to next sc, sc in same st and in each of next 14 (14,16) sc; do not work over rem 13 (15,16) sc. Ch 1, turn. With A, rpt Rows 3 and 4 over these 15 (15,17) sts. Continue in rib pat for 6 (6,8) more rows. Break off and fasten.
Flower Side: Following Chart 2, work same as for Rainbow Side.
Sleeve And Shoulder (Make 2): Start at sleeve edge with H, ch 26 (28,30). Having 25 (27,29) sts on each row, work same as for Rainbow Side until Row 9 has been completed. Break off and fasten; attach B, ch 1, turn. Mark each end of last row for end of sleeve seam. **Row 10:** With B sc in each of first 7 (8,9) sc, *make raised tr around post of st directly below next sc on 2nd row below, sk next sc (covered by tr) on last row, sc in next sc; rpt from * 5 more times; sc in each of rem 6 (7,8) sc. Ch 1, turn. **Row 11:** Sc in each st across. Ch 1, turn. **Rows 12 through 15:** rpt Rows 10 and 11. Ch 1, turn. **Row 16:** Sc in each of first 6 (7,8) sc, sc in next sc, changing to F, drop B to wrong side of work; with F work in rib pat as established over center 13 sts, changing to another strand of B in last sc, drop

F, with B sc in each rem sc. Ch 1, turn. **Row 17:** Working colors as established on last row, sc in each st across. Break off F. Ch 1, turn. Using C instead of F, work same as for Rows 16 and 17 for 4 (6,8) rows. Break off C. Using G instead of F, work 1 more row same as Row 16. Break off all colors and fasten.
FINISHING: Pin pieces to measurements on a padded surface; cover with a damp cloth and allow to dry; do not press. Sew side seams; sew sleeve seams up to markers. Fit rem portion of sleeve and shoulder piece over top edges of back and front and along side edges of center ribbed sections as illustrated. Sew in place. Block sweater.
HAT: Start at center top with A, ch 6. Join with sl st to form ring. **Rnd 1:** 12 sc in ring. Do not join rnds, but mark end of each rnd. **Rnd 2:** 2 sc in each sc around. **Rnd 3:** Sc in each sc around — 24 sc. **Rnd 4:** *Sc in next sc, 2 sc in next sc; rpt from * around — 36 sc. **Rnd 5:** Rpt Rnd 3. **Rnd 6:** *Sc in each of next 3 sc, 2 sc in next sc; rpt from * around, — 45 sc. At end of this rnd join with sl st to next sc. Break off and fasten; attach H to same sc used for joining. **Rnd 7:** Sc in same sc as joining, sc in each sc to last sc, 2 sc in last sc. Join with sl st to first sc — 46 sc. Break off and fasten. Hereafter join at end of each rnd, as directed. Attach E to same sc as joining, ch 1, turn. **Rnd 8:** With E sc in same sc as joining, sc in each sc around. Join to first sc. Break off and fasten; attach F, ch 1, turn. Always change color in this manner. Working as for Rnd 8, work colors as follows: **Rnd 9:** F. **Rnd 10:** D. **Rnd 11:** C. **Rnd 12:** With A, sc in same sc as joining, sc in each sc around. Join. Ch 1, turn. **Rnd 13:** With A, sc in same sc as joining, *working in front of last rnd, make raised tr around st directly below next sc, sk next sc on last rnd (covered by tr), sc in next sc; rpt from * around, end with raised tr. Join to first sc. Ch 1, turn. **Rnds 14 through 17:** Rpt Rnds 12 and 13. Change to B at end of last rnd. Ch 1, turn. With B rpt Rnds 12 and 13 once more. Change to G, Ch 1, turn. With G, rpt Rnd 12. Break off.

CROCHETED RIBBED TUNIC AND HAT

(page 37)

Directions are given for Small (8-10) Size. Changes for Medium (12-14) and Large (16-18) Sizes are in parentheses.
MATERIALS: Bernat Danish Bulky: 15 (16,17) balls of #8093 Flagstone (A), 4 (5,5) balls of #8055 Copper Frost (B); crochet hook, Bernat Aero Size P OR ANY SIZE CROCHET HOOK WHICH WILL OBTAIN THE STITCH GAUGE BELOW.
GAUGE: 2 sts = 1"; 10 rows = 4".
MEASUREMENTS:

Size:	Small (8-10)	Medium (12-14)	Large (16-18)
Bust:	33"	36"	40"
Width across back or front at underarms:	16½"	18"	20"
Width across sleeve at upper arm:	13"	14"	15"

DIRECTIONS — TUNIC — BACK:
Row 1 (wrong side): Start at lower edge with A, ch 34 (38,42) to measure 17½ (19,21)". Sc in 2nd ch from hook, *ch 1, sk next ch, sc in next ch; rpt from * across — 17 (19,21) sc. Ch 1, turn. **Row 2:** Sc in first sc, *working over next ch-1, dc in skipped ch below on starting chain, sc in next sc on last row; rpt from * across — 33 (37,41) sts. Ch 1, turn. **Row 3:** Sc in first sc, *ch 1, sk next dc, sc in next sc; rpt from * across. Ch 1, turn. **Row 4:** Sc in first sc, *working over next ch-1, dc in top of dc below, sc in next sc on last row; rpt from * across. Ch 1, turn. Rpt last 2 rows (Rows 3-4) alternately for pat. Work in pat until length is about 17 (18,18)", end with a right-side row. Ch 1, turn.
Ribbed Section — Row 1: Sc in each st across. Break off and fasten. Attach B to end of row, ch 1, turn. **Row 2:** With B sc in first sc, *yarn twice around hook, working in front of last row, insert hook (from right to left) under post of dc directly below next sc, yarn over hook and draw loop through, (yarn over hook, draw through 2 loops on hook) 3 times — **raised tr made**; sk next sc on last row (covered by raised tr just made), sc in next sc; rpt from * across — 16 (18,20) raised tr. Ch 1, turn. **Row 3:** Sc in each st across. Ch 1, turn. **Row 4:** Sc in first sc, * working in front of last row, make raised tr around post of raised tr directly below next sc, sk next sc on last row (covered by raised tr just made), sc in next sc; rpt from * across. Ch 1, turn. Rpt last 2 rows (Rows 3-4) for rib pattern 2 (3,4) more times. At end of last row, break off and fasten. Attach A, ch 1, turn.
Neck Shaping — Row 1: With A sc in first sc, *ch 1, sk next st, sc in next sc; rpt from * 4 (4,5) more times; do not work over rem sts — 11 (11,13) sts, including ch sts. Ch 1, turn. **Row 2:** Sc in first sc, *working over next ch-1, make dc in st directly below, sc in next sc on last row; rpt from * across. Ch 1, turn. **Row 3:** Sc in first sc, *ch 1, sk next dc, sc in next sc; rpt from * across. Ch 1, turn. **Row 4:** Rpt Row 2 of Neck Shaping. Ch 1, turn.
Shoulder Shaping: Row 1: Sl st in each of first 4 sts, sc in each rem st. Ch 1, turn. **Row 2:** Sc in each of first 3 (3,4) sc, sl st in next sc. Break off and fasten. Sk center 11 (15,15) sts on last row made before neck shaping; attach A to next st, sc in same st, work to correspond with opposite side, reversing shoulder shaping.
FRONT: Work same as Back.
SLEEVES: Start at lower edge with A, ch 28 (30,32). Having 14 (15,16) sc on Row

1 and 27(29-31) sts on Row 2, work as for Back until Row 4 has been completed. Rpt Rows 3-4 for pat until total length is about 16(17,17½)", end with a right-side row.

Ribbed Section: Work same as Ribbed Section of Back until Row 4 has been completed. Ch 1, turn. Rpt last 2 rows 0(1,2) times. **Next Row:** 2 sc in first sc, sc in each st across to last sc, 2 sc in last sc—inc made at each end. Ch 1, turn. **Next Row:** Working inc sts in sc, work same as Row 4 of rib pat. Rpt last 2 rows 1 more time.—31(33,35) sts. Break off and fasten.

FINISHING: To block, pin pieces to measurements specified on a padded surface; cover pieces with a damp cloth and allow to dry; do not press. Leaving 7" from lower edge open for side slits and top 7(8,9)" open for armholes, sew side seams. Sew shoulder and sleeve seams. Sew top edge of sleeves to armholes, adjusting to fit. With B, work 1 row of sl sts across center front and 1 row across center back of neck.

Belt: With A ch 112(120,126). Work same as for Back until Row 4 has been completed. Ch 1, turn. Sl st in each st across. Break off and fasten.

HAT: Starting at center top with A, ch 6. Join with sl st to form ring. **Rnd. 1:** 12 sc in ring. Do not join rnds; mark end of each rnd. **Rnd 2:** 2 sc in each sc around—24 sc. **Rnd 3:** Sc in each sc around. **Rnd 4:** *Sc in next sc, 2 sc in next sc; rpt from * around—36 sc. **Rnd 5:** Rpt Rnd 3. **Rnd 6:** *Sc in each of next 2 sc, 2 sc in next sc; rpt from * around—48 sc. At end of this rnd, join with sl st in next sc. Ch 1, turn. Hereafter, join rnds as directed. **Rnd 7:** Sk joining, sc in next sc, *ch 1, sk next sc, sc in next sc; rpt from * around. Join with sl st to first sc—47 sts, including ch sts. Ch 1, turn. **Rnd 8:** Sk joining, sc in next sc, *working over next ch-1, dc in skipped st directly below, sc in next sc on last rnd; rpt from * around, end with sc in same sc as joining of last rnd. Join to first sc. Joining is center back seam. Ch 1, turn. **Rnd 9:** Sk joining, sc in next sc, *ch 1, sk next dc, sc in next sc; rpt from * around, end with sc in same sc as joining of last rnd. Join to first sc. Ch 1, turn. **Rnds 10, 11 and 12:** Rpt rnds 8,9 and 8. Ch 1, turn.

Ribbed Section: Joining at end of each rnd, work same as for Ribbed Section of Back until Rnd 4 has been completed. Rpt Rnds 3-4 once more. Ch 1, turn. **Last Rnd:** Sl st in each st around, easing in edge to desired size. Break off and fasten loose ends.

CROCHETED EDGING FOR COAT AND BERET

(page 54)

Directions for Beret are given to fit all sizes.

MATERIALS FOR CROCHET: Bernat Knitting Worsted (4 oz. balls): 1 ball each of Dk. Grey (A) and Lt. Grey (B); crochet hook, Size I OR ANY SIZE HOOK WHICH WILL OBTAIN THE STITCH GAUGE BELOW. A round piece of Chinchilla 10" in diameter for beret.

(**Note:** Check weight of packaged yarn carefully before buying.)

GAUGE: 4 sts = 1".

DIRECTIONS—EDGING FOR COAT: Make holes along edges of sections as directed. Do not make holes along lower edges of back and fronts.

Sleeve Edging: With right side facing, attach A with sc in any hole along edge, ch 1, make sc and ch 1 in each hole around. Join last ch-1 with sl st to first sc. Break off and fasten. **Rnd 2:** Attach B with sc in first sc, work sc in each ch and in each sc around, making 3 sc in each corner st. Be sure to have same number of sts along corresponding edges. Join to first sc. Break off and fasten.

Back Edging: Start at lower end of side edge omitting joining of rnds, work same as for Sleeve Edging along side, armholes, top and other side edge; do not work across lower edge.

Front Edging: With right side facing, work same Edging along side, armhole, top and front edge of each front. Work edging around each pocket; then with A work 1 row across top edge only.

Joining: With a darning needle and A, working through back loop only of each st, sew side, shoulder and sleeve seams with an overcast st, matching corners. Sew in sleeves. **Next Row:** With A, starting at lower end of front edge and working in back loop only of each sc, work 1 row of sc along right front to next corner at neck, 3 sc in corner st, * sc in each of next 4 sc. *draw up a loop in each of next 2 sc, yarn over and draw through all 3 loops on hook — dec made;* rpt from * across neck to next corner, 3 sc in corner st, sc in each sc along left front edge. Break off and fasten.

Neckband — Row 1: With right side facing, attach A to center sc of 3-sc group at corner, sc in each sc across neck edge to center of next corner, making 10 decs evenly spaced across. Ch 1, turn. **Row 2:** Sc in each sc across. Ch 1, turn. **Row 3:** Rpt last row. Break off and fasten. Turn. **Next 3 Rows:** Working as for Row 2, make 1 row B and 2 rows A. Break off and fasten.

Front Bands (Make 2) — Row 1: With right side facing, with B, working in back loop only of each st, work 1 row sc along entire front edge, including neckband. Break off and fasten. Do not turn. **Row 2:** With A, work same as last row. Ch 1, turn. **Next 2 Rows:** Sc in each sc across. Ch 1, turn. At end of last row, break off and fasten.

Sleeve Band — Rnd 1: With right side facing, attach A to sleeve seam, working in back loop of each st, sc in each sc around. Join to first sc. **Next 3 Rnds:** Ch 1, working through both loops of each st, sc in same sc as joining, sc in each sc around. Join. At end of last rnd, break off and fasten.

BERET: Cut a circle of Chinchilla, 10" in diameter; make holes, as for Coats, ½" apart along outer edge of circle, making 54 holes. **Rnd 1:** With A, make a loop on hook, work 2 sc in each hole around. Join with sl st to first sc — 108 sc. **Rnd 2:** Ch 1, sc in same sc as joining, sc in each sc around. Join with sl st to first sc. **Rnds 3 and 4:** Rpt Rnd 2. **Rnd 5:** Ch 1, sc in same sc as joining, sc in each of next 4 sc, * 2 sc in next sc — inc made; sc in each of next 5 sc; rpt from * around, end with 2 sc in last sc. Join — 126 sc. **Rnds 6,7 and 8:** Rpt Rnd 2. Break off and fasten. **Rnd 9:** Attach B with sl st in joining, ch 1, *draw up a loop in same sc as joining and in next sc, yarn over hook, draw through all 3 loops on hook — dec made; * dec over next 2 sc; rpt from * around. Join — 63 sts. **Rnds 10 through 15:** Rpt Rnd 2. **Rnd 16:** Ch 1, sc in same sc as joining, sc in each sc, making 6 decs evenly spaced around. Join — 57 sts. **Rnd 17:** Rpt Rnd 2. **Rnd 18:** Ch 1, working over last rnd, make sc in each sc around Rnd 16. Join. **Rnd 19:** Sl st in each st around. Join. Break off and fasten.

PLAID NEEDLEPOINT BAG

(page 55)

MATERIALS: Butterick pattern #4530; ½ yard navy felt; 3¼ yards 1⅛"-wide navy fold-over tape; ¼ yard 10-mesh needlepoint canvas; piece of plaid desired for needlepoint; 1 ounce persian yarn in each color required for the plaid selected; masking tape.

DIRECTIONS: Select pattern pieces #13 and #14 from the Butterick pattern. Using the felt, cut one #13. Cut a second #13, except eliminate the flap end by cutting along the stitching line indicated for the fold nearest the flap. Fold back ⅝" seam allowance on straight side of pattern piece #14. Consider this edge a fold, and cut out a felt piece accordingly. Press this fold flat and edge stitch along crease. Cut the flap end (including both stitching lines) of #13 out of the needlepoint canvas. Cover all edges of the canvas with masking tape. Place canvas over the plaid fabric you wish to duplicate and trace off any lines necessary to guide you in reproducing the plaid. Using either half-cross or the continental stitch, needlepoint canvas ¼" beyond the ⅝" stitching lines of outer edges. When needlepoint is complete, block it. Take the felt piece of #13 that is minus the flap end, and fold under ½" along the straight edge on the fold stitching line. Place this folded edge along the top of the needle-pointed flap so that the entire shape fits the original whole shape of #13 pattern piece. Edge stitch along the folded edge of the felt to join the felt and needlepoint together. Pin the all-felt piece of #13 to the back of the felt-and-needlepoint #13. Pin the #14 double thickness of felt to the all-felt side of #13, matching notches. Bind off the entire outer edge with the fold-over tape. Using the remaining fold-over tape, sew the open side closed with an edge stitch to form shoulder strap. Knot each end. Find the mid-point of the strap and tack along stitching lines under bag flap. Close with a snap under the flap if desired.

CHILD'S DRESS AND CAP

(page 60)

Directions are given for Size 4. Changes for Sizes 6, 8 and 10 are in parentheses. Hat will fit all sizes.

MATERIALS: Bernat Knitting Worsted (4 oz. skns): For Dress: 3(4,4,5) skns of Natural. For Hat: 1 skn of same color. Knitting needles, 1 pair each Nos. 6 and 8 OR ANY SIZE NEEDLES WHICH WILL OBTAIN THE STITCH GAUGE BELOW; double-pointed needles, 1 set each Nos. 6 and 8; crochet hook, Size G.

GAUGE: Pats—11 sts = 2"

MEASUREMENTS:

Sizes:	4	6	8	10
Width across back or front at underarms:	12"	13"	14"	15"
Width across sleeve at upperarm:	9½"	10"	10¾"	11½"

PATTERN STITCHES

PATTERN 1: Worked over 12 sts. **Row 1:** P 3 *place next 3 sts on a d p needle and hold in front of work, k next 3 sts from d p needle—front cable made*; p 3. **Row 2:** K 3, p 6, k 3. **Row 3:** P 3, k 6, p 3. **Rows 4 through 7;** Rpt Rows 2 and 3 alternately twice. **Row 8.** Rpt Row 2. Rpt these 8 rows for Pat 1.

PATTERN 2: Worked on 7 sts. **Row 1:** K 1, p 2, *in next st k 1, p 1 and k1—3 sts made in one st*; p 2, k 1. **Row 2:** P 1, k 2, p 3, k 2, p 1. **Row 3:** K 1, p 2, k 3, p 2, k 1. **Row 4:** P 1, k 2, p 3 tog, k 2, p 1. Rpt all 4 rows for Pat 2.

PATTERN 3: Worked over 5 sts. **Row 1:** P 5, **Row 2:** K 5. **Rows 3 and 4:** Rpt Rows 1 and 2. **Row 5:** P 2, *in next st (k 1, p 1) twice; then k 1—5 sts made in one st*; p 2. **Row 6:** K 2, p 5, k 2. **Row 7:** P 2, k 5, p 2. **Rows 8 through 11:** Rpt Rows 6 and 7 alternately twice. **Row 12:** K 2, p 5 tog, k 2. **Row 13:** P 5. **Row 14:** K 5 Rpt these 14 rows for Pat 3.

PATTERN 4: Worked over 21 sts **Row 1:** P 3, *place next 3 sts on a d p needle and hold in back of work, k next 3 sts, k 3 ts from d p needle—back cable*; p 3, *place next 3 sts on d p needle and hole in front of work, k next 3 sts, k 3 sts from*

dp needle—front cable; p 3. **Row 2:** (K 3, p 6) twice; k 3. **Row 3:** (P 3, k 6) twice; p 3. **Rows 4 through 7:** Rpt Rows 2 and 3 alternately twice. **Row 8.** Rpt Row 2. **Row 9:** P 3, work front cable over next 6 sts, p 3, back cable over next 6 sts, p 3. **Rows 10 through 16:** Rpt Rows 2 through 8. Rpt these 16 rows for Pat 4.

DRESS—BACK: Start at lower edge, with No. 8 long needles, cast on 85(89,95,101) sts. P 1 row. Now establish pats as follows: **Row 1 (right side):** K 1(3,6,9), following Row 1 of each pat, work pat 1 over next 12 sts, pat 2 over 7 sts, pat 3 over 5 sts, pat 2 over 7 sts, pat 4 over center 21 sts, pat 2 over 7 sts, pat 3 over 5 sts, pat 2 over 7 sts, pat 1 over 12 sts, k 1(3,6,9) sts. **Row 2:** P 1(3,6,9), work Row 2 of each pat as established to at 1(3,6,9) sts, p rem sts. Working 1(3,6,9) sts at each end of each row in sts t (k 1 row, p 1 row), work other sts in pats as established until 1(2,3,5)" from beg, end with a wrongside row. **Note:** While shaping, if not enough sts rem at each end to complete cable pat, work rem sts of panel in reverse st st (p on right side, k on wrong side). Keeping continuity of pats as established, dec one st at each end of next row and every 2" 2 more times; then every 1½" 2(4,6,6) times. Dec one st at each end every 1" 4(2,0,0) times—67(71,77,83) sts. Keeping in pats, work even until length is 13(15,17,19)" from beg, end with a wrong-side row.

Armhole Shaping: Keeping continuity of pats throughout, bind off 4(5,5,6) sts at beg of next 2 rows. Dec one st at each end every other row 3(3,4,4) times—53(55,59,63) sts. Work even until length from first row of armhole shaping is 4½(5,5½,6)".

Shoulder Shaping: Bind off 8(8,9,9) sts at beg of next 4 rows. Place rem 21(23,23,27) sts on a st holder for back of neck.

FRONT: Work same as for Back until length above first row of armhole shaping is 2½(3,3½,3½)", end on wrong-side —53(55,59,63) sts.

Neck Shaping: Work in pat over first 20(21,23,24) sts. Place rem sts on a st holder. Working in pat over sts on needle only, dec one st at neck edge every other row 4(5,5,6) times. If necessary, work even until length of armhole is same as on Back, end at armhole edge.

Shoulder Shaping: At armhole edge, bind off 8(8,9,9) sts at beg of next row. Work 1 row even. Bind off rem 8(8,9,9) sts. Leaving center 13(13,13,15) sts on front holder, sl rem 20(21,23,24) sts onto No. 8 needle; attach yarn and work to correspond with opposite side, reversing shaping.

SLEEVES: With No. 6 long needles, cast on 37(37,39,41) sts. **Row 1:** K 1, * p 1, k 1; rpt from * across. **Row 2:** P 1, * k 1 p 1; rpt from * across. Rpt these 2 rows of ribbing for 1½(1½,2,2)". Change to No. 8 needles and p 1 row. Establish pats

as follows: **Row 1(right side):** K 1(1,2,3); following Row 1 of each pat, work pat 2 over next 7 sts, pat 4 over center 21 sts, pat 2 over next 7 sts, k 1(2,3). **Row 2:** P 1(2,3), work Row 2 of pat 2 over 7 sts, pat 4 over 21 sts, pat 2 over 7 sts, p 1(2,3). Working 1(2,3) sts at each end in st st and all other sts in pats as established throughout, work 2 more rows. Working inc sts in st st, inc one st at each end of next row and every 5th(5th,6th,6th) row thereafter 8(9,10,11) times in all—53(55,59,63) sts. Work even until length is 10(11½,13,14½)" from beg, end with a wrong-side row.

Top Shaping: Keeping in pats, bind off 4(5,5,6) sts at beg of next 2 rows. Dec one st at each end every other row 4(5,6,7) times; then at each end every row 4 times. Bind off 2 sts at beg of next 4 rows. Bind off rem sts.

FINISHING: Pin pieces to measurements on a padded surface, cover with a damp cloth and allow to dry; do not press. Sew left shoulder seam. **Neckband:** With right side facing and No. 6 needles, pick up and k 74(78,80,84) sts along entire neck edge, including sts on holders. Work in k 1, p 1 ribbing for 11(11,13,13) rows. Bind off loosely in ribbing. Fold neckband in half to wrong side and stitch loosely in place. Sew right shoulder seam, including neckband. Sew side and sleeve seams. Sew in sleeves. With right side facing, starting at lower end of a side seam, sc evenly along lower edge, being careful to keep work flat. Join with sl st to first sc. Break off and fasten.

BERET: Start at lower edge with No. 6 d p needles, cast on loosely 108 sts. Divide sts evenly on 3 needles. Being careful not to twist sts, join. Mark end of each rnd. Work in rnds of K1, P1 ribbing for 6 rnds, increasing 6 sts evenly spaced on last rnd. Change to No. 8 d p needles, work in pat over 114 sts as follows: **Rnd 1:** * P 6, k 6, p 6, k 1; rpt from * around. **Rnd 2:** P 6, *sl next 3 sts on a No. 6 d p needle and hold in front of work, k next 3 sts, k 3 sts from No. 6 needle—front cable*; p 6, k 1; rpt from * around. **Rnd 3:** Rpt Rnd 1. **Rnd 4:** P 6, *k in bar between last st used and next st—inc made*; k 6, k in bar between sts, p 6, k 1; rpt from * around — 12 sts increased. **Rnd 5:** * P 7, k 6, p 7, k 1, rpt from * around — 126 sts. **Rnd 6:** Rpt Rnd 5. **Rnd 7:** * P 7, inc one st as before, k 6, inc one st, p 7, k 1; rpt from * around — 138 sts. **Rnds 8 and 9:** * P 8, ki 6, p 8, k 1; rpt from * around. **Rnd 10:** * P 8, front cable over next 6 sts, p 8, k 1; rpt from * around. **Rnds 11 through 17:** Rpt Rnd 8. Rpt last 8 rnds (Rnds 10 through 17) 2 more times. **Next Rnd:** Rpt Rnd 10. **Next 2 Rnds:** Rpt Rnd 8.

Top Shaping—Rnd 1: * P 6, p 2 tog, k 6, p 2 tog, p 6, k 1; rpt from * around —12 sts decreased. **Rnd 2:** * P to within cable panel, k 6, p to next k-1 ridge, k 1; rpt from * around. **Rnd 3:** P to within 2 sts before cable panel, p 2 tog, k 6, p

2 tog, p to k-1 ridge; k 1; rpt from * around. Making front cables in 8th row from last cable rnd, continue to dec before and after each cable panel every other rnd as before until 54 sts rem on needles. **Next Rnd:** P 1, (k 6, p 3 tog) 5 times; k 6, p 2 tog—43 sts. Leaving a 10″ length, break off. Using a darning needle, draw end of yarn through rem sts, pull sts tog and fasten off securely. **Pompon:** Cut 2 cardboard circles, each 2″ in diameter. Cut a hole 1½″ in diameter at center of each circle. Cut 4 strands of yarn, each 9 yds long. Place cardboard circles tog and wind yarn around the double circle, drawing yarn through center opening and over edge until center hole is filled. Cut yarn around outer edge between circles. Double ½-yd length of yarn and slip between the 2 cardboard circles, tie securely around strands of pompon. Remove cardboard and trim evenly.

ZIP-FRONT JACKET, HAT AND SCARF

(page 60)

Directions are given for size 4. Changes for sizes 6,8 and 10 are in parentheses. Hat will fit all sizes.
MATERIALS: Bucilla deluxe 4-Ply Knitting Worsted (4 oz. skns): For Sweater: 3(4,4,5) skns of #375 Winter White. For Hat and Scarf: 2 skns of same color. Knitting needles, 1 pair each Nos. 6 and 8 OR ANY SIZE NEEDLES WHICH WILL OBTAIN THE STITCH GAUGE BELOW: crochet hook, Size F; 1 d p needle, No. 8; zipper, 10(12,14,16)″ length.
GAUGE: Pat Sts—11 sts = 2″.
MEASUREMENTS:

Sizes:	4	6	8	10
Width across back at underarms:	12″	13″	14″	15″
Width across each front at underarm:	6½″	7″	7½″	8″
Width across sleeve at upper arm:	9″	9½″	10½″	11½″

Scarf measures 8″ × 34″, plus fringe.
PAT A: Garter st (k each row), worked over any given number of sts.
PAT B: Double Twist worked over 6 sts. **Row 1 (right side):** P 1, sl next st onto d p needle and hold in back of work, k next st, k st from d p needle—right twist: sl next st onto d p needle and hold in front of work, k next st, k st from d p needle —left twist; p 1. **Row 2:** K 1, p 4, k 1. **Row 3:** P 1, make left twist, right twist, p 1. **Row 4:** Rpt Row 2. Rpt these 4 rows for Pat B.
PAT C: Bobble worked over 8 sts. **Row 1 (right side):** P 8. **Row 2:** K 1, in next st make (k 1, p 1) twice; p next 4 sts tog, in next st make (k 1, p 1) twice; k last st. **Row 3:** P 11. **Row 4:** K 1, p next 4 sts tog, in next st make (k 1, p 1) twice; p next 4 sts tog, k 1. Rpt these 4 rows for Pat C.
PAT D: Cable twist worked over 11 sts.

Row 1 (right side): P 1, sl next 3 sts onto d p needle and hold in back of work, k next st, k the 3 sts from d p needle, k 1, sl next st onto d p needle and hold in front of work, k next 3 sts, k st from d p needle, p 1. **Row 2:** K 1, p 9, k 1. **Row 3:** P 1, k 9, p 1. **Row 4:** Rpt Row 2. Rpt these 4 rows for Pat D.
PAT E: First half of Pat D worked over 7 sts. **Row 1(right side):** P 1, sl next 3 sts onto d p needle and hold in back of work, k next st, k the 3 sts from d p needle, k 2. **Row 2:** P 6, k 1. **Row 3:** P 1, k 6. **Row 4:** Rpt Row 2. Rpt these 4 rows for Pat E.
PAT F: Last half of Pat D, worked over 7 sts. **Row 1 (right side):** K 2, sl next st onto d p needle and hold in front of work, k next 3 sts, k st from d p needle, p 1. **Row 2:** K 1, p 1. **Row 3:** K 6, p 1. **Row 4:** Rpt Row 2. Rpt all 4 rows for Pat F.
DIRECTIONS—SWEATER—BACK: Start at lower edge with No. 6 needle, cast on 67(73,77,83) sts. **Row 1:** K 1, * p 1, k 1; rpt from * across. Work 6 more rows in k 1, p 1 ribbing as established. change to No. 8 needles and establish pats as follows: **Row 1 (right side):** Following Row 1 of each pat, work 7(10,12,15) sts in pat A, p 1, 6 sts pat B, 8 sts pat C, 6 sts pat B, 11 sts pat D, 6 sts pat B, 8 sts pat C, 6 sts pat D, 6 sts pat B, 8 sts pat C, 6 sts pat B, p 1, 7(10,12,15) sts pat A. Working in pats as established and working one st between pats A and B at each end in reverse st st (p on right side, k on wrong side) continue in pats until length is 6½(7½,9,10)″ from beg, end with a wrong-side row.
Armhole Shaping: Keeping continuity of pats throughout, bind off 3(3,4,4) sts at beg of next 2 rows. Dec one st at each end every other row 3(4,4,5) times—55(59,61,65) sts. Work even in pats until length is 4½(5,5½,6)″ from 1st row armhole shaping, end on wrong-side row.
Shoulder Shaping: Keeping in pat, bind off 8(8,9,9) sts at beg of next 2 rows; then 9(10,10,11) sts at beg of following 2 rows. Place rem 21(23,23,25) sts on a st holder for back of neck.
LEFT FRONT: Start at lower edge with No. 6 needles, cast on 35(38,40,43) sts. Work in k 1, p 1 ribbing for 7 rows, same as for Back. Change to No. 8 needles and establish pats as follows: **Row 1 (right side):** Following first row of each pat, work 7(10,12,15) sts in pat A, p 1, 6 sts pat B, 8 sts pat C, 6 sts pat B and 7 sts pat E. Working in pats as established, and working one st between pats A and B in reverse st st, continue in pts until length is 6½(7½,9,10)″ from beg, end at side edge.
Armhole Shaping: Keeping continuity of pats throughout, at side edge bind off 3(3,4,4) sts at beg of next row, dec one st at same edge every other row 3(4,4,5) times—29(31,32,34) sts. Work even until length is 3(3½,4,4½)″ from first row of

armhole shaping, end at front edge.
Neck Shaping: Keeping continuity of pats, at front edge bind off 6(7,7,8) sts at beg of next row, at same edge bind off 2 sts every other row twice; then dec one st every other row twice—17(18,19,20) sts. If necessary, work even in pat until length of armhole is same as on Back, end at armhole edge.
Shoulder Shaping: At armhole edge bind off 8(8,9,9) sts; complete row. Work 1 row even. Bind off rem 9(10,10,11) sts.
RIGHT FRONT: Work as Left Front until ribbing has been completed. change to No. 8 needles and establish pats. **Row 1:** Work 7 sts pat F, 6 sts pat B, 8 sts pat C, 6 sts pat B, p 1, 7(10,12,15) sts pat A. Working pats as established, complete to correspond with Left Front, reversing shaping.
SLEEVES: With No. 6 needles, cast on 39(39,43,45) sts. Work 7 rows of ribbing same as for Back. Change to No. 8 needles and establish pats as follows: **Row 1 (right side):** Work 0(0,2,3) sts pat A, 8 sts pat C, 6 sts pt B, 11 sts pat D, 6 sts pat B, 8 sts pat C, 0(0,2,3) sts pat A. Keeping in pats as established and working inc sts in pat A, work even for 1″. Inc one st at each end of next row and every 1″ thereafter 6(7,7,8) times in all—51(53,57,61) sts. Work even in pats until length is 11½(12½,14,16)″, end with a wrong-side row.
Top Shaping: Keeping in pat, bind off 3(3,4,4) sts at beg of next 2 rows. Dec one st at each end every other row 10(12,13,14) times. Bind off 3 sts at beg of next 2 rows. Bind off rem sts.
FINISHING: Pin pieces to measurements on a padded surface; cover with a damp cloth and allow to dry; do not press. Sew shoulder seams.
Neckband: With right side facing and No. 6 needle, pick up and k 17(17,18,18) along right front neck edge, k sts from back holder, pick up and k 17(17,18,18) sts along left front neck edge—55(57,59,61) sts. Work in k 1, p 1 ribbing same as Back ribbing for 7 rows. Bind off in ribbing. Fold ribbing in half to right side at turning ridge and stitch in place. With right side facing and crochet hook, work 1 row of sc along each front edge. Sew side and sleeve seams. Sew in sleeves. Sew in zipper.
HAT: Start at cuff edge with No. 6 needles, cast on 86 sts. Work in k 1, p 1 ribbing for 2½″. change to No. 8 needles and establish pats as follows: **Row 1 (right side):** P 1, * work 6 sts pat B, 8 sts pat C; rpt from * across to last st, p 1. Keeping continuity of pats B and C as established and working first and last st in reverse st st (p on right side, k on wrong side), work even until length is about 8″ from beg, end with Row 4 of each pat.
Top Shaping—Row 1: P 1, * k 2 tog, k 2, k 2 tog, (P2 tog, p 2) twice; rpt from * across to last st, p 1. **Row 2:** K 1, * k 1, in next st make (k 1, p 1) twice; p

86

next 4 sts tog, k 1, p 2, k 1; rpt from * across, end k 1. **Row 3:** P 1, * (k 2 tog) twice; p 6; rpt from * across, end p 1. **Row 4:** K 1, * k 1, p next 3 sts tog; rpt from * across, end k 1. Leaving a 20" length, break off. Using a darning needle, sl rem sts onto end of yarn, pull tightly, secure and sew center back seam. Turn ribbing to right side for cuff.

Pompon: Cut 2 cardboard circles, each 3½" in diameter. Cut a hole 1¾" in diameter in center of each circle. Cut 4 strands of yarn each about 9 yards long. Place cardboard circles tog and holding the 4 strands tog, wind around double circles, drawing yarn through center opening and over edge until center hole is filled. Cut yarn around edge, between circles. Slip a double strand of yarn between 2 cardboard circles and tie securely around strands of pompon. Remove cardboard; trim, unraveling ends of strands. Tack to center top of hat.

SCARF: With No. 8 needles, cast on 46 sts. **Row 1:** P 3, (k 8, p 8) twice; k 8, p 3. **Row 2:** K 3, p 8, place next 2 sts on d p needle and hold in back of work, k next 2 sts, k 2 sts from d p needle—**right cable twist made** place next 2 sts on d p needle and hold in front of work, k next 2 sts, k 2 sts from d p needle—**left cable twist made**; p 8, k 8, p 8, k 3. **Row 3:** P 3, make right cable twist, left cable twist, p 8, k 8, p 8, right twist, left twist, p 3. **Rows 4 through 7:** Rpt Rows 2 and 3 twice. **Row 8:** K 3, p 8, k 8, p 8, left twist, right twist, p 8, k 3. **Row 9:** P 3, k 8, p 8, left twist, right twist, p 8, k 8, p 3. **Rows 10 through 13:** Rpt Rows 9 and 9 twice. **Row 14:** K 3, p 8, left twist, right twist, p 8, k 8, p 8, k 3. **Row 15:** P 3, left twist, right twist, p 8, k 8, p 8, left twist, right twist, p 3. **Rows 16 through 19:** Rpt Rows 14 and 15 twice. **Row 20:** K 3, p 8, k 8, p 8, right twist, left twist, p 8, k 3. **Row 21:** P 3, k 8, p 8, right twist, left twist, p 8, k 8, p 3. **rows 22 through 25:** Rpt Rows 20 and 21 twice. Rpt last 24 rows (Rows through 25) for pat until length is about 34" from beg, ending with Row 13, 19 or 25 of pat. Bind off. With crochet hook, crochet 1 row of sc along each long edge.

Fringe: Wind yarn several times around a 2" square of cardboard, cut at one end, making 4" strands. Continue to cut strands as needed. Hold 5 strands tog and fold in half to form a loop, insert hook from back to front in first st on a short edge of scarf and draw loop through, draw loose ends through loop and pull tightly to form a knot. Tie 5 strands in same way in every 4th st across end in same way. Trim evenly. Steam lightly.

CHILD'S MIDDY SWEATER AND TAM

(page 61)

Directions are given for size 4. changes

for sizes 6, 8 and 10 are in parentheses. Cap will fit all sizes.

MATERIALS: Spinnerin "Wintuk" Sport (2 oz. ball): For Blouse: 3(4,4,5) balls of Navy (A), 1 ball White (B) and a few yards Scarlet (C). For Cap: 1 ball A; a few yards of B and C. Knitting needles, 1 pair each of Nos. 4 and 5 OR ANY SIZE NEEDLES WHICH WILL OBTAIN THE STITCH GAUGE BELOW; crochet hook, Size G for cap; 2 small red stars and a sleeve ornament; if desired.

GAUGE: Blouse—6 sts = 1". Cap—11 sc = 2".

MEASUREMENTS:

Sizes:	4	6	8	10
Width across back or front at underarms:	12"	13"	14"	15"
Width across sleeve at upper arm:	9"	9¾"	10¼"	11¼"

DIRECTIONS—SWEATER—BACK: Start at lower edge with No. 4 needles and A, cast on 72(78,84,90) sts. Work in st st (k 1 row, p 1 row) for 5 rows for hem, ending with a k row. Knit next row for hemline. change to No.5 needles and starting with a k row, work in st st until length is 9(9½,10,10½)" from hemline. **Armhole Shaping:** Continuing in st st throughout, bind off 4(5,5,6) sts at beg of next 2 rows. Dec one st at each end every other row 2(3,4,4) times—60(62,66,70) sts. Work even until length from first row of armhole is 4½(5,5½,6)".

Shoulder Shaping: Bind off 8(8,9,9) sts at beg of next 4 rows. Bind off rem 28(30,30,34) sts.

FRONT: Work same as for Back until length from hemline is 8½(9,9½,10)", end with a p row.

Armhole and Neck Shaping—Row 1: Continuing in st st throughout, k 36(39,42,45); place rem sts on a st holder. Work over sts on needle only. **Row 2:** P across. **Row 3:** At side edge, bind off 4(5,5,6) sts; complete row, decreasing one st at end of row—neck edge. Dec one st at each end every other row 2(3,4,4) times. Keeping armhole edge straight, continue to dec one st at neck edge every other row until 18(18,20,20) sts rem; then every 4th row until 16(16,18,18) sts rem. If necessary, work even until length of armhole is same as on Back, end at armhole edge.

Shoulder Shaping—Row 1: At armhole edge, bind off 8(8,9,9) sts; complete row. **Row 2:** Work across. bind off rem sts. Place sts from holder on a No.5 needle; attach A at neck edge and work to correspond with opposite side, reversing shaping.

SLEEVES: With No.4 needles and A, cast on 38(40,42,44) sts. Work 5 rows in st st for hem. K next row for hemline. Change to No.5 needles. Starting with a k row, work in st st, increasing one st at each end every 1", 8(9,10,12) times—

54(58,62,68) sts. Work even in st st until length from hemline is 11(12,13½,15½)", end with a p row.

Top Shaping: Continuing is st st, bind off 4(5,5,6) st at beg of next 2 rows. Dec one st at each end every other row 8(9,11,13) times; then at each end of every row 5 times. Bind off 2 sts at beg of next 4 rows. Bind off rem 12 sts.

Collar: With No.4 needles and B cast on 61(61,65,65) sts. **Row 1:** K 1, * p 1, k 1; rpt from * across. **Next 3 Rows:** Work in k 1, p 1 ribbing as established. **Next Row:** Work in ribbing over first 5 sts for side border, place these 5 sts on a safety pin; break off B; attach A and change to No.5 needles; with A, cast on one st, k across to within last 5 sts, cast on one st; place rem 5 sts on another safety pin —53(53,57,57) sts on needle. P across sts on needle. Work in st st until A portion measures 4½(4½,5,5)" end with a p row. **Neck Shaping—Row 1:** K 13(13,15,15); place these sts just worked on a separate safety pin; bind off center 27 sts; complete row. **Row 2:** P across 13(13,15,15) sts on needle. **Row 3:** *Inc in first st—inc made at neck edge;* k across. Working in st st, inc one st at neck edge every 6th row 2 more times—16(16,18,18)sts. P next row. Now shape both edges as follows: Continuing to inc one st at neck edge every 6th row as before 3 more times **at the same time,**dec one st at outer edge of collar on next row and every other row thereafter 13(13,15,15) times in all—6 sts. Dec one st at outer edge on every row until 2 sts rem. Bind off. S1 the 13(13,15,15) A sts from safety pin onto a No.5 needle,attach A and work to correspond with opposite side, reversing shaping. S1 the 5 B border sts from first safety pin onto a No.4 needle; attach B and cast on one st at inner edge. Work in k 1, p 1 ribbing as established over these 6 sts until strip fits (slightly stretched) along entire side edge of collar. Bind off in ribbing. Work other side rib border in same way. Sew B borders along side edges of collar.

Tie: With No.4 needles and B, cast on 15 sts. Work in k 1, p 1 ribbing same as for beg of collar, for 8 rows; mark first row for right side; break off B; attach C. With C k 1 row; then work in ribbing as established for 5 rows. Break off C; attach B. With B, k 1 row, then work in ribbing until length is 25(26,26½,27)" from beg, end on wrong side. Break off B; attach C. With C, k 1 row, then work in ribbing for 5 rows Break off C. With B, k 1 row, work in ribbing for 7 rows. Bind off in ribbing.

Tie Loop: With A, cast on 3 sts. **Row 1:** K 1, p 1, k 1. Work in ribbing as established for 3". Bind off.

FINISHING: Pin pieces to measurements on a padded surface; cover with a damp cloth and allow to dry; do not press. Sew side, shoulder and sleeve seams. Sew in sleeves. Turn hems to wrong side at hemlines and stitch in place. Sew collar to neck edge, adjusting to fit. Sew tie loop to center front, ½" below neck edge. Place tie around neck, under collar and draw ends through loop. Sew ornament to center of uppper section of left sleeve; sew a star to each corner of collar.

CAP: Start at center top with crochet hook and A, ch 4. Join with sl st to form ring. **Rnd 1:** 8sc in ring; do not join. Mark end of each rnd. **Rnd 2:** 2 sc in each sc around—16 sc. **Rnd 3:** *Sc in next sc, 2 sc in next sc; rpt from * around 24 sc. **Rnd 4:** *Sc in each of next 2 sc, 2 sc in next sc rpt from * around—8 sc increased. Being careful not to have incs fall directly above previous inc, continue to inc 8 sc evenly spaced on each rnd until there are 136 sc in rnd. **Next Rnd:** Sc in each sc around. Rpt last rnd 4 more times. **Next Rnd:** *Sc in each of next 15 sc, *draw up a loop in each of next 2 sc, yarn over hook and draw through all 3 loops on hook—dec made; rpt from * around—8 decs made. Dec 8 sc evenly spaced around in each of next 4 rnds— 96 sc. Break off A; attach C. With C,

sc in each sc around—96 sc. Break off C; attach B. With B, sc in each sc around. Break off B; attach A. With A, Work 2 rnds even. **Next Rnd:** Working in back loop only of each sc, sc in each sc around —turning ridge. Working over both loops, work 4 more rnds with A. Join last rnd with sl st in next sc. Break off and fasten. Turn last 5 rnds under to wrong side and stitch in place, allowing for stretching.
Pompon: Cut 2 cardboard circles, each 2½" in diameter. Cut a hole 1¼" in diameter in center of each circle. Cut 2 strands B and 2 strands C each 8 yards long. Place cardboard circles tog and holding 2 B and 2 C strands tog, wind yarn around double circle, drawing yarn through center opening and over edge until center hole is filled. Cut yarn around outer edge, between circles. Double ½-yard length of B; slip between 2 cardboard circles and tie securely around strands of pompon. Remove cardboard circles and trim yarn strands evenly. Tack finished pompon securely to center top of cap.

CHILD'S FISHERMAN TURTLENECK PULLOVER

(page 61)

Note: This sweater is suggested for experienced knitters only.
Directions are given for Size 4. Changes for Sizes 6 and 8 are in parentheses.
MATERIALS: Coats & Clark's Red Heart "Wintuk" Sport Yarn, 2 Ply (2 oz. PullOut skns): 6(7,8) skns of #111 Eggshell; circular needles, Nos. 4 and 6, 24" length; double-pointed needles, 1 set each Nos. 4 and 6 OR ANY SIZE NEEDLES WHICH WILL OBTAIN THE STITCH GAUGE BELOW.
GAUGE: St st—9 sts = 2"
Pat—11 sts = 2"
MEASUREMENTS:

SIZES:	4	6	8
Chest:	26"	28"	30"
Width across back or front at underarms:	13"	14"	15"
Width across sleeve at upper arm:	10"	11"	12"

DIRECTIONS—BODY: Start at lower edge with No. 4 circular needle, cast on 134(146,158) sts. Being careful not to twist sts, join. Place a marker on needle to indicate end of rnd; sl marker on every rnd. **Rnd 1:** * K in back of next st, p 1; rpt from * around. Rpt this rnd of ribbing for 2". Change to No.6 circular needle and set up pat as follows: **Rnd 1:** * K 2, p 3(6,3), k 5, P 3, k 1, p 4, (k 2, p 4) 1(1,2) times; k 1, p 3, *in next st k, p and k—2 sts increased;* (p 5, in next k st, k, p) twice; p 3, k 1, p 4, (k 2, p 4) 1(1,2) times; k 1, p 3, k 5, p 3(6,3); rpt from * once more for front section— 146(158,170) sts. 3 sets of cross pat

started at center of back and front. **Rnd 2:** * k 2, p 3(6,3) k 5, p 3, *sl next st onto a d p needle and hold in front of work, p next 2 sts, k st from d p needle **left trellis made;** sl next 2 sts onto dp needle and hold in back of work, k next st, p 2 sts from dp needle—right trellis made;* make (left trellis, then right trellis) 1(1,2) more times; p 3, (k 3, p 5) twice; k 3, p 3, (left trellis, then right trellis) 2(2,3) times; p 3, k 5, p 3(6,3); rpt from * once more.
Rnd 3: * *Sk next st, from back of work k in back of next st, k skipped st and drop both sts off left-hand point of needle— baby cable made;* p 3(6,3), make (baby cable over next 2 sts) twice; k 1, p 5, k 2, (p 4, k 2) 1(1,2) times; p 5, (k 1, p 1, k 1, p 5) 3 times; k 2, (p 4, k 2) 1(1,2) times; p 5, (baby cable over next 2 sts) twice; k 1, p 3(6,3); rpt from * once more. **Rnd 4:** * K 2, p 3(6,3), k 5, p 5, k 2, (p 4, k 2) 1(1,2) times; p 5, (k 3, p 5) 3 times; k 2, (p 4, k 2) 1(1,2) times; p 5, k 5, p 3(6,3); rpt from * once more. **Rnd 5:** * Baby cable, p 3(6,3), k 1, 2 baby cables, p 5, k 2, (p 4, k 2) 1(1,2) times; p 5, (k 1, p 1, k 1, p 5) 3 times; k 2, (p 4, k 2) 1(1,2) times; p 5, k 1, 2 baby cables, p 3(6,3); rpt from * once more. **Rnd 6:** Rpt Rnd 4. **Rnds 7, 8 and 9:** Rpt Rnd 3, 4 and 5. **Rnd 10:** * K 2, p 3(6,3), k 5, p 3, (right trellis, left trellis) 2(2,3) times; p 3, (k 3, p 5) twice; k 3, p 3, (right trellis, left trellis) 2(2,3) times; p 3, k 5, p 3(6,3); rpt from * once more. **Rnd 11:** * Baby cable, p 3(6,3), 2 baby cables, k 1, p 3, k 1, p 4, (k 2, p 4) 1(1,2) times; k 1, p 3, *sl next sts onto d p needle and hold in back of work, k next st, sl 2nd st from d p needle back onto left-hand point of needle and p this st, k st from d p needle —right cross over 3 sts made;* (p 5, make right cross st over next 3 sts) twice; p 3, k 1, p 4, (k 2, p 4) 1(1,2) times; k 1, p

3, 2 baby cables, k 1, p 3(6,3); rpt from * once more. **Rnd 12:** * K 2, p 3(6,3), k 5, p 3, k 1, p 4, (k 2, p 4) 1(1,2) times; k 1, p 2, *sl next next st onto d p needle and hold in back, k next st, p st from d p needle — **right cross over 2 sts;** p 1, sl next st onto d p needle and hold in front, p next st, k st from d p needle — **left cross over 2 sts,** (p 3, make right cross over next 2 sts, left cross over next 2 sts) twice; p 2, k 1, p 4, (k 2, p 4) 1(1,2) times; k 1, p 3, k 5, p 3(6,3); rpt from * once more. **Rnd 13:** * Baby cable, p 3(6,3), k 1, baby cables, p 3, k 1, p 4, (k 2, p 4) 1(1,2) times; k 1, p 1, make (right cross over 2 sts, p 3, left cross over 2 sts, p 1) 3 times; k 1, p 4, (k 2, p 4) 1(1,2) times; k 1, p 3, k 1, 2 baby cables, p 3(6,3) from * once more. **Rnd 14:** * K 2, p 3(6,3), k 5, p 3, k 1, p 4, (k 2, p 4) 1(1,2) times; (make right cross over 3 sts, p 5) 3 times; right cross over 3 sts, p 4, (k 2, p 4) 1(1,2) times; k 1, p 3, k 5, p 3(6,3); rpt from * once more. **Rnd 15:** * Baby cable, p 3, 2 baby cables, k 1, p 3, k 1, p 4, (k 2, p 4) 1(1,2) times; k 1, p 1, (left cross over 2 sts, p 3, right cross over 2 sts, p 1) 3 times; k 1, p 4,(k 2, p 4) 1(1,2) times; k 1, p 3, 2 baby cables, k 1, p 3(6,3); rpt from * once more. **Rnd 16:** * K 2, p 3, k 5, p 3, k 1, p 4, (k 2, p 4) 1(1,2) times; k 1, p 2, (left cross over 2 sts, p 1, right cross over 2 sts, p 3) twice; left cross over 2 sts, p 1, right cross over 2 sts, p 2, k 1, p 4, (k 2, p 4) 1(1,2) times; k 1, p 3, k 5, p 3(6,3); rpt from * once more. **Rnd 17:** * Baby cable, p 3(6,3), k 1, 2 baby cables, p 3, k 1, p 4, (k 2, p 4) 1(1,2) times; k 1, p 3, (right cross over 3 sts, p 5) twice; right cross over 3 sts, p 3, k 1, p 4, (k 2, p 4) 1(1,2) times; k 1, p 3, k 1, 2 baby cables, p 3(6,3); rpt from * once more. Rpt last 16 rnds (Rnds 2 through 17) for pat until length is about 9(10,11)" from beg, end with an odd numbered rnd, put aside.
SLEEVES: With No.4 d p needles, cast on 44(48,54) sts. Divide sts evenly on 3 needles; being careful not to twist sts, join. Place marker on needle to indicate end of rnd, sl marker on every rnd. Work ribbing same as for Body for 4", inc 11(13,13) sts evenly spaced in last rnd — 55(61,67) sts. Change to No.6 d p needles and set up pat as follows: **Rnd 1:** K 2, p 3(6,3), k 5, p 3, k 1, p 4, (k 2, p 4) 1(1,2) times; k 1, p 3, *in next st k, p and k — 2 sts increased for center cross pat;* p 3, k 1, p 4, (k 2, p 4) 1(1,2) times; k 1, p 3, k 5, p 3(6,3) — 57(63,69) sts. **Rnd 2:** K 2, p 3(6,3), k 5, p 3, (make left trellis over next 3 sts; right trellis over next 3 sts) 2(2,3) times; p 3, k 3, p 3, (left trellis, right trellis) 2(2,3) times; p 3, k 5, p 3(6,3). Starting with Rnd 3, continue in pat as established same as for Body **EXCEPT** work only one set of crosses at center instead of 3 sets as indicated on back and front of body. Work even in pat until length is about 11(12,13)" from beg, end with same pat rnd as Body. Work first 5 sts of next rnd; sl these 5 sts plus last

3 sts from previous rnd (8 sts in all) onto a large safety pin for underarm. The baby cable from beg of each rnd will be centered on safety pin. Place rem 49(55,61) sts of Sleeve on a large st holder (or on any spare needle). Work other Sleeve in same way.

YOKE: Rnd 1 (Joining rnd): Pick up circular needle with Body sts; work first 5 sts of next rnd of Body; sl these 5 sts plus last 3 sts of previous rnd onto another safety pin (8 sts in all) for underarm. Keeping continuity of pat over each section throughout, work across to within 3 sts before single baby cable at other underarm; sl next 8 sts onto another safety pin for underarm. With same yarn, right side facing, work in pat across sts of one Sleeve; work across front sts of Body, then across second Sleeve — 228(252,276) sts on needle. These are 49(55,61) sts for each sleeve and 65(71,77) sts for front and back. **Rnd 2:** Keeping continuity of pat over each section, * work across to within 2 sts before next underarm junction, place a marker on needle; rpt from * around, end 2 sts before right back seam, place a different color marker on needle to indicate end of rnd; do not work over rem 2 sts. Remove original end-of-rnd marker. There are 4 markers; sl markers in every rnd. **Rnd 3:** * P 1, k 2, p 1; work even across to next marker; rpt from * around. **Rnd 4:** * P 1, make baby cable over 2 sts for raglan seam, p 1, work even to next marker; rpt from * around, end last rpt 2 sts before last marker. **Rnd 5(Dec Rnd):** * Dec one st before marker (to dec either p 2 tog or k 2 tog according to pat), p 1, k 2, p 1, dec one st, work across to within 2 sts before next marker; rpt from * around — dec made before and after each raglan seam. Rpt Rnds 4 and 5 alternately until there are 76(76,84) sts on needle, end with a dec rnd.
Note: When sts no longer fit on circular needle, change to No.6 d p needles.
Neck Shaping — Row 1: Change to No.4 d p needles. **Row 1:** Work in k 1, p 1 ribbing same as for bottom ribbing across back to next marker. Turn. **Row 2:** Work in ribbing as established across last row of ribbing, plus 2 extra sts. Turn. Rpt last row 5 more times. Turn. **Turtleneck:** With wrong side facing, work in rnds of k 1, p 1 ribbing (do not turn at end of rnds) until length is 3" from center front of neck. Bind off loosely in ribbing.
FINISHING: Weave underarms tog as follows: Sl sts off safety pins onto 2 separate d p needles; hold needles tog; thread a tapestry needle with a separate piece of yarn and attach to right end st on back needle, draw yarn through first st on front needle as if to p, leave st on needle, * draw yarn through next st on back needle as if to k, leave st on needle, draw yarn through same st on front needle as if to k, drop st off needle, draw yarn through next st on front needle as

if to p, leave st on needle, draw yarn through same st on back needle as if to p, drop st off needle; rpt from * until all sts are woven tog. Fasten off; with same strand pull tog triangle spaces at each end. Pin sweater to measurements on a padded surface, cover with a damp cloth; allow to dry: do not press but let air-dry.

EMBROIDERED TABLECLOTH

(page 78)

Finished embroidered center measures 26" in diameter.
MATERIALS: #18 tapestry needle; 21-threads-to-the-inch evenweave linen or homespun fabric, or purchased tablecloth (size depends on table size). Note: Use embroidery needle for homespun or purchased tablecloth. DMC #3 coton perlé in the following amounts and colors: 6 skeins #443 brown, 3 skeins #890 dark green, 5 skeins #909 medium green, 5 skeins #913 light green, 2 skeins #605 light pink, 2 skeins #603 medium pink, 2 skeins #718 dark pink, 2 skeins #552 dark purple, 1 skein #321 red, 1 skein #815 dark red, 1 skein #402 gold; transfer pencil; large embroidery hoop; basting needle and thread; tracing paper for pattern.
DIRECTIONS—Enlarging and Transferring the Pattern: Fold fabric in half lengthwise; press. Baste along fold; press out fold. Repeat for width. (These will be guidelines for centering design on fabric.) Following directions on page 18, enlarge pattern; transfer onto tracing paper (design given repeats in quarters). Retrace this enlarged design on large sheet of tracing paper which has been folded in quarters; repeat original tracing in each of the quarters until circular design is complete, making sure front half of bird matches back half where

sections meet, and pine branches also match. Turn tissue over; on reverse side, redraw all lines with transfer pencil. With this side down, center the pattern on the basting lines on tablecloth. Pin securely to the right side of the tablecloth. Pin in place around edges, smoothing paper out from center to remove any wrinkles or pleats. Press paper with hot iron in a circular motion to transfer the design to the fabric. Unpin and remove pattern. **To embroider:** Using hoop, embroider as follows, using photo and diagram as guides: Chain and Lazy Daisy Stitches (or Single Chain) are used throughout (see page 7 for Basic Embroidery Stitches). Place fabric in embroidery hoop (since the design is large, you will have to work it a section at a time). With chain Stitch, embroider the birds. Use the photo as a color guide. (Positions of dark purple and dark pink are switched on every other bird.) Birds' eyes and red berries are pairs of Chain Stitches worked in opposite directions. Work pine branches in brown Chain Stitch; work pine needles in Lazy Daisy or Single Chain Stitches, working dark green closest to center, then medium green, then lightest green. Work each section of stitches from the center (near branch) outward. (Note: To conserve floss, do not carry it across back of large floss frequently.) **To finish:** Remove basting stitches; fold edges of cloth over once and over again; press and hemstitch. For optional edging: Cut all leftover thread into equal lengths (approximately 21" each). Count out how many of each there are and separate into equal piles. Separate colors as to how you would like to see them alternate. Work Blanket or Buttonhole edging Stitch over 2 threads wide and 6 threads (¼") high, tying one color to the next as you get to the end of each color. Press entire cloth on wrong side over towel or padding to finish.

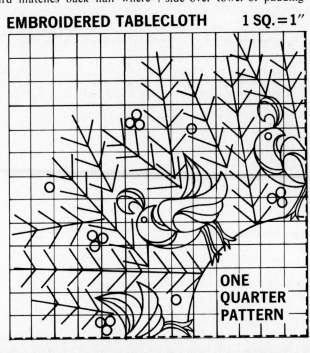

EMBROIDERED TABLECLOTH   1 SQ.=1"

ONE QUARTER PATTERN

(Continued from page 18.)
design makes squaring off easier.
2. Transfer the original design to clear, acetate graph paper.
3. Use Printing Technology Institute's "Craft Plan"™.

PILLOW DOLLS

(page 4)

MATERIALS: For all dolls, polyester fiberfill and white glue. **For Soldier:** ½ yd. of stiff red cotton duck for body, arms and coat front; felt in the following sizes and colors: 4″ × 6″ piece of white felt for face; 9″ × 9″ gold for visor, plume, epaulets, buttons, hands and stripes; 9″ × 8″ black for eyes, mustache, sideburns, boots and hat button; pinking shears; six-strand black embroidery floss. **For Daniel Boone:** ⅜ yd. of double-faced non-raveling vinyl suede cloth for body, tunic front, front fringe and arms; 6″ × 18″ of fake raccoon fur for hat and hat tail; felt in the following sizes and colors: 5″ × 6″ piece of white felt for face and hands; 6″ × 8″ brown for hair back, sideburns and mustache; 8″ × 8″ black for eyes, belt and boots. **For Engineer:** ½ yd. of stiff navy and white cotton ticking for body, arms and bib; 5″ × 5″ piece of red cotton bandana print for kerchief; felt in the following sizes and colors: 4″ × 6″ piece of white felt for face; 4″ × 7″ red for hands and visor; 5″ × 8″ black for eyes, boots, sideburns and mustache; 1½″ × 2½″ gold for buttons (2); pinking shears; six-strand black embroidery floss.

GENERAL DIRECTIONS: Following directions on page 18, enlarge and cut out all pattern pieces. Pin pieces to fabric, using materials list as a reference; cut out fabric, using pinking shears where indicated on pattern pieces. Cut fringe on lines as marked. If felt is very thin, cut four hand pieces for each doll and glue two together with rubber cement. All trim and detailing is applied to right side of fabric and seam allowance is ¼″ unless otherwise indicated. Use photo on page 4 as a guide for assembling all three dolls.

DIRECTIONS—For Soldier: Sew epaulets to top of arm pieces, ⅛″ from edge; sew stripes ½″ up from bottom edge. Fold arms in half lengthwise, right sides together; place flat edge of hand along bottom edge, facing inside of arm, thumb away from fold. Sew along bottom edge; turn and press with iron at lowest steam setting. Turn raw edges of underarm seam to inside; topstitch close to edge. Turn under ¼″ on top and side edges of coat front and pin to body front, matching notches at center bottom. Topstitch around three folded edges. Pin buttons to coat front and sew an "X" through all thicknesses with embroidery floss. Pin face to body, ¼″ up from top of coat front; stitch around face close to all edges. Pin sideburns in place, tops touching top edge of face; stitch close to all edges. Pin mustache in place; stitch close to all edges. Pin visor so top is ¼″ above top of face; stitch close to top edge. Pin plume in place in center of visor; place hat button over bottom of plume and topstitch around button, slightly in from pinked edges. Pin both arms to right side of body front, arms facing in toward center, fold at top, lining up with notch. Stitch arms in place close to edge, making sure fringe on epaulets is free. Pin boots to right side of body front, centered from bottom notch, ¼″ apart, toes pointing out. Sew in place across bottom edge with a ⅜″ seam. Pin body back piece to body front, right sides together with arms and boots inside; stitch around sides and top. Turn and stuff with polyester fiberfill; turn under ⅜″ on bottom of body back piece and slipstitch bottom opening closed. Glue eyes on face with white glue.

For Daniel Boone: Fold arms in half lengthwise from top point and bottom notch. Finish arms, following directions for soldier, turning under raw edge of underarm only on side without fringe. Sew face, sideburns and mustache to body front, following directions for soldier. Pin tunic to body front, wrong side of tunic to right side of body, with bottom edge of fringe ¼″ up from bottom of body front; sew along top edge. Pin and sew belt over

PILLOW DOLLS
S - CUT HERE FOR BODY
S - SLEEVE STRIPE CUT 2
1 SQ. = 1″
S-COAT FRONT CUT 1
E - CUT HERE FOR BODY
DB - CUT HERE FOR BODY
S-EPAULETS & PLUME CUT 3
S/E - NOTCHES
DB - NOTCHES
DB - NOTCHES
⅜″
BODY FRONT AND BACK
⅜″
S - HAT BUTTON CUT 1
S - BOOT CUT 2
EYE - CUT 2
CENTER STITCHING LINE
S/E - ARM CUT 2
S/E BUTTON CUT 6/2
E - BIB CUT 1
S/E - VISOR CUT 1
E - KERCHIEF CUT 1
E - MUSTACHE CUT 1
S/E SIDEBURNS CUT 2
PINKED EDGES
DB - HAT CUT 2
S/E - CUT HERE
FACE CUT 1
DB - CUT HERE
DB-HAIR BACK CUT 1
DB - FRONT TUNIC CUT 1
DB - SLEEVE CUT 2
DB-FRONT FRINGE CUT 1
DART
DB/S - MUSTACHE CUT 1
⅜″
E/DB - BOOT
CUT 2
HAND CUT 2
DB - SIDEBURNS CUT 2
DB - BELT CUT 2
DB -HAT TAIL CUT 1

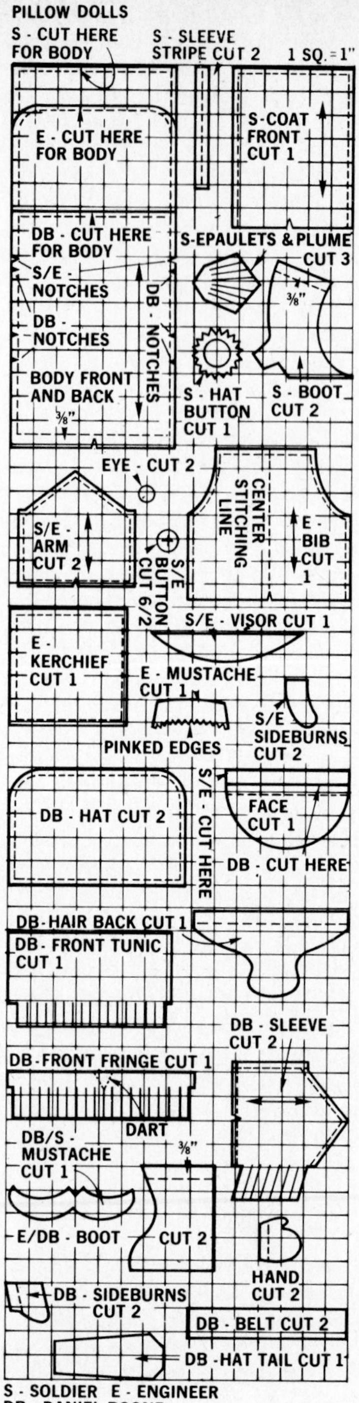

S - SOLDIER E - ENGINEER
DB - DANIEL BOONE
⟷ LENGTHWISE GRAIN OF FABRIC
ALL SEAMS ¼″ UNLESS OTHERWISE NOTED

HOW TO TAKE BODY MEASUREMENTS:

It's easy to determine the correct size for any crocheted or knitted garment. First, make sure the person you're measuring is wearing the usual undergarments. For all women's and girls' sizes, measure at the fullest part of natural waistline, hips and bust. We've made allowances for ease to insure a proper fit. If you have to make adjustments between the measurements and size differential, do it during the blocking and finishing. Determine men's sizes by loosely holding the tape around the fullest part of the chest.

STANDARD BODY MEASUREMENTS:

All measurements in inches.

JUNIORS

Size	7	9	11	13	15
Bust	31	32	33½	35	37
Waist	22½	23½	24½	26	28
Hip	33	34	35½	37	39

TEENS

Size	7/8	9/10	11/12	13/14
Bust	29	30½	32	33½
Waist	23	24	25	26
Hip	32	33½	35	36½

MISSES

Size	8	10	12	14	16	18
Bust	31½	32½	34	36	38	40
Waist	23	24	25½	27	29	31
Hip	33½	34½	36	38	40	42

WOMEN

Size	38	40	42	44	46	48
Bust	42	44	46	48	50	52
Waist	34	36	38	40½	43	45½
Hip	44	46	48	50	52	54

MEN

Size	34	36	38	40	42	44
Chest	34	36	38	40	42	44
Waist	30	32	34	36	38	40

raw top edge of tunic, matching belt to lower notches on body sides; stitch close to top and bottom edges. Repeat for sewing back belt to body back piece. Fold front fringe in half crosswise, right sides together; make a small dart where marked on pattern piece. Pin fringe in place on body front piece with center of "V" at center of body; topstitch along upper edge. Pin hair back to body back piece, matching top edges; stitch close to edge. With right sides together, sew hat pieces to body front and back, top edges of back and front pieces lined up with bottom edges of hat. Push fur away from seam to stitch. Finish doll, following directions for soldier. Sew hat tail on by hand, wrong side of tail to right side of hat, lengthwise center of tail lined up along left side seam.

For Engineer: Make arms, following directions for soldier. Turn under ¼" along top and pocket curves of bib, clipping if necessary; topstitch ⅛" from fold. Pin bib to body front, matching bottom notches. Sew down center line from top to bottom of bib; stitch again over first stitching. Topstitch across top and along side edges of bib, leaving pockets open. Sew face, sideburns, mustache and visor to body front, following directions for soldier. Pin buttons to top edge of bib and sew an "X" through all thicknesses with embroidery floss. Finish doll, following directions for soldier. Hem raw edges of kerchief and place in bib pocket.

CHEVRON RAINBOW SWEATER

(page 6)

Directions are given for size Small (8-10). Changes for sizes Medium (12-14) and Large (16-18) are in parentheses.

MATERIALS: Brunswick "Windrush" 4 oz. skeins, *for each size:* 1 skein each of Dk. Green #9044 (A), Lime #9093 (B), Misty Lime #90921 (C), Med. Aqua #90392 (D), Dk Aqua #90393 (E), Royal #9012 (F), Purple #9014 (G), Bright Scarlet #9025 (H), Orange #9006 (I), Honey #9027 (J); crochet hook, Size H OR ANY SIZE HOOK WHICH WILL OBTAIN THE STITCH GAUGE BELOW.
GAUGE: 3 dc = 1"; 3 rows (measuring straight up) = 2". One complete pattern = 3½ (4, 4)".
MEASUREMENTS:

Sizes:	Small (8-10)	Medium (12-14)	Large (16-18)
Bust:	33"	37"	41"
Width across back or front at underarms (including edging)	16½"	18½"	20½"
Width across sleeve at upper arm (including edging):	13"	14"	15"

DIRECTIONS—BACK: Starting at lower edge with A, ch 57 (65, 71) to measure 19 (21, 23½)". **Row 1:** Dc in 4th ch from hook, dc in each of next 3 (3, 6) ch, * sk next 2 ch sts, dc in each of next 4 (5, 5) ch, 3 dc in next ch, dc in each next 4 (5, 5) ch; rpt from * across to within last 6 (6, 9) ch, sk next 2 ch, dc in each of next 3 (3, 6) ch, 2 dc in last ch—54 (62, 68) dc, counting chain at beg of row as 1 dc. Ch 3, turn. Mark Row 1 for right side. **Row 2:** Dc in first dc, dc in each of next 3 (3, 6) dc, * sk next 2 dc, dc in each of next 4 (5, 5) dc, 3 dc in next dc, dc in each of next 4 (5, 5) dc; rpt from * across to within last 6 (6, 9) dc, counting chain at end of row as 1 dc, sk next 2 dc, dc in next 3 (3, 6) dc, 2 dc in top of turning chain—same number of sts as on last row. Last row forms the Chevron pattern stitch. Ch

3, turn. **Row 3:** Rpt Row 2. Ch 3, turn. **Row 4:** Work same as for Row 2 to within ch-3, 1 dc in top of ch-3; *holding back on hook last loop of dc, make another dc in top of ch-3; cut A, leaving a 2" end; attach B and draw a B loop through the 2 loops on hook—color change made;* (always make color change in this manner), with B, ch 3 to count as first dc of next row, turn. **Row 5:** With B, work as for Row 2 to within ch-3, 2 dc in top of ch-3, changing to C in last dc; ch 3, turn. Always count turning ch-3 as first dc of following row. **Row 6:** With C, work as Row 2, changing to D at end of row, as before; ch 3, turn. Continuing to work as for Row 2, change color at end of each row as directed and ch 3, turn, using colors in the following sequence: **Row 7:** D. **Row 8:** E. **Row 9:** F. **Row 10:** G. **Row 11:** H. **Row 12:** I. **Row 13:** J. Working in pattern st, rpt last 9 rows (Rows 5 through 13) for color sequence until total length, along side edge, is approximately 16½", or desired length to underarms. Change to next color at end of last row; with new color, ch 52 (56, 56) for Sleeve, turn.
SLEEVES—Row 1: Dc in 4th ch from hook, dc in each of next 48(52, 52) ch, 2 dc in first dc on last row, work in pattern across, ending with 2 dc in top of ch-3 (do not change color). Drop loop from hook; attach a separate strand of same color being used in same st as last dc, ch 50(54, 54) for other Sleeve, cut this strand and fasten; pick up dropped loop, working along chain just made, dc in each of 50(54, 54) ch sts, changing to next color in last dc—154(170, 176) dc, counting chain at beg of row as 1 dc. Ch 3, turn. **Row 2:** With new color, sk first dc, dc in each of next 49(53, 53) dc on sleeve, 2 dc in next dc; work in pattern across to within the 50(54, 54) sts of other Sleeve, ending with 2 dc

---

HOW TO ESTIMATE YARDAGE

The fabrics we sew today come in many widths. Since the space on the pattern envelope is limited, at times the fabric width chosen may not be included in the yardage chart provided for each pattern.
The Fabric Conversion Chart reprinted below was developed by Rutgers, The State University of New Jersey, Cooperative Extension Service, to help estimate the yardage for different fabric widths.

FABRIC CONVERSION CHART

FABRIC WIDTH	32"	35"-36"	39"	41"	44"-45"	50"	52"-54"	58"-60"
Yardage*	1⁷	1¾	1½	1½	1³	1¼	1¹	1
	2¼	2	1¾	1¾	1⁵	1½	1³	1¼
	2½	2¼	2	2	1¾	1⁵	1½	1³
	2¾	2½	2¼	2¼	2¹	1¾	1¾	1⁵
*Add an additional ¼ yd. for wide span conversion in fabric, for nap or one directional prints, for styles with sleeves cut in one piece with body of garment.	3¹	2⁷	2½	2½	2¼	2	1⁷	1¾
	3³	3¹	2¾	2¾	2½	2¼	2	1⁷
	3¾	3³	3	2⁷	2¾	2³	2¼	2
	4	3¾	3¼	3¹	2⁷	2⁵	2³	2¼
	4³	4¼	3½	3³	3¹	2¾	2⁵	2³
	4⁵	4½	3¾	3⁵	3³	3	2¾	2⁵
	5	4¾	4	3⁷	3⁵	3¼	2⁷	2¾
	5¼	5	4¼	4¹	3⁷	3³	3¹	2⁷

Reprinted courtesy of: New Jersey Cooperative Extension Service, Rutgers, The State University

in last dc before Sleeve; dc in each dc across Sleeve, dc in top of turning chain, changing to next color. Ch 3, turn. Continuing to work in same color sequence, rpt last row until Sleeves measure approximately 6(6½, 7)″ from chains at underarms. End last row with dc in top of ch-3. Cut yarn and fasten.

Edging: With right side facing, starting at end of first row on right-hand side edge of body, attach A to end st of Row 1; working along ends of rows, ch 3, dc over end of same row, work 2 dc over end of each row along right side edge to underarm, dc in each ch across chain at underarm of sleeve, ending with 3 dc in corner st; along sleeve edge make * sc over end of next row, 3 dc over end of next row; rpt from * across sleeve edge to next corner, end with 3 dc in either corner st or over end of last row; working across top row, make (dc in each dc to within one dc before next 3-dc group, hdc in next dc, sc in next 3 dc, hdc in next dc) 4 times; dc in each rem dc to end of row; now work across sleeve edge, along underarm of sleeve and along left side edge to correspond with opposite side. Cut yarn and fasten.

FRONT: Work same as Back, including Edging. (Start edging at lower corner of left side.)

FINISHING: Pin each section to measurements on a padded surface; cover with a damp cloth, allow to dry; **do not press.** Sew side and underarm of sleeve seams, matching sts. Leaving center 8(8½, 8½)″ open for neck, sew shoulder and top of sleeve seams.

Drawstring: Make a chain the desired length. Sl st in 2nd ch from hook and in each ch across. Cut yarn and fasten. Run drawstring through spaces at waist.

BOAT NECK SWEATER

(page 6)

Directions are given for size Small (6-8). Changes for sizes Medium (10-12) and Large (14-16) are in parentheses.

MATERIALS: Lion Brand ''Pamela'' 4-ply 4 oz. skeins worsted weight, 1(1, 2) Navy (A); 1(1, 2) Red (B); 2(2, 3) Yellow (C); 1(1, 2) Orange (D); knitting needles No. 8 OR ANY SIZE NEEDLES WHICH WILL OBTAIN THE STITCH GAUGE BELOW; crochet hook No. H.

GAUGE: On No. 8 needles 4 sts = 1″; 5 rows stockinette stitch = 1″.

MEASUREMENTS:

	Small	Medium	Large
Size:	(6-8)	(10-12)	(14-16)
Bust:	34″	37″	40″
Width across			

back or front
at under arm: 17″ 18½″ 20″
Width of sleeve at
upper arm: 14″ 15½″ 17″

(**Note:** Sweater is knitted in one piece beginning at lower edge of front.)

DIRECTIONS—FRONT: With A, cast on 68(74, 80) sts. **Rows 1-10:** Work in garter st for 10 rows. **Row 11:** Right side k. **Row 12:** K 6, p 56(62, 68) sts, k 6. Rpt rows 11 and 12 as Pattern. Work 38(40, 42) rows, cut A and attach B. Work 38(40, 42) rows B. Cut B and attach C. Work 10(12, 14) rows ending with a p row. **Shape Sleeves:** At beginning of next row, cast on 62(68, 74) sts. Knit right across row. At beginning of second row, cast on 62(68, 74) sts. Now k 68(74, 80) sts. P 56(62, 68) sts and k 68(74, 80) sts. There should be 192(210, 228) sts on needle. Repeat these two rows 8 times (5 ridges of garter stitch). Now working 6 sts at beginning and end of each row in garter st and center 180(198, 216) sts in stockinette st, continue straight until 34(36, 38) rows have been worked in C. Cut C and attach D. Continue in stockinette st with 6 sts at beginning and end of each row in garter stitch for 9(11, 13) rows, ending with a k row.

Shape Neck: *With work side facing k 6, P 72(77, 85) sts, K 40(44, 48) sts. P 72(77, 85) sts, k 6 sts. Next row k.* Repeat these 2 rows 7 times—5 ridges.

Bind off for Boat Neck: K 6. P 72(77, 85) sts. K 8(8, 10) sts. Bind off 24(28, 28) sts. K 8(8, 10) sts, p 72(77, 85) sts. K 6. **Next Row:** K 84(91, 100) cast on 24(28, 28) sts. K to end of row. Now work from * to * of neck shaping 9 times. Continue in stockinette st working 6 sts at beginning and end of each row in garter stitch for 9(11, 13) rows. Cut D and rejoin C, work 14 rows. Still using C, work 1 row knit. **Next Row:** K 68(74, 80) sts. P 56(62, 68) sts. K 68(74, 80) sts. Repeat these two rows 8 times. Bind off 62(68, 74) sts at beginning of next 2 rows. Now finish Back to correspond to Front.

FINISHING: Steam lightly using a damp cloth and warm iron. **Tie Bands:** Using double yarn, make a chain to measure 10″. Make 8 ties in C, 4 in A and 4 in B. Attach to sweater at side and sleeve edges as shown in photograph.

LAVENDER V-NECK CARDIGAN

(page 10)

Directions are given for size Small (8). Changes for sizes 10, 12 and 14 are in parentheses.

MATERIALS: Unger's ''Darling'' 1 4/10 oz. balls: 6 (7, 8, 8) balls color No. 09; knitting needles size 6 OR ANY SIZE NEEDLES WHICH WILL OB-

TAIN THE STITCH GAUGE BELOW; steel crochet hook size 3; tapestry needle.

GAUGE: 5 sts = 1″.

DIRECTIONS—BACK: Cast on 76 (80, 84, 88) sts. K 1 row, p 1 row for 7 rows (hem). K 1 row on wrong side (hemline). Change to Stockinette St. Work even 16 rows. Inc 1 st each end of next row, then every 10th row 4 times more—86 (90, 94, 98) sts. Work even until 12½″ from hemline, or desired length to underarm. Place a marker at each end for armhole. Work even until armhole measures 4½ (4¾, 5, 5¼)″, ending with a p row. **Shape Neck and Shoulders.** Work 36 (37, 38, 39) sts, attach a 2nd ball of yarn, bind off center 14 (16, 18, 20) sts loosely, work 36 (37, 38, 39) sts. Working both sides at same time, at each neck edge, bind off 2 sts every other row 5 times, dec 1 st every row 5 times—21 (22, 23, 24) sts. Work even until armhole measures 7 (7¼, 7½, 7¾)″. At each arm edge, bind off 7 sts every other row 2 times, 7 (8, 9, 10) sts once.

LEFT FRONT: Cast on 40 (42, 46, 50) sts. Work hem and hemline as for Back. Change to Stockinette St. Work even 16 rows. Inc 1 st at side edge, then every 10th row 4 times more—45 (47, 51, 55) sts. Work to within 1″ of armhole. **Shape Neck:** K to within 3 sts from front edge, k 2 tog (neck dec), k 1. Repeat neck dec every other row 23 (24, 25, 26) times more, every row 0 (0, 2, 4) times—21 (22, 23, 24) sts. **At the same time,** when same length as Back to underarm, place a marker at arm edge. Work to shoulder as for Back. **Shape Shoulder:** At arm edge, bind off 7 sts every other row twice, 7 (8, 9, 10) sts once.

RIGHT FRONT: Work to correspond to Left Front, reversing shaping.

SLEEVES: Sew shoulder seams. With right side facing, pick up 70 (72, 76, 80) sts across armhole edge from marker to marker. Work Stockinette St (start with a p row), decreasing 1 st each end every 10th row 9 (9, 8, 8) times, every 6th row 0 (0, 2, 3) times—52 (54, 56, 58) sts. Work even until 13 (13½, 14, 14)″ from beg, or desired length. Bind off.

FINISHING: Sew side seams. Turn lower hem to wrong side and sew in place. **Front Border:** Attach yarn at lower right front corner. Work 1 row of sc along right front, around neck and along left front (make sure to keep work flat). Ch 1, turn. Work 1 sc in each sc to start of V-neck of left front. Ch 1, turn. Work 1 sc in each sc along left front. **Next Row:** With right side facing, working backwards from left to right, sc in each sc to start of V-neck. Fasten off. Mark for 10 buttons evenly spaced along left front edge. With wrong side facing, attach yarn at start of V-neck of right front. Work 1 row of sc along right front edge, working in 10 buttonholes opposite markers for buttons. **Buttonhole:** Ch 2, skip 1 sc, sc in next sc. Ch 1, turn. Work 1 row of sc along right front, working 1 sc under each ch-2. Work last row as for last row of left front. **Buttons:** Make 10. Ch 2, 6 sc in 2nd ch from hook. **Next rnd:** 2 sc in each sc—12 sc. Fasten off, leaving a long strand. With tapestry needle, draw edge tog to form a small ball-like button. Fill button with yarn and sew back tog securely. Sew on buttons. **Do not block or press.** Wet block. (Wet with cold water. Lay on a towel to measurements. Dry away from heat and sun.)

POPCORN PEASANT BLOUSE

(page 10)

Directions are given for size Small (6-8). Changes for sizes Medium (10-12) and Large (14-16) are in parentheses.

MATERIALS: Coats & Clark "Red Heart" Sock & Sweater Yarn, 3-ply, 2 oz. skeins: 7 (8, 8) skeins of color #767 "Rose Nova"; crochet hook, size F OR ANY SIZE HOOK WHICH WILL OBTAIN THE STITCH GAUGE BELOW; ½ yd. round elastic.
GAUGE: 7 spaces or popcorn sts = 3"; 7 rows = 3".
MEASUREMENTS:

Sizes:	Small (6-8)	Medium (10-12)	Large (14-16)
Body bust size:	30½-31½"	32½-34"	36-38"
Width across back or front at underarm:	19"	22"	24½"
Length from shoulder to lower edge:	20½"	21½"	22½"
Width across sleeve at upper arm:	17½"	18¼"	19"
Length of sleeve seam:	18"	19"	19"

DIRECTIONS—BACK: Starting at lower edge, ch 94 (106, 118), having 14 ch sts to 3". **Row 1 (right side):** Dc in 6th ch from hook to make first sp; * ch 1, skip next ch, dc in next ch. Repeat from * across—45 (51, 57) sps. Ch 4, turn. **Row 2:** *Dc in next dc—* **starting sp over sp made;** * ch 1, dc in next dc—sp over sp made. Repeat from * across to turning chain sp, ch 1, skip next ch, dc in 3rd ch of turning chain—45 (51, 57) sps. Ch 4, turn. **Row 3:** Make 4 (1, 4) sps, *make 4 dc in next sp, drop loop from hook, insert hook from front to back in first dc of

the 4-dc group and draw dropped loop through, ch 1 to fasten—**front pc st over sp made;** dc in next dc; make 5 sps. Repeat from * across, end last repeat with 4 (1, 4) sps. Ch 4 (3, 4), turn. **Row 4:** Make 3 (0, 3) sps, *make 4 dc in next sp, drop loop from hook, insert hook from back to front in first dc of the 4-dc group and draw dropped loop through, ch 1 to fasten—**back pc st over sp made;** dc in next dc, ch 1, skip next pc st, dc in next dc—sp over pc st made; back pc st over next sp, sp over next 3 sps. Repeat from * across, end last repeat with 2 (0, 2) sps, ch 1 (0, 1), dc in 3rd ch of turning chain. Ch 4, turn. Repeat Rows 3 and 4 alternately for pattern. Work in pattern until 36 (38, 40) rows in all have been completed. Ch 4, turn.

Neck and Shoulder Shaping—Next Row: Work in pattern over first 9 (11, 13) sps or pc sts. Ch 4, turn. Continue in pattern for 11 more rows. Break off and fasten. With right side facing, skip center 27 (29, 31) sps or pc sts on last long row worked before Neck Shaping; attach yarn to next dc, ch 4, complete in pattern across—9, (11, 13) sps or pc sts. Ch 4, turn. Complete as for other side.

FRONT: Work as for Back.

SLEEVES: Starting at lower edge, ch 86 (90, 94), having 14 ch sts to 3". **Row 1:** Work as for Back—41 (43, 45) sps. **Row 2:** Work as for Row 2 of Back. **Row 3:** Make 2 (3, 4) sps, * front pc st in next sp, sp over each of next 5 sps. Repeat from * across, end last repeat with 2 (3, 4) sps over each of last 2 (3, 4) sps. Ch 4, turn. **Row 4:** Make 1 (2, 3) sps, * back pc st over next sp, sp over next pc st, back pc st over next sp, sp over next 3 sps. Repeat from * across, end last repeat with sp over each of last 1 (2, 3) sps. Ch 4, turn. Work in pattern as established until 42 (44, 44) rows in all have been completed. Break off and fasten. Pin pieces to measurements on a padded surface; dampen and leave to dry; **do not press.** Sew shoulder seams.

FINISHING—Neck Edging: With right side facing, attach yarn to any shoulder seam, ch 1, sc in same place where yarn was attached; * ch 2, sc in end st of each row or in each dc. Repeat from * around, end with ch 2. Join to first sc. Break off and fasten. Starting at lower edge, matching rows, sew first 11½" (12", 13") for side seams. Sew sleeve seams. Sew in sleeves.

Sleeve Edging: Attach yarn to sleeve seam; working over elastic, sc in each st around, along starting chain. Break off and fasten. Adjust elastic to desired length, allowing ½" for sewing, cut overlap ends, sew together.

Bottom Tie: Make a chain to measure 60" (66", 70") long. Sl st in 2nd ch from

hook and in each ch across. Break off and fasten. Lace through first row of sps to tie in front. Knot at each end. **Neck Tie:** Make a chain to measure 50" (52", 54"). Complete as for Bottom Tie. Lace through sps on neck edging, to tie in front. Knot at each end.

PINK CLUTCH BAG

(page 13)

MATERIALS: M E Enterprises "Warp and Woof Weaving Board" Kit. (Kit includes: Weaving board measuring 13½"×18"; one 15" shuttle; one 6" shuttle; one large weaving needle.)
(**Note:** It would be advisable to purchase an additional large weaving needle.) Bucilla yarns: 1 skein "Warp Cotton" color #200 Natural, for warp; 1 skein "Multi-Craft," color #10 Bright Rose (A); 1 ball "Rustique," color #1 Natural White (B); 1 skein "Mimosa," color #3 Red (C); 1 skein "Persian Needlepoint and Crewel," Art. 4612, color #43 French Blue (D); 1 skein "Fruitwood," color #7 Blue (E); 1 skein each "Persian Needlepoint and Crewel," color #3 Dk. Yellow (F), color #15 Dk. Pink (G), color #30 Violet (H); ⅜ yd. lightweight fabric for lining; Velcro® fasteners.
DIRECTIONS: Use Warp Cotton to warp, following directions in weaving kit. To weave, follow general directions in kit. Note that your woof should be loosely woven to avoid pulling the warp lines. Use small shuttle or weaving needle. Allow 3" of yarn at beginning and end of each row for fringe.(**Note:** All colors except A are used with yarn double on needle or shuttle.) **Step 1:** Beginning at bottom, weave 7 rows A (single ply). **Step 2:** Weave 1 row B. **Step 3:** Weave 1 row C. **Step 4:** Weave 2 rows D. **Step 5:** Weave 1 row E. **Step 6:** Weave 2 rows F. **Step 7:** Repeat Step 6. **Step 8:** Repeat Step 5. **Step 9:** Repeat Step 4. **Step 10:** Repeat Step 3. **Step 11:** Repeat Step 2. **Step 12:** Weave 4 rows G. **Step 13:** Weave 1 row H. **Step 14:** Weave 1 row C. **Step 15:** Weave 1 row H. **Step 16:** Repeat Steps 12-15 seven times. **Step 17:** Weave 4 rows G. **Step 18:** Repeat Steps 2-10. **Step 19:** Weave 7 rows A (single ply). To remove weaving from board, see directions for WOVEN PILLOW, page 109.

FINISHING: With zigzag stitch, staystitch weaving along edge of fringe. Cut lining same size as weaving (excluding fringe). Press long edges of lining under scant ¼". Pin lining to weaving, right sides together; seam short edges. Turn right sides out; press. Fold bag in half, right sides out, with fringe on sides.

Do two rows of topstitching at sides, ¼" and ⅜" from fringe, catching in lining. Close top with Velcro® fasteners.

(**Note:** This design could also be turned into a pillow, following directions for WOVEN PILLOW, page 109.)

GREY CLUTCH BAG

(page 13)

Materials and weaving directions for bag are the same as for WOVEN PILLOW, page 109. Directions below are for finishing bag.

FINISHING: Cut fabric for lining same size as weaving. Pin weaving to lining, right sides together. Stitch seams at short sides. Re-fold lining and weaving along center lines so that seams match. Stitch sides, leaving an opening in one side for turning. Turn right side out; slipstitch opening. Push lining into bag. Make tassel (see WOVEN PILLOW, page 109) and attach to one upper corner. If desired, close with Velcro® fasteners.

INFANT'S MARY-JANE SOCKS

(page 16)

Measurements are given for 5" from heel to toe; 7" stretched at top.

MATERIALS: Small amounts of Fingering Weight yarn in green, pink and white, or desired colors; knitting needles, one pair each, No. 2 and No. 0 OR ANY SIZE NEEDLES WHICH WILL OBTAIN THE STITCH GAUGE BELOW; two ⅜" buttons; two stitch holders.

GAUGE: 7 sts = 1" on No. 2 needles.

DIRECTIONS—SOCK: Starting at top with pink and No. 2 needles, cast on 42 sts. Break off pink, join white and work in k 1, p 1 rib for 2 rows; then p one row.

Begin Pattern St—Row 1 (right side): K 1, * k 2 tog, yo, k 1, yo, sl 1, k 1, psso, k 5 *, rpt from *, end k 6. **Row 2:** P 8, * sl 1 purlwise, p 9 * rpt from *, end p 3. **Row 3:** Rpt Row 1. **Row 4:** Rpt Row 2. **Row 5:** K. **Row 6:** P. **Row 7:** K 1, * k 5, k 2 tog, yo, k 1, yo, sl 1, k 1, psso, * rpt from *, end k 1. **Row 8:** P 3, * sl 1 purlwise, p 9 *, rpt from *, end p 8. **Row 9:** Rpt Row 7. **Row 10:** Rpt Row 8. **Row 11:** K. **Row 12:** P. Repeat pattern Rows 1-12 once more. Work 2 rows st st, or desired length to ankle. Change to No. 0 needles and work 4 rows k 1, p 1 rib. Break off white, leaving 12" end for back seam.

Shape Instep: Slip 1st 15 sts to holder; join white and with No. 2 needles, k across next 12 sts; slip remaining 15 sts to 2nd holder. Continue in st st on center 12 sts for 15 rows (about 1½"), ending with p row. Break off white. **Shape Foot:** With green, k 15 sts from

1st holder; pick up and k 15 sts along right side of instep; k across 12 sts on left needle; pick up and k 15 sts along other side of instep; k 15 sts from 2nd holder — 72 sts. K 2 rows.

Shape Toe — Inc Row (wrong side): K 31, inc 1 st in each of next 10 sts, k 31 — 82 sts. Continue in Garter st for 12 rows (about 1" from 1st ridge of garter section), end at right side.

Dec Row: K 25, k 2 tog 16 times, k 25. — 66 sts. K 1 row.

Shape Sole — Row 1: K 2 tog, k 29, k 2 tog twice, k 29, k 2 tog (4 sts dec). **Rows 2, 4, 6:** K. **Row 3:** K 2 tog, k 27, k 2 tog twice, k 27, k 2 tog (4 sts dec). **Row 5:** K 2 tog, k 25, k 2 tog twice, k 25, k 2 tog (4 sts dec). **Row 7:** K 2 tog, k 23, k 2 tog twice, k 23, k 2 tog — 50 sts. **Row 8:** K 2 tog, k 23, fold in half, wrong sides tog, and graft sts together for sole seam as follows: Cut yarn, leaving 32" length. With darning needle, * insert in first st on back needle as to p; insert in first st of front needle as to k and slip front st off needle; insert in 2nd st on front needle as to p; insert in 1st st on back needle as to k and slip off needle, * rpt from *, working sts off needles one at a time until 2 sts remain on back-needle and work these off together. Weave remainder of garter section seam for heel. Fasten off green.

FINISHING: Weave in ends on wrong side. With 12" end and darning needle, weave back sock seam.

Strap: With green and No. 2 needles, cast on 42 sts. **Row 1:** K 2, bind off 2 sts for buttonhole, k to end. **Row 2:** K across, casting on 2 sts over bound-off sts. **Row 3:** Bind off. Sew on button. Tack strap at back seam, so that button end comes at side of shoe.

BABY'S DYED T-SHIRT

(page 16)

MATERIALS: 1 T-shirt (Carter's) with side snaps; 1 package Rit Dye, color Purple; 1 package Rickrack (Talon), color Turquoise; 1 spool orange thread.

DIRECTIONS: Dye T-shirt according to directions on Rit Dye package. To trim, place rickrack *under* edge of T-shirt and topstitch in place. Use a decorative stitch with orange thread.

BABY'S SUNDRESS OR BIB

(page 16)

MATERIALS: 2 lightweight face cloths in color of your choice; 1 yd. of 1"-wide novelty trim; 1½ yds. washable ribbon.

DIRECTIONS: Place cloths together, wrong sides facing. Topstitch narrow side seams, leaving 3½" open

at top and bottom. At each top corner, take a ¾" tuck toward curved outside edge; stitch firmly in place. Divide the ribbon into 4 pieces and stitch in place for shoulder ties. Add novelty trim approximately 2" up from bottom edge.

INFANT'S CROCHETED-COLLAR SAQUE

(page 16)

MATERIALS: J. & P. Coats "Knit-Cro-Sheen" Mercerized knitting and crochet, Art. A. 64; steel crochet hook, Size 7 OR ANY SIZE HOOK WHICH WILL OBTAIN THE STITCH GAUGE BELOW; purchased layette-sized saque (ours, Carter's).

GAUGE: 5 dc = 1".

DIRECTIONS: Starting at neck edge, ch 94. **Row 1:** Dc in 5th ch from hook, * ch 1, skip 1 ch, dc in next ch. Repeat from * ending row with dc in last ch — 46 dc. Ch 4, turn. **Row 2:** Dc in 1st dc, ch 1, (dc, ch 1, dc) in next dc and in each dc across row ending with dc, ch 1, dc in 3rd ch of ch-4 — 92 dc. Ch 4, turn. **Row 3:** Dc in 2nd dc, * ch 1, dc in next dc. Repeat from * ending row with dc in 3rd ch of ch-4. Ch 4, turn. **Row 4:** Repeat Row 3. **Row 5:** Dc in 2nd dc, * ch 2, sl st in dc just made (picot formed), ch 1, dc in next dc, ch 1, dc in next dc. Repeat from * across row. Fasten off.

FINISHING: Slipstitch crocheted ruffle to saque. For embroidery, write "Bebe" on tissue paper in longhand and transfer to saque. Baste a piece of batiste on back edge of area to be embroidered to prevent stretching. Hand embroider in a chain stitch, or use a decorative stitch on the sewing machine.

CROCHETED SWEATER AND HAT

(page 19)

Directions are given for size Small (6-8). Changes for Medium (10-12) and Large (14-16) are in parentheses.

MATERIALS: Unger's "Britania", 1 6/10 oz balls: 10 (12, 14) balls of color #553 for sweater, and 4 balls for hat; aluminum crochet hook, size J OR ANY SIZE NEEDLES WHICH WILL OBTAIN THE STITCH GAUGE BELOW.

GAUGE: 5 dc = 2"; 4 rows = 3".

DIRECTIONS—SLEEVES AND TOP YOKE: With double strand, ch 40 (42, 44). **Row 1:** Dc in 4th ch from hook, dc in each ch across — 38 (40, 42) dc, counting turning ch as a st. Ch 3, turn. **Row 2:** Ch 3 on turn is always counted as first st, dc in each st. Ch 3, turn. Repeat Row 2 for pattern. Work even until 16" from beg, or 1" less than desired length to underarm. Place a marker at each side for end of sleeve.

Work even 7 (8, 9) rows from sleeve marker for shoulder—shoulder should measure approx 5 (5½, 6)". **Split For Neck:** Work 13 (14, 15) sts, ch 3, turn (neck edge). Work even on these sts for 9 (9, 11) rows more—10 (10, 12) rows in all. Place a marker at center of neck. Go back to row that you split for neck, leave out 12 sts at neck edge to go over shoulder, attach double strand and work remaining 13 (14, 15) sts for 10 (10, 12) rows as for other side. Join each side of 13 (14, 15) sts with a ch 12 in between. Fasten off. **Next row:** Reattach double strand at beg of row and work dc in all sts and 1 dc in each of the 12 chs—38 (40, 42) sts. Work even for same number of rows to correspond to other shoulder. Place a marker at each end for start of sleeve. Work even same number of rows to correspond to other sleeve. Fasten off.
BACK: With right side facing, attach double strand at underarm marker, ch 3, work 47 (49, 51) dc more across yoke edge to other underarm marker—24 (25, 26) dc on each side of center neck, counting ch 3 as a st. Work even in dc for 5". Dec 1 st each end to dec. Ch 3 on turn is first st, yo draw up a loop in next st and retain 3 loops on hook, draw up a loop in next st, yo draw through 2 loops, yo draw through remaining loops, work across to within 3 sts from end, dec 1 st over next 2 sts, work last st—46 (48, 50) sts. Work even until 14" from underarm, or 1" less than desired length. Fasten off.
FRONT: Work same as for Back on other side of yoke.
FINISHING: Weave undersleeve and side seams. **Sleeve Trim:** Attach double strand at seam. Work 2 rnds of sc, having a multiple of 3 sts. **Last rnd:** * Ch 3, skip 2 sc, sc in next sc; repeat from * around. Fasten off. **Lower Trim:** Work same as for Sleeve Trim around lower edge of sweater. **Neck Trim:** Work as for Sleeve Trim, taking in slightly to fit on first rnd. **Do not block.**
HAT—Crown: (Note: One size fits average head sizes.) Ch 3, join with a sl st to form a ring. **Rnd 1:** 6 sc in ring. Mark beg of rnd. **Rnd 2:** 2 sc in each st—12 sc. **Rnd 3:** * Sc in next st, 2 sc in next st; repeat from * around—18 sc. **Rnd 4:** * Sc in each of 2 sts, 2 sc in next st; repeat from * around—24 sc. Continue to inc 6 sc on each rnd, keeping work flat until piece measures 6" in diameter. Work even in sc until piece measures 6½" from center top, or desired depth. Fasten off.
CUFF: (Note: Cuff is worked in length.) With double strand, ch 29. **Row 1:** Sc in 2nd ch from hook, sc in each ch across—28 sc. Ch 1, turn. **Row 2:** Sc in back loop of each sc. Ch 1, turn. Piece should measure ap-

prox 9". Repeat Row 2 until piece is long enough to fit around lower edge of crown. Fasten off.
FINISHING: Weave back seam of cuff. Sew cuff to crown. Roll cuff as desired.

TINTED UNDERWEAR

(page 20)

Tint underwear following directions in dye package, using ¼ tsp. Grey and ½ tsp. Old Rose.

TURTLENECK SWEATER AND HAT

(page 26)

Directions are given for size Small (8-10). Changes for sizes Medium (12-14) and Large (16-18) are in parentheses.
MATERIALS: Columbia-Minerva "Icelandia" 3-ply, 1¾ oz. skeins: 8 (8, 9) color Winter Wheat (A); Lion Brand "La Difference" 4-ply, 85 grams (3 oz. balls): 4 (4, 5) color #4 "Neutrals" (B); hat requires 3 oz. of "Icelandia" and 2 oz. of "La Difference"; knitting needles, 1 pair No. 10 OR ANY SIZE NEEDLES WHICH WILL OBTAIN THE STITCH GAUGE BELOW.
GAUGE: 4 sts = 1"; 12 rows = 2".
PATTERN: 6 rows (3 ridges) Garter St (A); 6 rows Stockinette St (B).
DIRECTIONS—BACK: With No. 10 needles and A, cast on 68 (76, 82) sts. K 1, p 1 for 2¼". **Start pattern:** With B, work 6 rows in stockinette st. With A, work 6 rows in garter st. Continue in pattern until piece measures 17" from beginning, ending with stockinette stripe.
ARMHOLE: Continuing in pattern, bind off 4 st at beg of next 2 rows. Dec 1 st each side every 2d row 4 times—52 (60, 66) st on needle. Work straight in pattern until armhole measures from bound off stitches 7½" (8", 8½"), ending with stockinette stripe.
SHOULDER: At beg of next 2 rows, bind off 12 (14, 16) sts. Place remaining 28 (32, 34) st on needle for turtleneck.
FRONT: Same as BACK.
SLEEVES: With A cast on 36 (38, 40) sts. Work in garter st for 2¼". Change to B, increasing 1 st each side. Continue in pattern increasing 1 stitch each side every stockinette stripe 5 (6, 7) times more, having 48 (52, 56) sts on needle until sleeve measures 17" (18", 19") from beginning, ending with stockinette stripe.
ARMHOLE: Bind off 4 st at beg of next 2 rows. Dec 1 st each side every 3rd row until 10 st remain. Bind off.
MEDIUM: Dec 1 st each side every 4th row (2 times); then every 2nd row 19 times. When 10 st remain, bind off.
LARGE: Dec 1 st each side every 3rd

row (2 times); then every 2nd row until 10 st remain. Bind off. Sew pieces together.
TURTLENECK: With A and right side facing, pick up stitches on back needle and stitches on front needle 56 (64, 68) sts. Work in garter stitch until collar measures 5". Bind off loosely.
HAT: With No. 10 needles and A, cast on 6 st. Inc in every st (12st) working in garter st and continue increasing 6 times every 2d row, until 3 ridges. Change to B and stockinette st, and continue in pattern, increasing 6 times across row every 2nd row, until there are 66 st on needle. Work without increasing until 7" from beginning, ending with stockinette stripe. Change to A and garter st and increase evenly across row 10 st every 2nd row until 106 st. Work until 5 ridges have been completed. Bind off on wrong side (making 6th ridge).

RIBBED GREY TWEED SWEATER

(page 27)

Directions are given for size Small (6-8). Changes for sizes Medium (10-12) and Large (14-16) are in parentheses.
MATERIALS: Tahki Imports "Super Heavy Donegal Tweed Homespun" (3.6 oz. skeins): 8 (9, 9) skeins color #312; knitting needles, No. 7 OR ANY SIZE NEEDLES WHICH WILL OBTAIN THE STITCH GAUGE BELOW.
GAUGE: 5 sts = 1"; 11 rows = 2".
MEASUREMENTS:

Sizes:	Small (6-8)	Medium (10-12)	Large (14-16)
Bust:	34"	36"	38"
Width across back or front at underarms:	17"	18"	19"
Width Across sleeves at upper arm:	16"	16"	16"

Complete sweater is worked in basic ribbed pattern of k 2, p 2.
DIRECTIONS—BACK: With No. 7 needles, cast on 108 (110, 112) sts.
Row 1 (wrong side)—Small: (K 2 p 2) 27 times, to measure 21½". **Medium:** P 2, (k 2 p 2) 27 times, to measure 22". **Large:** (K 2 p 2) 28 times, to measure 22½".
Row 2 (right side): K the p sts and p the k sts of previous row. **Rows 3 thru 94 (100, 110):** Repeat rows 1 and 2. Work should measure 17 (18, 20¼)". **Row 95 (101, 111):** As Row 1, binding off all stitches.
Back Ribbing: At lower edge, with right side facing, pu evenly across 68 (72, 76) sts. **Row 1 (wrong side):** K 1, (p 2 k 2) 16 (17, 18) times, p 2, k 1. **Row 2 (right side):** P 1, (k 2 p 2) 16 (17, 18) times, k 2, p 1. **Rows 3 thru 16:** Repeat Rows 1 and 2. **Row 17:** Work as Row 1, binding off all sts. (Work should mea-

95

sure 3".)

FRONT: Same as Back.

SLEEVES: Cast on 80 (80, 84) sts. **Row 1 (wrong side):** (K 2 p 2) 20 (20, 21) times. **Row 2:** K the p sts and p the k sts of previous row. **Rows 3 thru 84:** Repeat Rows 1 and 2 (15½" all sizes). **Row 85:** Work as Row 1, binding off all sts.

Sleeve Ribbing: With right side facing, pu evenly across row 32(32,36) sts. **Row 1 (wrong side):** K1, (p2 k2) 7(7,8) times, p2, k1. **Row 2 (right side):** K the p sts and p the k sts of previous row. **Rows 3 thru 16:** Repeat Rows 1 and 2. **Row 17:** As Row 1, binding off all sts.

HIGH NECK: Place Back and Front flat on table. Measure 5", or 28 rows from sides towards center of top edge of Front and Back (opposite edge of ribbed cuff), and place markers. Neck opening should measure 8" — all sizes. With right side facing, pu 38 sts along edge of Front neck, 38 sts along edge of Back neck, or 76 sts (all sizes). **Row 1:** P 1 (k 2 p 2) 18 times, k 2, p 1. **Row 2:** K the p sts and p the k sts of previous row. **Rows 3 thru 40:** Repeat Rows 1 and 2. **Row 41:** As Row 1, binding off all sts loosely.

FINISHING: Matching ribs carefully, seam back and front of sweater. Sew sleeve seams, leaving 8" (42 sts — all sizes) from shoulder for armhole opening. Set in sleeves.

PULLOVER, LEGWARMERS AND HAT

(page 28)

Directions are given for size Small (6-8). Changes for sizes Medium (10-12) and Large (14-16) are in parentheses.

MATERIALS: Reynolds Icelandic Lopi, 100 grams (3½ oz. skeins): 4 (4, 5) skeins #51 Natural (A); 3 (4, 4) skeins each of #78 Red (B) and #75 Green (C); set of DP needles No. 6, No. 8 and No. 10; 2 long stitch holders; 29" circular needles No. 10 OR ANY SIZE NEEDLES WHICH WILL OBTAIN THE STITCH GAUGE BELOW.

GAUGE: On No. 10 needles, 7 sts = 2"; 4 rnds = 1".

MEASUREMENTS:

	Small (6-8)	Medium (10-12)	Large (14-16)
Fits bust size:	30½-31½"	32½-34"	36-38"
Knitted bust measurement:	32"	36½"	41"
Length from lower edge to back of neck:	23½"	24"	24½"
Width of sleeve at upper arm:	11½"	13½"	13½"

DIRECTIONS — Pattern Notes: Change colors on wrong side, lock strands by picking up new color from under dropped color. Carry colors not being used loosely across back of work. Cut and join colors as needed.

PULLOVER — Body: Beg at lower edge of front and back, with A and No. 10 circular needle, cast on 112 (128, 144) sts. Put and keep a marker on needle between last and first sts of rnd. **Hem:** With A, join with care not to twist sts and work around in stockinette st (k each rnd) for 7 rnds. **Next Rnd:** With A, p for turning rnd.

PULLOVER, LEG WARMERS AND HAT

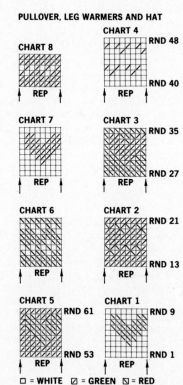

CHART 8 — **RND 48**
CHART 4 — **RND 40**
REP — REP

CHART 7 — **RND 35**
CHART 3 — **RND 27**
REP — REP

CHART 6 — **RND 21**
CHART 2 — **RND 13**
REP — REP

CHART 5 — **RND 61**
CHART 1 — **RND 9**
RND 53 — **RND 1**
REP — REP

☐ = WHITE ▨ = GREEN ◪ = RED

Pattern — Rnds 1-9: Follow chart 1 working in stockinette st. **Rnds 10-12:** P 1 rnd each of C, B and A. **Rnds 13-21:** Follow chart 2 working in stockinette st. **Rnds 22-26:** P 1 rnd of A, 2 rnds B, 1 rnd C, 1 rnd A. **Rnds 27-35:** Follow chart 3 working in stockinette st. **Rnds 36-39:** P 2 rnds A, 1 rnd each of C and B. **Rnds 40-48:** Follow chart 4 working in stockinette st. **Rnds 49-52:** P 2 rnds B, 1 rnd each C and A. **Rnds 53-61:** Follow chart 5 working in stockinette st. **Rnds 62-64:** P 1 rnd A, 2 rnds B.

Divide for Underarms — Rnd 65: P with A binding off first 8 sts for underarm, p until 48 (56, 64) sts beyond bound-off sts and put sts on st holder for front, bind off next 8 sts for underarm, p to end of rnd and put these 48 (56, 64) sts on st holder for back.

Sleeve Length Note: Sleeve is planned for 19" to underarm with cuff unfolded. For shorter length, work less garter st rnds on cuff.

SLEEVES: With A and No. 10 dp needles, cast on 40 (48, 48) sts; divide on 3 dp needles. Mark end of rnd. **Cuff:** Join with care not to twist sts and work around with A in garter st (k 1 rnd, p 1 rnd) for 22 rnds (11 ridges) or less if shorter sleeve length is desired. **Pattern — Rnds 1-64:** Follow Rnds 1-64 on Body.

Divide for Underarm — Rnd 65: P with A, binding off first 8 sts. Put remaining 32 (40, 40) sts on a strand of yarn. Work 2nd sleeve.

Yoke: From right side, put on No. 10 circular needle sts of front, one sleeve, back and 2nd sleeve — 160 (192, 208) sts. **Pattern — Rnds 1-9:** Follow chart 6 working in stockinette st. **Next 3 (4, 5) Rnds:** P 2 (3, 4) rnds C, 1 rnd A. **First Dec Rnd:** With B [p 3 (4, 4), p 2 tog] 16 times, [p 3 (4, 5), p 2 tog] 16 times — 128 (160, 176) sts. **Next 8 Rnds:** Follow chart 7 working in stockinette st for 8 rnds. **2nd Dec Rnd:** Working last rnd of chart 7, with A [p 2 (3, 3), p 2 tog] 16 times, [p 2 (3, 4), p 2 tog] 16 times — 96 (128, 144) sts. (**Note:** Change to No. 10 dp needles as sts get crowded.) **Next 3 (4, 5) Rnds:** P 1 rnd B, 2 (3, 4) rnds C. (**3rd Dec Rnd:** With A [p 2 (2, 1), p 2 tog] 12 (16, 16) times, (p 2, p 2 tog) 12 (16, 24) times — 72 (96, 104) sts. **Next 5 Rnds:** Follow chart 8 working in stockinette st for 5 rnds. **4th Dec Rnd:** Working last rnd of chart 8, with C [p 3 (1, 1), p 2 tog] 12 (24, 24) times, [p 4 (1, 2), p 2 tog] 2 (8, 8) times — 58 (64, 72) sts.

Neckband: With A and No. 6 dp needles, work around in garter st (k 1 rnd, p 1 rnd) for 8 rnds, dec 0 (2, 6)sts evenly spaced across first rnd — 58 (62, 66) sts. Bind off loosely.

FINISHING: Weave bound-off underarm sts tog. Run in yarn ends on wrong side. Steam pullover lightly on wrong side. Turn hem to wrong side of body; sew in place.

LEG WARMERS — Cuff: With A and No. 6 dp needles, cast on 40 sts; divide sts on 3 dp needles. Mark end of rnd. With A, work around in k 2, p 2 ribbing for 4½". Change to No. 8 dp needles. **Pattern — Rnds 1-61:** Follow Rnds 1-61 as on Body, ending on last rnd of chart 5, changing to No. 10 dp needles on Rnd 49. **Rnds 62-71:** P 1 rnd each of A, B, C, A, B, A, 2 rnds C, 2 rnds B. With B, bind off loosely in p. Run in all yarn ends on wrong side.

HAT: With A and No. 10 dp needles, cast on 56 sts; divide sts on 3 dp needles. Mark end of rnd. **Brim:** Join with care not to twist sts and work around with A in garter st (k 1 rnd, p 1 rnd) for 22 rnds (11 ridges). **Pattern — Rnds 1-9:** Work Rnds 27-35 on chart 3 in stockinette st. **Rnds 10-12:** P 1 rnd each of A, C, B. **Rnds 13-18:** Work 6 rnds of chart 8 working in stockinette st. **Rnds 19-20:** P 1 rnd each of A and C. **Rnds 21-28:** Work Rnds 1-8 of chart 1 working in stockinette st. **Dec Rnd:** Working last rnd of chart 1, with A k 2 tog around—28 sts. **Next 3 Rnds:** P 1 rnd each of C, B, C. Change to No. 6 dp needles. **Dec Rnd:** With B, p 2 tog around—14 sts. Leaving a 10″ end, cut B. Run end through all sts, draw sts tog. Fasten securely on wrong side. Run in ends on wrong side.

RUST KNITTED SWEATER

(page 29)

Directions are given for size Small (8-10). Changes for sizes Medium (12-14) and Large (16-18) are in parentheses.

MATERIALS: Tahki Yarn "Michelaine" 100% Wool (3.6 oz. skeins): 10(12, 14) skeins of color #11; knitting needles, a pair each No. 9 and No. 10 OR ANY SIZE NEEDLES WHICH WILL OBTAIN THE STITCH GAUGE BELOW.
GAUGE: Pattern on No. 10 needles—7 sts=2″; 4 rows=1″.

MEASUREMENTS:

Sizes:	Small (8-10)	Medium (12-14)	Large (16-18)
Bust:	33″	36″	41″
Width across back or front at underarms:	16½″	18″	20½″
Width across sleeve at upper arm:	13¼″	14¼″	15¼″

DIRECTIONS—BACK: Starting at lower edge with No. 9 needles, cast on 58(66, 74) sts. Work in garter st (k each row) for 1½″. Change to No. 10 needles and work pattern as follows:
Row 1 (right side): K 1, * p 3, k 1; rpt from * across, ending with p 3, k 2.
Row 2: K 1, *in next st make k 1, p 1 and k 1—3 sts made in one st; P 3 tog; rpt from * across, ending with k 1.
Row 3: K 2, * p 3, k 1; rpt from * across to end of row. **Row 4:** K 1, * p 3 tog, in next st make k 1, p 1 and k 1; rpt from * across, ending with k 1. Rpt last 4 rows (Rows 1 through 4) for pattern until total length is 18½(18½, 19½)″ from beg, ending with Row 4 of pattern.
Armhole Shaping: Keeping continuity of pattern throughout, bind off 4 sts at beg of each of next 2 rows. Work even in pattern over 50(58, 66) sts until length from bound-off sts at underarms is 7(7½, 8)″, ending with Row 4 of pattern.
Shoulder Shaping: Keeping in pattern, bind off 8 sts at beg of next 4 rows; then bind off 0(4, 6) sts at beg of following 0(2, 2) rows. Bind off rem 18(18, 22) sts for back of neck.
FRONT: Work same as for Back until total length is 15½(15½, 16½)″ from beg, ending with Row 4.
To Start Collar—Row 1 (right side): Work in pattern over first 21(25, 29) sts; k 15, inc one st in next st; place

rem 21(25, 29) sts on a st holder—38(42, 46) sts on needle. **Row 2:** K 16, inc one st in next st, place a marker on needle, work in pattern to end of row, ending with k 1—39(43, 47) sts.
Row 3: Work in pattern to marker, slip marker, k 18. Slip marker in every row. **Short Row 1:** K 18; do not work over rem sts. Turn. **Short Row 2:** Sl 1, k 17. Turn. **Row 4 (long row):** K 18, slip markers, work in pattern over rem sts on needle. Keeping the 18 sts of collar in garter st (k each row), and working all other sts in pattern, work even (no short rows) until total length is 18½(18½, 19½)″, ending at side edge.
Armhole Shaping—Row 1: Bind off 4 sts, work in pattern to marker, slip marker, k 18. Work 2 short rows same as before. Repeating the 2 short rows every 3″, 2 more times, work even as before over 35(39, 43) sts until length of armhole is same as on Back, ending at side edge.
Shoulder Shaping: Keeping collar sts in garter st, and working other sts in pattern, from armhole edge bind off 8 sts 2 times; then remove marker; from same edge bind off 1(5, 5) sts—18(18, 20) sts remain on needle for collar.
Back Section of Collar—Rows 1 through 4: K 18(18, 20). **Row 5:** K 12; do not work over rem sts. Turn. **Row 6:** Sl 1, k 11. Turn. Rpt these 6 rows (Rows 1 through 6) 6 (6, 7) more times; then k 1 row across all sts. Bind off—this completes half of back portion of collar.
Opposite Side—Row 1: Slip sts from holder onto a No. 10 needle; attach yarn and work in pattern over these 21(25, 29) sts. **Row 2:** Work in pattern across sts on needle; with wrong side facing, pick up and k one st in each of the 17 sts across first row at base of collar. **Row 2:** Inc one st in first st, k 16, place a marker on needle, work in pattern to end of row—39(43, 47) sts. Work to correspond with opposite side (including back section of collar), reversing shaping.
SLEEVES: Starting at lower edge with No. 9 needles, cast on 44(46, 50) sts. Work in garter st (k each row) for 1½″. **Next Row:** K, increasing 2(4, 4) sts evenly spaced across—46(50, 54) sts. Change to No. 10 needles and work in pattern, same as for Back, until length is 19½(20½, 20½)″ from beg, ending with Row 4 of pattern.
Top Shaping: Keeping continuity of pattern, bind off 4 sts at beg of next 8 rows. Bind off rem 14(18, 22) sts.
FINISHING: Pin each section to measurements on a padded surface; cover with a damp cloth and allow to dry; do not press. Sew side, shoulder and sleeve seams. Sew sleeves into armholes, adjusting to fit. Sew center back seam of collar; adjust inner edge of back of collar to fit back neck and

sew in place. Fold back section of collar in half to right side as photographed. Fold garter st sections at lower edges of sleeves to right side for cuffs.

LOOPY SWEATER AND CAP

(page 29)

Directions are given for size Small (6-8). Changes for sizes Medium (10-12) and Large (14) are in parentheses.
MATERIALS: Coats & Clark Red Heart "Fabulend" knitting worsted type yarn: 11 (12, 13) 4-ply, 3½ oz. skeins, color #111 Eggshell; crochet hooks, sizes I and K OR ANY SIZE HOOK WHICH WILL OBTAIN THE STITCH GAUGE BELOW: 7 buttons.
GAUGE: Crochet hook K, 2 sc = 1″; 2 rows = 1″.

MEASUREMENTS:

Sizes:	Small (6-8)	Medium (10-12)	Large (14)
Body bust size in inches	30½-31½″	32½-34″	36″
Width across back or front at underarm:	19½″	20½″	21½″
Length from shoulder to lower edge:	22″	23½″	25″
Length of side seam:	12″	13″	14″
Length of sleeve seam excluding cuff	15″	15″	16″
Width across sleeve at upper arm:	15″	16″	17″

DIRECTIONS: Having 5 ch sts to every 1″, with Size I hook, make a chain using up an entire skein and wind this chain into a ball. Hereafter, this will be referred to as cord. Work 5 more skeins in same way—6 balls of chains. If additional chains are needed, work chain as necessary.
BACK: With Size K hook, ch 42 (44, 46) *loosely* to measure 21″ (22″, 23″).
Beading Row: Dc in 6th ch from hook, * ch 1, skip next ch, dc in next ch. Rpt from * across—19 (20, 21) sps. Ch 1, turn. **Now work in pattern as follows—Row 1 (right side):** Holding cord in front of work, *insert hook through first ch st on cord and through first dc on last row, yarn over and draw loop through, yarn over and draw through 2 loops*—**joint sc made;** * skip next 4 ch on cord, insert hook through next ch on cord and through next ch on last row and complete a joint sc, skip next 4 ch on cord, insert hook through next ch on cord and through next dc on last row and complete a joint sc. Rpt from * to last sp, (skip next 4 ch on cord, joint sc

through next ch on cord and next ch of last row) twice—39 (41, 43) joint sc. Ch 1, turn. **Row 2:** Holding cord in back of work, skip next 4 ch on cord, insert hook through first sc of previous row and through following ch on cord and complete a joint sc, * skip next 4 ch on cord, make a joint sc as before through next sc on row and following ch on cord. Rpt from * across—39 (41, 43) joint sc. Ch 1, turn. **Row 3:** Holding cord in front of work, work as for Row 2. Ch 1, turn. Repeating last 2 rows alternately for pattern, work in pattern until total length is 12" (13", 14"), end on wrong side. Turn.

Armhole Shaping—Row 1: Sl st in first sc, ch 1, work in pattern to last sc. Do not work over last st—37 (39, 41) joint sc. Ch 1, turn. Continue in pattern until length from armhole shaping is 10" (10½", 11"), end on wrong side. Cut and secure. Turn.

Shoulder Shaping—Row 1: Sl st in first 6 sc, ch 1, with cord in front, make a joint sc in same place where last sl st was made; work in pattern to last 5 joint sc. Cut cord and secure. Turn **Row 2:** Sl st in first 6 sc, ch 1, then with cord in back, work as for previous row. Cut cord and secure. **Row 3:** Sl st in first 5 (6, 7) joint sc, with cord in front, work as before to last 4 (5, 6) joint sc. Fasten off.

FRONT: Work as for Back until Row 1 of Armhole Shaping has been completed. Work 1 row even.

Front Opening—Next Row: Work in pattern across first 18 (19, 20) sts. Do not work over remaining sts. Ch 1, turn. Continuing in pattern, work over the 18 (19, 20) joint sc only, until length from Row 1 of Armhole Shaping is 7½" (8", 8½"), end at front edge. Cut and secure cord. Turn.

Neck Shaping—Row 1: From front edge, sl st across first 3 sts, ch 1, make joint sc in same st and in each st across. Ch 1, turn. **Row 2:** Work in pattern across to last 2 sts, skip next sc, joint sc in last sc. Ch 1, turn. **Row 3:** Joint sc in first sc, skip next sc; complete row in pattern. Work even until length of armhole is same as on back end at armhole edge. Cut cord and secure.

Shoulder Shaping—Row 1: Sl st in first 6 sts, joint sc in last sl st, complete row. Ch 1, turn. **Row 2:** Work in pattern to last 5 sts. Fasten off. Skip next joint sc on last long row worked, attach yarn in next joint sc and complete row—18 (19, 20) joint sc. Ch 1, turn. Complete as for opposite side, reversing shapings.

SLEEVES: Starting at lower edge, with size K hook, ch 31 (33, 35) loosely to measure 15½" (16½", 17½"). **Row 1 (right side):** With cord in front, insert hook in 2nd ch from hook and in first ch on cord and

complete a joint sc, * skip next 4 ch on cord, joint sc through next ch of starting chain and next ch on cord. Rpt from * across. Ch 1, turn. Starting with Row 2, work in pattern as for Back until total length is 15" (15", 16"), end on wrong side. Cut and secure.

Top Shaping (Note: Cut cord and secure at end of every row.)—Row 1: Sl st in first 3 joint sc, ch 1, make joint sc in same place as last sl st was made, work in pattern to last 2 joint sc. Ch 1, turn. **Rows 2-6:** Rpt last row. Fasten off.

Cuff: With Size I hook, ch 16 to measure 5¾". **Row 1:** Sc in 2nd ch from hook and in each ch—15 sc. Ch 1, turn. **Row 2:** Working through **back** loops of each sc, sc in each sc across. Ch 1, turn. Rpt Row 2 until piece measures 8" (8½", 8½"). Fasten off. Sew side, sleeve and shoulder seams.

Collar: With Size I hook, ch 22 to measure 8". Work same as for Cuff over 21 sc until piece reaches around entire neck edge. Ch 1, turn.

Next Row (Buttonhole Row): Sc in first 2 sc, (ch 3, skip next 3 sc, sc in each of next 4 sc) twice; ch 3, skip next 3 sc, sc in last 2 sc. Fasten off. Gathering lower edge of sleeve to fit, sew sleeve to cuff. Sew in sleeves. With size I hook, work 1 row of sc around neck edge, easing in to fit.

Button Band—Row 1: With right side facing, attach yarn at corner at neck on left front. Being careful to keep work flat, sc along front edge to lower corner. Ch 1, turn. **Row 2:** Sc in each sc across. Fasten off. With pins mark the position of 4 buttons evenly spaced on button band, having first pin ½" from top edge and last pin 1" above front opening.

Buttonhole Band—Row 1: Attach yarn at lower corner of right front, sc evenly to corner at neck edge. Ch 1, turn. **Row 2:** (Sc in each sc to next pin, ch 3, skip next 3 sc, sc in next sc) 4 times; sc in each remaining sc. Fasten off. Sew collar to neck edge. Sew on buttons.

Tie: With size I hook, make a chain 80" long. Sl st in each ch across. Fasten off. Weave tie through beading row. Make 4 knots on each end of tie. Tie ends into bow.

HAT: Directions are given to fit all sizes. With size I hook, ch 19 loosely to measure 9½". **Rows 1 and 2:** Work same as for Sleeve. **Row 3:** Work in pattern across 14 sts, drop chain; sc in each of next 4 sts. Ch 1, turn. Mark end of last row for top of cap. **Row 4:** Sc in first 4 sc; work in joint sc pattern across remaining 14 sts. Ch 1, turn. **Row 5:** Work in pattern across. Rpt Rows 2-5 seven more times; then rpt rows 2-4 once. Fasten off. Sew last row to starting chain for back seam. Draw sts together at top and fasten securely.

CARDIGAN SWEATER AND HAT

(page 29)

Directions are given for 36" blocked bust size. Changes for 38", 40", 42" blocked bust sizes are in parentheses.
MATERIALS: Plymouth Combo-Set (4 ply; 100 gram balls): 8 (9, 10, 10) balls color #1201 (A); and Combo (4-ply 100 gram balls): 3, (3, 4, 4) balls color #8268 (B); knitting needles, 1 pair each No. 9 and No. 10 OR ANY SIZE NEEDLES WHICH WILL OBTAIN THE STITCH GAUGE BELOW.
GAUGE: On No. 10 needles, 3 sts = 1"; 4 rows = 1".

DIRECTIONS—Back: Cast on with B on No. 9 needles 53 (55, 57, 59) sts. Work in st st for 2", end with p row. **Picot turning edge:** K1, *yo, k2 tog*, repeat across, ending with k1. Continue in st st for 2 additional inches. Change to No. 10 needles and increase 8 (10, 10, 12) sts evenly across. There will be 61 (65, 67, 71) sts. Break off B and join A. **Work in pattern row:** *K2, p2* repeat across, ending with k1, (k1, p1, p1). Repeat this row for pattern, always starting with k2. Continue in pattern until 17 (17, 18, 18)" from start of garment.
Armhole: Bind off 2 sts at the beg of next 2 rows. **Decrease for raglan:** K1, k2 tog through back of sts, work across in pattern, ending with k2 tog, k1. Continue decreasing every other row, while maintaining pattern, until 21 (21, 21, 23) sts remain. Bind off.
Pockets (Make 2): Cast on with No. 9 needles in A 17 sts. Work in st st 5 inches. Put on holder.
LEFT FRONT: Cast on with B on No. 9 needles 24 (25, 27, 28) sts. Work border to match back. Change to No. 10 needles and increase 5 (6, 6, 7) sts evenly across. There are 29 (31, 33, 35) sts. Break off B and join A and work in pattern until 9" from start of garment.
Pocket: Work across 6 (7, 8, 9) sts, bind off next 17 sts, work to end of row. Next row, work in pattern st across with the sts of the pocket in place of the bound-off sts. Work until piece measures back to underarm, ending on wrong side.
Armhole: Bind off 2 sts on following row and continue decreasing to match back until 16 (16, 17, 18) sts remain. Continue to decrease for the armhole while binding off every other row for the neck edge as follows: **Row 1:** 3 sts at beg of row. **Row 3:** 2 sts at beg of row. **Row 5:** 1 (1, 2, 2) sts at beg of row. **Row 7:** 1 st at beg of row. **Row 9:** Repeat Row 7. **Row 10:** 0 (0, 0, 1) st at beg of row. When only 2 sts remain, k2 tog and bind off remaining st.
RIGHT FRONT: Work to match Left Front, reversing shapings.

7. When collar measures 6″ from beginning, work across 26 (26, 26) sts, bind off 20 (21, 20) sts (for back of collar), work across remaining 26 (25, 26) sts. At inside edge of collar, bind off 1 st every 2nd row until 2 sts remain and piece measure 12¼″ from beginning. Bind off. Work other side in same way, dec at inside edge.
FINISHING: Sew side seams. Sew sleeve seams. Set in sleeve. Sew collar to neck, matching back of neck to bound-off sts of collar, being careful to have right side of collar next to inside of sweater, so that when the collar is lying back, the right side faces the outside.

KNITTED HAT

(page 31)

MATERIALS: Worsted weight yarn: Main color, Gold (MC), 2 oz; contrasting colors, Blue (CCB), ½ oz,; Red (CCR), ½ oz.; White (CCW), ½ oz.; knitting needles, No. 13; crochet hook, size I.
GAUGE: On no. 13 needles—3 sts = 1″; 4 rows = 1″.
(**Note:** Hat is worked in stockinette st; brim is worked in single crochet throughout.)
DIRECTIONS:—Hat: With CCB, cast on 48 sts. P 1 row, *K 1 row, p 1 row, rpt from * once (5 rows). Change to CCW and rpt between *s once (7 rows). **Triangle Pattern—Row 1:** *K 4 CCW, 1 CCR, 3 CCW; rpt from * across. **Row 2 and all even rows:** P back, working colors same as in previous row. **Row 3:** *K 3 CCW, 3 CCR, 2 CCW, rpt from * across. **Row 5:** *K 2 CCW, 5 CCR, 1 CCW; rpt from * across. **Row 7:** *K 1 CCW, 7 CCR; rpt from * across. **Row 8:** Rpt Row 2. Continuing in st st, work 2 rows in CCR, then 4 rows in CCW, then 2 rows in MC. **Alternating Colors —Row 1:** *K 1 CCR, sl 1 MC; rpt from * across. **Row 2:** *Sl 1 MC, p 1 CCR; rpt from * across. Work 2 rows st st with MC. **Row 5:** *Sl 1 MC, k 1 CCR; rpt from * across. **Row 6:** P 1 CCR, sl 1 MC; rpt from * across. Work 2 rows st st with MC. Change to CCB and work **1st dec row:** *K 2, k 2 tog; rpt from * across. P 1 row. **2nd dec row:** *K 1, k 2 tog; rpt from * across. P 1 row. **3rd dec row:** K 2 tog across. Break yarn, leaving 12″. Weave yarn through rem sts and fasten to inside. Hat should measure approx. 7½″. Sew back seam; matching patterns.
Brim: Starting at lower edge, with crochet hook, work 1 sc in each st around (48 sts). **Rnd 1:** Work sc around; inc 5 sts evenly spaced (53 sts). Repeat Rnd 1—5 times more (78 sts). Crochet 1 rnd even. Fasten off. (**Note:** The yarn colors called for in

Materials are merely suggestions. Other color combinations can be substituted, if you wish.)

KNITTED SCARF

(page 30 and 31)

Finished size approximately 7″x62″, not including fringe.
MATERIALS: Worsted weight yarn, 4 oz., in colors of your choice; knitting needles, No. 13.
DIRECTIONS: This garter stitch scarf is a challenge to the knitter. You can create your own design by choosing contrasting colors and determining yourself where to place the stripes. With No. 13 needles, cast on 24 sts. Work in garter st (k every row). Work until scarf measures 62″ long, or any length that you choose. Bind off loosely.
Fringe: Wind main color and contrasting color yarn around an 8″ piece of cardboard. Cut yarn at one end. (Colors used are optional. Experiment with different color combinations, if you wish.) Fold in half and knot a loop in every 3rd st across both narrow ends of scarf. Trim evenly.

COILED RUG

(page 32)

Finished size approximately 22½″ x 36″.
MATERIALS: 7 skeins (3½ oz. each) American Thread's "Dawn Sayelle" yarn, color#390 Plumberry; Susan Bates' "Knitting Knobby" (available in variety stores and notions departments); large-eyed tapestry (blunt) needle. (**Note:** If more than one person at a time will be working on rug, purchase additional Knitting Knobbies.)
DIRECTIONS: Following instructions packaged with Knitting Knobby, make 40 cords, each 54″ long, and 28 cords, each 10″ long. Coil each cord into a disc, slipstitching with matching yarn. (You will get 4½″ discs from the 54″ cords and 2″ discs from the 10″ cords.) Arrange the 4½″ discs into 5 rows of 8 discs each; place the 2″ discs into the spaces between the large discs. Slipstitch all discs together for about 1″ at the points where they touch. Steam rug lightly to block.

"BLESS THIS HOUSE" RUG

(page 33)

This is an authentic hooked rug, made with strips of wool fabric pulled up through a burlap backing.
MATERIALS: (See Note for all items marked *.) 1 yd. 50″-wide burlap fab-

ric; dressmaker's carbon paper (or pre-printed burlap*); new or used tightly-woven wool fabrics* (see color photo on page 33 and instructions below for colors and amounts); primitive rug hook* (not a latch hook); 3¾ yds. of 1½″-wide twill tape; sharp scissors; frame, approximately 16″×18″ or larger (this can be a frame especially intended for rug-hooking or one made from artists' stretcher bars, available in art-supply stores).
DIRECTIONS: Following directions on page 18, transfer design onto burlap, leaving excess burlap all around design. (If you purchase pre-printed burlap, you can eliminate this step.) Collect the wool fabrics. As a guide to amounts, estimate that you will need 5 sq. ft. of fabric for 1 sq. ft. of rug—cover each hooking area with 5 layers of fabric. If you are unable to find fabric in the colors you need, you may dye colors.* If you recycle old clothes, rip out the seams and hems, remove any lining, padding or interfacing. Cut out buttonholes, remove buttons, zippers, hooks and eyes. Every piece of fabric, new or old, must be washed before using. This will remove any fabric sizing and will make wool softer and easier to manage. Use a washing machine on delicate setting with warm or cold water. A few pieces may feel thick after washing. Dry these pieces on a line. Throw the remainder in the dryer, again on a delicate setting. Washing sometimes shrinks loosely woven or basketweave materials enough to make them useable. If your loosely woven material remains too loose after washing and drying, don't discard it until you try shrinking it in a hot dryer. Attach twill tape to rug base by hand or machine: Pin the edge of tape along the outside edge of the design, with the tape extending in toward the center. Start the tape by folding the end in about ½″. Sew about ⅛″ from edge; press tape back. When you have your frame together, wrap 4 sides with 2″ strips of strong fabric. Use tacks or staples to hold the beginning and end of each strip. Corners do not have to be covered. Place design over frame. The area you wish to work on should be in the center of the frame. Start at one side with long pins or T-pins. Use about six across this side and pin firmly. Now pin the opposite side, pulling burlap firmly across. Then pin the third side, pulling firmly as you work. Now pin the fourth side, again pulling firmly so that your working area is taut. If it loosens while hooking, re-pin.
Cut strips and hook: If this is your first rug, you will need to practice your stitch before starting to hook

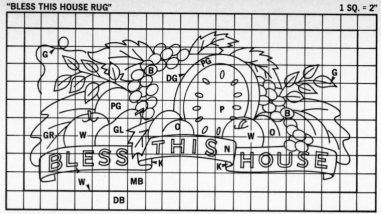

"BLESS THIS HOUSE RUG"

1 SQ. = 2"

- **B** - BLUE (3 SHADES)
- **GR** - GREEN (TWEEDS & 3 SHADES)
- **W** - WINES & BROWNISH PINKS
- **GL** - GOLDS (2-3 SHADES)
- **O** - ORANGE/RUST
- **N** - NATURAL
- **P** - BRIGHT PINK - TWEED & SOLID
- **DG** - DARK GREEN
- **PG** - PALE GREENS
- **MB** - MEDIUM BROWN
- **DB** - DARK BROWN
- **K** - KHAKI

your design. Cut a ¼"-wide strip on the straight of the fabric. Strips cut on the bias will break. Fasten your burlap on your frame as indicated above, leaving some space to practice between the burlap edge and the design edge. You should learn how to hook curves and straight lines in all directions. Hold fabric strip in your left hand between thumb and forefinger, touching *underside* of burlap. Hold wooden hook handle in palm of your right hand with thumb and forefinger pointing to shank of hook. From the topside, push the hook down through the burlap and pull end of strip up to the topside. The following stitches will be loops pulled up about ¼" above burlap. As the strip comes through the burlap, pull slightly toward the previous completed loop. This will help you achieve a uniform height. If you pull a loop too high, pull it down with your left hand. Your right hand is the working hand on the top of the pattern. Your left hand guides the strip on the bottom of the pattern and lets it feed through two fingers. All strips should start and end on top. Cut them off, even with top of your loops. Your finished rug should be springy and soft. A hard rug is the result of tight packing—loops too close together. This puts a strain on your burlap and uses more wool than is necessary. Loops should touch, covering the burlap, but should not be crowded. In the beginning, pull a loop through every second mesh until you get the "feel" of what you are doing. Then you may want to pass over more spaces or hook closer. Thin wool requires more loops closer together. Have a neat underside—do not let strips twist and do not cross over from one spot to another. Cut the strip on top and start again when you have to work another spot. When you have mastered your stitch, begin hooking your rug near the center of the design. Outline each motif, then hook its interior. After each section is

hooked, hook two rows of background around it. After design is finished, hook two straight rows around the edge of the entire rug, then fill in the remaining background with gentle curving rows. Include your initials, if you wish.

FINISHING: After your hooking is completed, cut the outside edge of your burlap 1" from stitching line. Fold twill tape to back of rug, covering excess burlap; slipstitch tape to back of rug.

(**Note:** This design is available pre-printed on burlap. To order, write and make check payable to Lib Callaway Patterns, 109 Shady Knoll Lane, New Canaan, Conn. 06840. Specify #67B, House Blessing, 22"×42", $8.00 (shipping paid). Also available are primitive rug hooks at $1.50 each. For dyeing, Ms. Callaway recommends Cushing's Perfection Dyes, available in craft shops. For dyeing tips, consult Ms. Callaway's catalog or *Rug Hooker's Dye Manual* by C. Charleson. A source for new wool, available in 60 colors, is Dorr

Mill Store, Guild, N.H. 03754. Write for a price list.

"MEXICAN" EMBROIDERED RUG

(page 34)

Finished measurements 26½" × 43", excluding fringe.

MATERIALS: 1¼ yds. 54"-wide Haitian cotton (Roth Imports—see Note); 1⅝ yds. jumbo tasseled fringe (Conso—see Note); Paternayan "Pat-Rug" yarn: 4 oz. each of colors #968 Orange, #237 Red, #259 Pink, #005 White and 2 oz. each of colors #122 Grey, #441 Yellow, #569 Green, #755 Blue; large-eyed (chenille) needle; heavy-duty thread.

DIRECTIONS: With basting stitches, mark the center line of the fabric, parallel to the selvages; this will be a fold line. Enlarge diagram, following directions on page 18, and transfer outlines to fabric 1½" from edge along either end, on one side of basted line. Work embroidery according to stitch key, except for yellow running stitches (these will be worked later). Fold rug along basted line, wrong sides together. Machine-stitch ½" from selvage edge through both layers; trim away bulky selvage. With heavy-duty thread, overcast the edges of the two open ends of rug together. Work yellow running stitches through both layers, to keep rug flat. Remove basting. With white rug yarn, work 1"-deep overcasting along both long edges. Cut fringe in half; baste one piece over each short edge of rug, turning under raw ends of fringe. Machine-stitch in place along each edge of fringe heading. (**Note:** Haitian cotton and jumbo tasseled fringe are commonly used for upholstery. Check the home decorat-

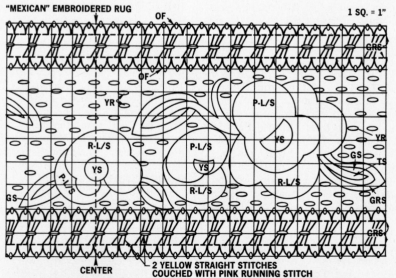

"MEXICAN" EMBROIDERED RUG

1 SQ. = 1"

2 YELLOW STRAIGHT STITCHES
COUCHED WITH PINK RUNNING STITCH

- **P-L/S** — PINK - LONG AND SHORT STITCHES
- **R-L/S** — RED - LONG AND SHORT STITCHES
- **YS** — YELLOW - STRAIGHT STITCH
- **GS** - GREEN - STEM STITCH
- **YR** — YELLOW - RUNNING STITCH
- **TS** — TURQUOISE - STEM STITCH
- **OF** — ORANGE - FLY STITCH
- **GRS** — GRAY - STEM STITCH

ing section of your local department store.)

CHECKED LATCH-HOOK RUG

(page 34)

Finished size approximately 33″ × 44½″.

MATERIALS: Reynolds' Pre-cut "Tapis Pengouin" (40 g. bundles): 25 bundles #105 white, 3 bundles each of colors #110 red, #134 royal, #151 hot pink, #152 orange, #155 turquoise, #157 purple, #158 kelly, #161 yellow, #162 magenta; Reynolds' Uncut "Tapis Pengouin": 2 (50 g) balls #05 white; latchet hook; large-eyed tapestry (blunt) needle; 1⅜ yds. 40″-wide (3.3 hole) rug canvas.

CHECKED LATCH-HOOK RUG
SHORT SIDE

ONE QUARTER OF RUG - REPEAT 3 MORE TIMES

☐-105 WHITE   T-155 TURQUOISE
R-110 RED   P-157 PURPLE
A-134 ROYAL   K-158 KELLY
H-151 HOT PINK   Y-161 YELLOW
O-152 ORANGE   M-162 MAGENTA

DIRECTIONS: Following color placement diagram, latch-hook squares six knots across and six knots deep. (Work in center of canvas, so 2″-3″ border remains all around hooked section of canvas.) To make knots, refer to diagrams and instructions packaged with latch hook. **Work in one direction only.** This is so all knots on rug will lie in the same direction. After finishing knots, cut away excess canvas, leaving a border 4 squares wide all around. Fold the border in half, and with a double strand of (uncut) white, overcast all around the rug, going into the second square of canvas and working over corners twice to be sure they are completely covered.

BARGELLO RUG

(page 35)

Finished size approximately 36″ x 51″.

MATERIALS: 1⅔ yds. 40″-wide #4 double mesh rug canvas; Paternayan Pat-Rug yarn: 2 lbs. Navy #365, ¾ lb. Red #233, ¾ lb. Cream #020; heavy tapestry needle; ruler; indelible marker. (For optional lining: 1½ yds. linen or burlap; 5 yds. 1¼″ rug binding tape; strong thread.)
DIRECTIONS: Unroll canvas over a flat surface and steam it lightly. Let it dry and machine stitch or tape edges to prevent ravelling. (**Note about**

BARGELLO RUG - STITCH A

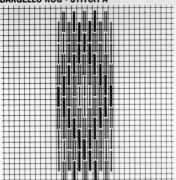

counting on canvas: Vertically, count canvas threads because the stitches are worked *over* counted threads. Horizontally, count canvas *spaces* because the stitches are *placed* in the spaces *between* the vertical canvas threads.) **All stitches are worked over four canvas threads with two strands of yarn.** Using the diagram as a guide, draw the six squares and the borders on the *threads* of the canvas. Center and stitch the patterns within the squares, following the stitch diagrams and the color photo on page

BARGELLO RUG - STITCH B

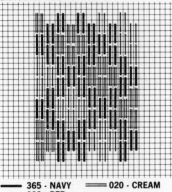

━━ 365 - NAVY   ═══ 020 - CREAM
━━ 233 - RED

35. Work stitches softly and guide the yarn so the strands lie side by side for better coverage. Work without knots and allow at least 2″ of tail end at the beginning and end of each strand of yarn, to be woven into the back later. Trim away the canvas four threads away from the large outer border. Fold back canvas on thread line of outside edge, matching canvas squares carefully; press with fingers to create a sharp edge. Clip and miter the corners and machine or hand stitch all around. After stitching,

BARGELLO RUG - STITCH C

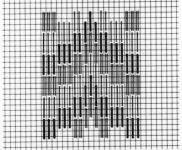

work all borders in brick stitch, through both layers of canvas where necessary. With a double strand of navy blue yarn, overcast the last thread around the edge, working extra stitches at corners if necessary to be sure they are covered.

FINISHING: If too many canvas threads show through or if the rug is too rigid, soften it by dipping it in warm water. (Half fill a bathtub with very warm water, dissolve ½ cup salt and soak the rug for five minutes.) Drain out the water and place the rug on the bathroom floor over a thick layer of newspapers on a plastic sheet. Straighten borders, but do not pull or pin down. Change newspapers every day until the rug is completely dry. Lining is optional. An unlined rug will hang better and will be easier to repair. If you wish, line rug with linen or burlap mitered and folded to be 1″ smaller all around than rug. Pin and baste wrong sides together and slipstitch with strong thread. Add 1¼″ rug binding tape all around the edge and slipstitch; binding should not show from right side of rug. Run a few lines of large basting stitches across the lining at regular intervals, catching some of the stitches in the rug. This will prevent the lining from ballooning.

BARGELLO RUG
8 SPACES   49 SPACES

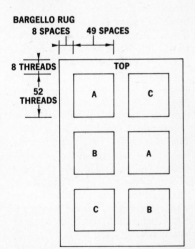

Band along front and bottom edge: With No. 5 needle and right side facing, pick up 1 st for each stitch along bottom fronts and back; at lower front curve edge pick up 10 sts, along remaining front edge pick up 1 st every other row, around neck edge pick up 11 sts, pick up 13 sts at center of back, continue down left side to match. Join. Work in garter st (k1 row, p1 row). On next row increase 4 sts along lower front curves. Continue in garter st for 5 rows. On 6th row work 4 horizontal buttonholes. For each buttonhole, bind off 3 sts and on following row cast on 3 sts over bound off sts. Count number of sts between top of curve and beginning of decreases for V-neck. Subtract 12 sts from this amount and divide remaining sts by 3, which will be the number of sts between buttonholes. Make buttonholes, starting at 5 sts above top of curve on right side. Continue in garter st for total of 10 rows. Bind off on 11th row.

HOOKED RUG WITH BRAIDED BORDER

(page 35)

Finished size is approximately 30" diameter. This rug is made from an 18" circular latch-hook canvas (from a kit), surrounded by wool fabric braids. Follow kit directions to work center circle; instructions below are for making and attaching braids. You may also adapt this technique to other size and shape rugs.

MATERIALS: Shillcraft latch-hook rug kit #268 "Pisces" or any other 18"-diameter hooked rug (order catalog from Shillcraft, address on page 126); approximately 1 ⅓ yds. (or 1 lb.) each of three new or used firmly-woven wool fabrics to coordinate with center, 4 yds. total (see "BLESS THIS HOUSE" Rug instructions, page 101, for preparing fabric); braid folders * (optional, see Note): lacing needle * or large tapestry needle; strong, heavy thread, preferably linen, for lacing braids together; braid clamp (optional); large-eyed darning needle.

DIRECTIONS: Follow kit directions to construct and bind the 18" circular rug. From wool fabrics, cut or tear crosswise strips 1¾" wide. Join strips of the same fabric with bias seams (see Fig. 1); roll finished strips with seams on the inside.

The T-start: To start the border, join two of the finished strips with a bias seam (see Fig. 1). Fold the raw edges of the third strip toward the middle, then fold the strip in half, raw edges inside (see Fig. 2). (Some people prefer to use braid folders to keep the braids folded—see Note. If you use them, follow directions included.) Place this strip, open edge to the left, at the seam of the joined strip and sew in place (see Fig. 3). Now fold the joined strips in thirds (see Fig. 4). Your T-start is now completed. Place your thumb firmly over the seam (see Fig. 5). Flip strand #1 up and over strand #3. All open edges now face left. Pull #2 firmly over #1 (See Fig. 6). The T-loop at top should be straight and look the same on the front and back, with the seam on the edge of the loop so that it will be completely hidden when the rug is laced.

Braiding: The key to successful braiding is firm, even tension. Braids should be fat, not pulled and flattened. Secure the T-start in the clamp

FIG. 1   T-START

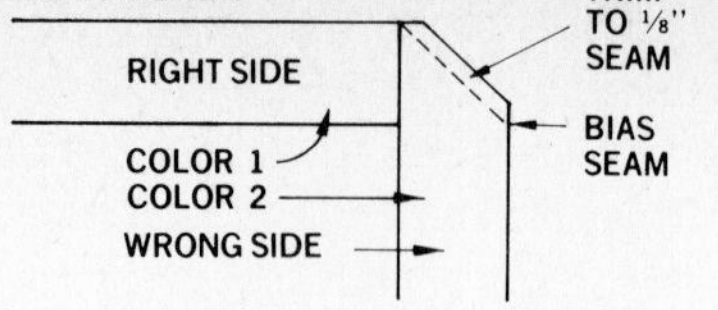

RIGHT SIDE

COLOR 1
COLOR 2
WRONG SIDE

TRIM TO ⅛" SEAM

BIAS SEAM

FIG. 2

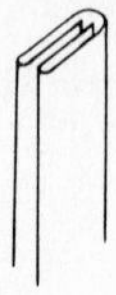

FIG. 3

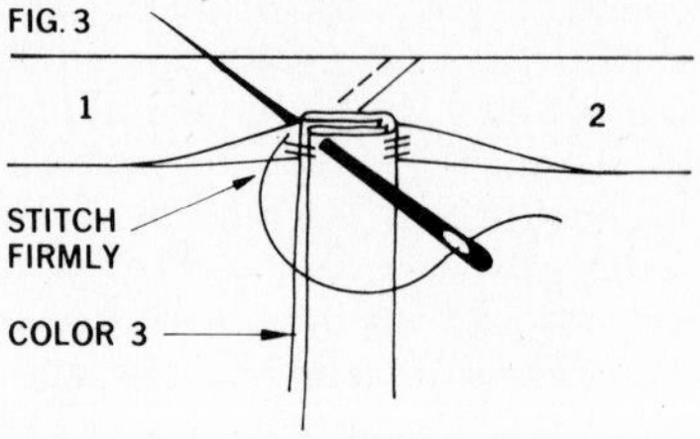

1 2

STITCH FIRMLY

COLOR 3

FIG. 4

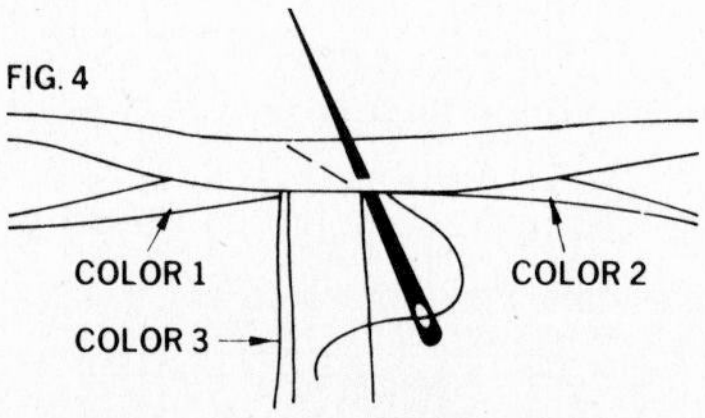

COLOR 1   COLOR 2
COLOR 3

FIG. 5

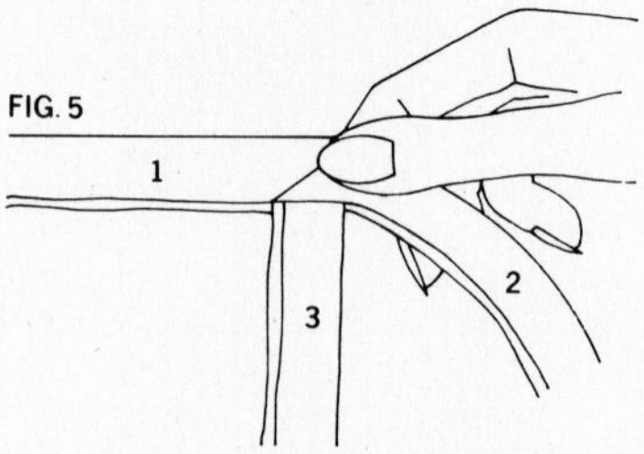

1

3   2

FIG. 6

SEAM   T

COLOR 2

3   1

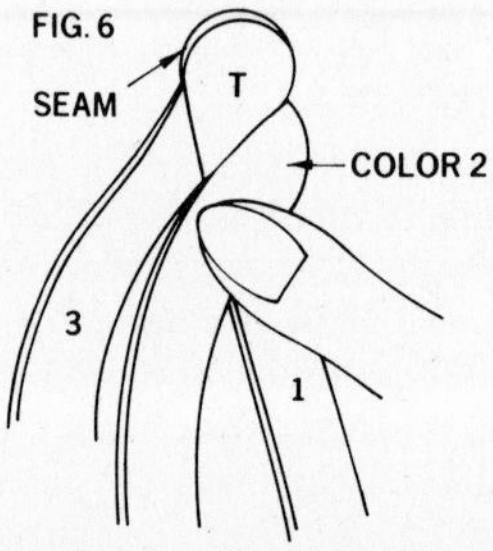

(or improvise by shutting it in a heavy drawer), open edges facing left (this is the rug's right side). Your thumbs are always on top of the strips keeping the tension even and the strips properly folded. Keep the open edges on the left as you braid (see Fig. 7). If little pleats, called tweeks, are occurring on the back, the strips are not evenly folded, the tension isn't even, or the fabric in that strip is a lighter weight than the two other strips.

Attaching the first braid to the hooked center: After you have finished braiding all but 8" of the strips, attach the first row of the border to the hooked center of the rug. To do this, thread the lacing thread through the darning needle and knot the thread. Sew

through the first loop of the T-start, making sure the knot is hidden inside the loop. Secure thread with a few more stitches, then remove thread from darning needle and place on lacing needle. Proceed as directed in Lacing (see below), but lace first row through the outer row of spaces on the rug canvas. Then proceed lacing remaining rows.

Lacing: Lacing is not the same as sewing. The lacing needle does not go into the fabric; it goes through the loops. The continuous braids are held together with a continuous lacing thread. Lace from right to left on the underside (with open edges toward center of rug), pulling firmly enough to conceal the thread inside the loops (sequence is shown in Fig. 8). Lace through every loop except when increasing. It is time to increase whenever the loop on the braid fails to match the loop on rug (see Fig. 9). To increase, lace through two loops on the braid and one on the rug, whenever necessary. Improper increasing causes two common problems: *First*, a ruffled or wavy edge results from too many increases. To correct this, gently stretch the braid in the next row and make fewer or no increases. *Second*, a cupped or buckled center results from too few increases. To correct this, unlace until the rug lies flat, then relace, adding more increases.

Tapering: When you have laced all but the last 8", trim the strips, taper-

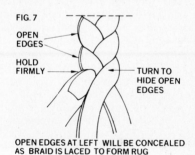

FIG. 7

OPEN EDGES

HOLD FIRMLY

TURN TO HIDE OPEN EDGES

OPEN EDGES AT LEFT WILL BE CONCEALED AS BRAID IS LACED TO FORM RUG

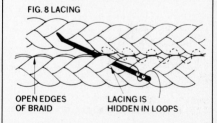

FIG. 8 LACING

OPEN EDGES OF BRAID

LACING IS HIDDEN IN LOOPS

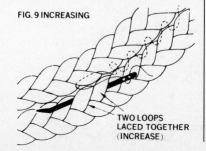

FIG. 9 INCREASING

TWO LOOPS LACED TOGETHER (INCREASE)

ing them to half their width. Braid for four more inches. Lace the entire tapered braid to the rug, then lace backward for six stitches to secure the thread. Use a crochet hook to weave the rest of the strips into the back of the rug and conceal the ends by tucking each one into a loop. (**Note:** a complete line of braiding equipment, including braid folders, lacing needles and clamps, is available from Braid-Aid 446 Washington St. Pembroke, MA 02359. Send one dollar for catalog.)

GREEN STRIPED CARDIGAN

(page 38)

Directions are given for size Small (6-8). Changes for sizes Medium (10-12) and Large (14-16) are in parentheses.

MATERIALS: Pinecroft knitting worsted, 2-ply, 4 oz. skeins: 3(4,4) skeins of Light Green (LG), one 4 oz. skein of Dark Green (DG) (see Note below to mail order yarn and matching fabric); knitting needles, No. 9 OR ANY SIZE NEEDLES WHICH WILL OBTAIN THE STITCH GAUGE BELOW; ½ yd. fabric.

(**Note:** Yarn and fabric are available by mail from Pinecroft, Dunbarton, NH 03301. Two-ply yarn is $2.50 per skein; coordinating hand-woven fabric, 33″ wide, is $10.00 per yard. Please include $1.50 per order for postage and handling. Send $1.00 to obtain complete fabric and yarn color card.)

GAUGE: 9 sts = 2″.

MEASUREMENTS:

Sizes	Small (6-8)	Medium (10-12)	Large (14-16)
	34″	38″	40½″
Width across back or front at underarms:	17″	19″	20¼″
Width across sleeve at upper arm:	12¾″	13¾″	14¾″

Sweater is made in stockinette stitch with garter border and/or fabric trim.

DIRECTIONS—BACK: With No. 9 needles and Light Green (LG), cast on 76(80,84) sts. **Rows 1 to 4 (Border):** K every row (garter st). Balance of Back is worked in stockinette st (k 1 row, p 1 row). **Rows 5 to 24:** LG. **Rows 25 & 26:** Dark Green (DG). **Rows 27 to 34:** LG. **Row 35:** With LG, slip 1 st, k 1, psso, k to last 2 sts, k 2 tog. **Row 36:** With LG, p 74(78,82) sts. **Rows 37 to 42:** With LG, work stockinette st. **Rows 43 & 44:** DG. **Rows 45 to 52:** LG. **Rows 53 & 54:** DG. **Rows 55 to 62:** LG. **Rows 63 & 64:** DG. **Rows 65 to 68:** LG. **Rows 69 & 70:** DG. **Rows 71 & 72:** LG. **Row 73:** LG same as Row 35. **Row 74:** LG p 72(76,80) sts. **Rows 75 to 78:** DG. **Rows 79 to 82:**

LG. **Rows 83 to 86:** DG. **Rows 87 & 88:** LG.
UNDERARM—Row 89: DG, bind off 5 st, k to end of row. **Row 90:** DG, p, bind off 5 st, p to end of row. **Row 91:** DG, k, bind off 4 st, k to end of row. **Row 92:** DG, p, bind off 4 st, p to end of row. **Rows 93 to 96:** DG stockinette on 54(58,62) sts. **Rows 97 & 98:** LG. **Rows 99 to 128:** DG.
RIGHT SHOULDER SHAPING: DG. **Row 129:** K, bind off 6(7,7) sts, k 7(7,8) sts, place 41(44,47) sts on holder for back neck and left shoulder. **Row 130:** P 7(7,8) sts. **Row 131:** Sl 1, k 1, psso, bind off all sts.
LEFT SHOULDER SHAPING: DG. **Row 129:** K 13(14,15) sts. **Row 130:** P, bind off 6(7,7) sts, p 7(7,8) sts. **Row 131:** K, bind off 7(7,8) sts.
BACK NECK: With left side facing, pick up 2 sts at left shoulder neckline, slip 28(30,32) sts from holder, pick up 2 sts at right shoulder neckline. With LG and garter st: **Row 129:** K 32(34,36) sts. **Row 130:** Sl 1, k 1, psso, k 28(30,32) sts, k 2 tog **Row 131:** K 30(32,34) sts. **Row 132:** Sl 1, k 1, psso, k 26(28,30) sts, k 2 tog. **Row 133:** K 28(30,32) sts. **Row 134:** K and bind off 28(30,32) sts.
LEFT FRONT: (**Note:** When changing color, twist threads to avoid making a hole). With LG, cast on 42(46,50) sts.
Rows 1 to 4: K every row (garter st). Begin stockinette st, keeping 4 st at neck edge in garter st and LG. **Row 5:** LG K across 42(46,50) sts. **Row 6:** LG K4, p 38(42,46) sts. **Rows 7 to 24:** Repeat Rows 5 & 6. **Row 25:** DG, k 38(42,46) sts **Rows 29 to 34:** LG same as Rows 5 and 6. **Row 35:** LG, k2 tog, k40(44,48) sts. **Row 36:** LG, k4, p 37(41,45) sts. **Rows 37 to 42:** LG, repeat Rows 5 and 6 over 37(41,45) sts. **Rows 43 & 44:** DG, as Rows 25 and 26, over 37(42,45) sts. **Rows 45 to 72:** Work color changes as for Back, keeping 4 border sts in LG and garter st. **Row 73:** LG same as Row 35. **Row 74:** Same as Row 36 on 36(40,44) sts. **Row 75:** DG, k36(40,44), LG k4. **Row 76:** LG, k4, DG p36(40,44). **Rows 77 and 78:** DG repeat Rows 75 and 76. **Row 79:** LG k40(44,48) sts. **Row 80:** LG k4, p36(40,44). **Rows 81 and 82:** LG same as Rows 79 and 80. **Rows 83 to 86:** Repeat Rows 75 to 78. **Rows 87 and 88:** Repeat Rows 79 and 80.
UNDERARM—Row 89: DG, k, bind off 5 sts, k 31(35,39), LG k4. **Row 90:** LG k 4, DG p 31(35,39). **Row 91:** DG, k and bind off 4 sts, k 27(31,35) sts, LG k 4. **Row 92:** LG k 4, DG p 27(31,35).
V NECK SHAPING—Row 93: DG k 25(29,33), k 2 tog, LG k4. **Row 94:** LG k 4, DG, P 26(30,34). **Rows 95 to 114:** Repeat Rows 93 and 94. Decrease 1 st every 2d row on inside of 4

st border until 20(24,28) sts remain (counting border sts) (10 dec) **Rows 115 to 126:** Continue with DG, dec 1 st every 4th row at inside of neck border 3 times, keeping border sts in LG, until 17(21,25) sts remain (counting border sts). **Row 127:** DG k 13(17,21), LG k 4. **Row 128:** LG k 4, DG P 13(17,21).
SHOULDER SHAPING—Row 129: DG k and bind off 6(7,8) sts, k 7(10,13), with LG k 4. **Row 130:** LG k 4, DG p 7(10,13) sts. **Row 131:** DG sl 1, k 1, psso, k 5(8,11) sts, LG k 4. **Row 132:** LG bind off 4 st, DG bind off remaining sts.
RIGHT FRONT: Work same as Left Front, reversing shaping.
SLEEVES— With LG, cast on 38(40,42) sts. **Rows 1 to 4:** LG k every row (garter st). **Rows 5 to 42:** LG work in stockinette, inc 1 st each end, every 12th row, 3 times to 44(46,48) sts. **Rows 43 to 106:** Following stripe pattern for Back Rows 25 to 88, inc 1 st each end, every 12th row, 4 times to 52(54,56) sts.
UNDERARM—Row 107: DG bind off 5 st, k to end of row. **Row 108:** DG bind off 5 st, p to end of row. **Row 109:** DG bind off 4 st, k to end of row. **Row 110:** DG bind off 4 st, p to end of row on 34(36,38) sts. **Row 111:** DG sl 1, k 1, psso, k to last 2 sts, k 2 tog. **Row 112:** DG p 32(34,36) sts. **Row 113:** LG as Row 111. **Row 114:** LG p30(32,34) sts. **Rows 115-136:** DG rpt Rows 111 and 112 until 8(10,12) sts remain. **Row 137:** DG bind off 8(10,12) sts.
FINISHING: Sew side seams, matching stripes. Sew sleeve seams, matching stripes. Set in sleeves, matching seams. Take the following sweater measurements for binding: front/neck edge; hem edge; sleeve hem edges. From fabric, cut bias strips 3″ wide, piecing to get above measurements. For sleeve bindings, sew a bias seam to make a cylinder. Finish one long edge of each binding with edgestitching, zigzag or a ¼″ fold. Press strips in half. Pin unfinished edges to sweater edges on right side of sweater. Machine stitch a ¼″ seam. Turn bindings to wrong side of sweater on fold lines; hand blind-stitch in place.

PINK RIBBED SWEATER

(page 39)

Directions are given for size Small (6-8). Changes for sizes Medium (10-12) and Large (14-16) are in parentheses.
MATERIALS: Pinecroft 2-ply knitting worsted: 5(6,7) 4 oz. skeins (see Note below to mail order yarn and matching fabric); knitting needles, one pair each No. 8 and No. 10 OR ANY

SIZE NEEDLES WHICH WILL OBTAIN THE STITCH GAUGE BELOW.

GAUGE: On No. 10 needles, 4 sts = 1″; 8 rows = 1″.

(**Note:** Yarn and fabric are available by mail from Pinecroft, Dunbarton, NH, 03301. 2-ply yarn is $2.50 per skein; coordinating hand-woven fabric, 33″ wide, is $10.00 per yard. Please include $1.50 per order for postage and handling. Send $1.00 to obtain complete fabric and yarn color card.)

MEASUREMENTS:

	Small	Medium	Large
Sizes:	(6-8)	(10-12)	(14-16)
Bust:	34″	38″	40½″
Width across back or front at underarms:	17″	19″	20¼″
Width across sleeve at upper arm:	12¾″	13¾″	14¾″

DIRECTIONS—PATTERN STITCH:
Row 1 (right side): P 1, *k 1 in row below, p 1, repeat from *. **Row 2:** Slip 1, *p 1, k 1 in row below, repeat from *.
BACK: With No. 8 needles, cast on 73(81,85) sts. **Row 1:** P 1, *k 1, p 1, repeat from * to end of row. **Row 2:** K 1, *p 1, k 1, repeat from * to end of row. Repeat these 2 rows of ribbing for 18 rows or 3″. Change to No. 10 needles and Pattern Stitch. Work 90(94,98) rows of Pattern St or 11(11½,12)″ from ribbing.
Armhole—Row 1: With right side facing, bind off 6 st at beg of row, continue in pattern to end of row. **Row 2:** Bind off 6 st at beg of row, continue in pattern to end of row. **Row 3:** Bind off 2 st at beg of row, continue in pattern to end of row. **Row 4:** Bind off 2 st at beg of row, continue in pattern to end of row. Work even in pattern on 57(65,69) sts for 56(60,64) rows, or 7(7½,8)″.
Shoulder Shaping: Continuing in pattern, with right side facing, bind off 7(8,10) sts at beg of next 2 rows. Then bind off 8(9,9) sts at be of next 2 rows. Place remaining 27(31,31) sts on holder for High Neck.
FRONT: Same as Back to underarm.
Underarm: Working in pattern, BO 6 st at beg of next 2 rows. BO 2 sts at beg of next 2 rows. Work even on 57(65,69) sts until work measures from underarm 5½(6,6½)″, or 44(48,52) rows.
LEFT FRONT—Right side: Continuing in pattern, work across 17(21,23) sts. Turn. **Next row:** Work across 17(21,23) sts. **Next row:** Work across 15(19,21) sts. Place 2 sts at neck edge on holder to be picked up for High Neck. **Next row:** Work on 15(19,21) sts. Work even on 15(19,21) sts for 8(12,16) more rows, or a total of 56,(60,64) from underarm.
Shoulder Shaping: At armhole edge, bind off 7(9,10) sts. **Next row:** Work in

pattern across 8(10,11) sts. **Next row:** Bind off remaining 8(10,11) sts.
RIGHT FRONT: Same as Left Front, placing 2 st at neck edge on holder.
Shoulder Shaping: Same as Left Front.
HIGH NECK: With No. 8 needles, working in ribbing of k1 p1, with right side of sweater facing, pick up 6(8,8) sts at front edge, place front center 27(31,31) sts on needle, pu 6(8,8) sts along right front edge, place center back 27(31,31) sts on needle. **Next row (wrong side facing):** (k1, p1) 13(16,16) times, k 2 tog, p 1, (k1, p1) 19(21,21) times. Work in ribbing of k 1, p 1 on 66(76,76) sts for 38 rows or 6½″ on all sizes.
SLEEVES: With No. 8 needles, cast on 37(39,41) sts. Work in ribbing of k 1 p1, as for Back. Change to No. 10 needles and pattern st. Work even for 14 rows. **Increase Row:** On 33rd row, working in pattern, increase 1 st at each side, k1, p1 in row below of same st (increase made), *k1 in row below, p 1, repeat from * to last st, p 1 in row below of last st, k in same st (increase made). **Rows 34 through 46:** Work even in pattern. **Row 47 (right side):** P1, k1 in row below of same st (increase), * p1, k1 in row below, * repeat from * in pattern to last st, k1 in row below, then p in same st (increase). **Rows 48 through 150:** Continue in pattern, inc every 14th row as above 7 more times until 55(57,59) sts. (For Medium and Large, if necessary, increase length of sleeve.)
Underarm—Row 151: BO 6 sts, work in pattern to end. **Row 152:** BO 6 sts, work in pattern to end. **Row 153:** BO 2 sts, work in pattern to end. **Row 154:** BO 2 sts, work in pattern to end. **Rows 155-186:** Work in pattern on 39(41,43) sts, decreasing 1 st at beg of every row by sl 1, k 1 in row below (or p, according to st), psso, work to end of row. **Row 187:** Bind off 7(9,11) sts.
FINISHING: Sew shoulder seams, side seams, sleeve seams, neck seam. Sew in sleeves, matching seams. Block lightly.

CROCHETED COAT-SWEATER

(page 41)

Directions are given for size Small (8-10). Changes for sizes Medium (12-14), Large (16-18) and Extra-Large (40-42) are in parentheses.
MATERIALS: Tahki Donegal Tweed (3.6 oz. skeins): 14(16,18,19) skeins of purple #811; crochet hook, size H, OR ANY SIZE HOOK WHICH WILL OBTAIN THE STITCH GAUGE BELOW.
GAUGE: 3 sts =1″, 5 rows = 2″.
MEASUREMENTS:

	Small	Medium	Large	Ex- Large
Sizes:	(8-10)	(12-14)	(16-18)	(40-42)
Bust:	43″	47″	52″	56″

Width across back at underarms:

21″	23″	26″	28″

Width across each front at underarm (*including Collar*):

11″	12″	13″	14″

Width across sleeve at upper arm:

14½″	15″	16″	17″

DIRECTIONS—(Note: Coat is started with Yoke and Sleeve sections worked all in one piece. Back, Fronts and Collar are added afterwards as specified in directions.)
YOKE (*worked vertically*): Starting at right side edge, ch 46(48,52,54) to measure 15(16,17,18)″. **Row 1:** Hdc in 3rd ch from hook, hdc in each ch across—44(46,50,52) hdc (do not count ch at beg of row as 1 hdc). Mark Row 1 for right side. Ch 2, turn. (Do not count ch-2 as 1 hdc). **Row 2:** Hdc in each hdc across—44(46,50,52) hdc. Ch 2, turn. Rpt Row 2 for pat until piece measures 5(5½,6,6½)″ from beg, ending with a row on right side (end of row is lower edge of Back Yoke). Mark each end of last row to indicate end of shoulder portion. Ch 2, turn.
CENTER BACK: Hdc in each of first 22(23,25,26) sts; do not work over rem sts (rem sts form right front edge of Yoke). Ch 2, turn. Continue in pat over back 22(23,25,26) sts until length from Row 1 of Center Back is 11(12,13,14)″, ending with a wrong-side row at top edge. Mark lower end of last row to indicate end of center back Yoke. Ch 24(25,27,28) for left front edge, turn. **Next Row:** Hdc in 3rd ch from hook, hdc in each ch and in each hdc across last row—44(46,50,52) hdc. Ch 2, turn. Work even in pat for 5(5½,6,6½)″ for other shoulder section. Mark each end of last row to indicate end of Yoke and underarms of sleeve.
LEFT SLEEVE: Work in pat until length of sleeve (from underarm markers) is 16½(17,17½,18)″ or desired length from underarm, allowing 1½″ for cuff. Cut yarn and fasten.
RIGHT SLEEVE: Working along opposite side of starting chain of Yoke with wrong side of Row 1 facing, attach yarn to corner ch st, ch 2, hdc in same ch and in each of next 43(45,49,51) ch. Mark each end of starting chain for underarms. Ch 2, turn. Work in pat st over 44(46,50,52) hdc until same length as Left Sleeve. Cut yarn and fasten.
Center Back Panel (*worked horizontally*)—**Row 1:** Working over ends of rows along lower edge of center back portion of Yoke, attach yarn at marker at beg of center back Yoke, ch 2, work 35(38,44,47) hdc, evenly placed along lower edge of center portion of Yoke to next marker (do not work along shoulder portions of Yoke). Ch 2, turn. Work in pat over these sts until length of back panel is 27(27,28,28)″. Cut yarn and fasten.

106

Left Side Panel (*worked vertically*): With right side facing, working along left side edge of center panel, attach yarn at top end of side edge, ch 2, work 81(81,84,84) hdc evenly spaced along left side edge to lower corner (*be careful to keep work flat*). Ch 2, turn. Work even in pat until side panel measures 5(5½,6,6½)"; mark last row for side seam; mark top end of same row for underarm; continue to work even in pat for 5(5½,6,6½)" more, measuring from (marked) seam row, end at top edge. Cut yarn and fasten.

Right Side Panel: Starting at lower corner, work right side panel along right side edge of center panel to correspond with Left Side Panel, ending at lower edge. Cut yarn and fasten.

Joining Sections: Fold Yoke and Sleeves in half crosswise (right side out), with folds at centers of sleeves. Starting at underarm markers, sew sleeve seams. Fold each side panel in half lengthwise (right side out), with fold at side seam (marked row). Matching underarm markers, sew top edges of side panels to corresponding lower edges of back and both front shoulder portions of Yoke, adjusting to fit, if necessary.

FRONTS, SHAWL COLLAR AND LOWER BAND: With right side facing, attach yarn to first st at lower corner of right side panel. **Rnd 1:** Ch 2, working along entire outer edge of coat, hdc in each st across right front edge of side panel, hdc in each st up right front edge of Yoke; work 38(41,44,47) hdc across neck edge of center back of Yoke, hdc in each st down left front edge of Yoke and in each hdc down front edge of left panel to lower corner, 3 hdc in corner st, hdc evenly along entire lower edge of coat *be careful to keep work flat*, end with 2 hdc in same st as first hdc. Join with sl st to top of first hdc. Ch 2, turn. **Rnd 2:** Making 3 hdc in center st of 3-hdc group at each corner, hdc in each hdc around. Join with sl st to first hdc. Ch 2, turn, Rpt last rnd 8 more times. Cut yarn and fasten.

Front and Collar Border: With right side facing, attach yarn in center st of lower right front corner group, ch 2. **Row 1:** Hdc in each hdc along right front edge, collar and left front edge to center st of lower left front corner; do not work across lower edge. Ch 2, turn. **Row 2:** Hdc in each hdc across last row. Ch 2, turn. At end of last row, ch 1, turn. **Last Rnd:** Sc evenly along entire outer edge of coat, making 3 sc in each corner st. Join to first sc. Cut yarn and fasten.

Pocket (*make two*): Starting at side edge, ch 29 for all sizes. **Row 1:** Hdc in 3rd ch from hook and in each ch across—27 hdc. Work in pat as for

coat until pocket measures 7". Cut yarn and fasten.

FINISHING: Pin coat to measurements on a padded surface; cover with a damp cloth and allow to dry; **do not press.** Sew pocket to center of each front, approximately 9" above lower edge. Turn 1½" cuff to right side at lower edge of each sleeve and stitch in place. Fold shawl collar in half to right side.

CAFTAN

(*page 41*)

One size fits all.
MATERIALS: 3½ yds. 44"-wide fabric; 8 yds. foldover braid.

FIG. 1 FACING PATTERN

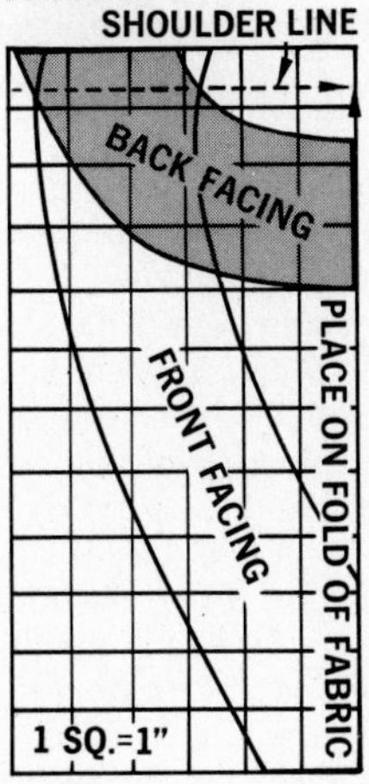

FIG. 2 CAFTAN: PLACE ON CROSSWISE FOLD OF FABRIC

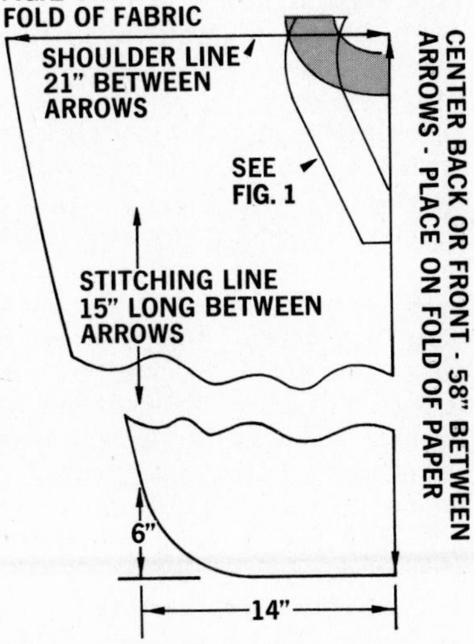

DIRECTIONS: Following directions in box on page 18, enlarge the patterns for Back Facing and for Front Facing (*see* Fig. 1). Set them aside. You do not need to trace the whole Caftan pattern. Fold the whole piece of fabric in half lengthwise, matching edges, and press the fold *lightly* to mark Center Back and Front. Unfold fabric and refold it in half *crosswise*, matching edges. Pin the two layers together along the lengthwise creases

and press the crosswise fold *lightly* to mark shoulderline. On the shoulderline mark Caftan outer edges 21" left of center. On the Center Front crease, mark Caftan bottom 58" from the shoulderline (or adjust to your own height). Draw a bottom edge left of, and at right angles to, Center Front line. On it measure 14" from center and at that point, draw a 6" upright. In this 6" corner, draw a curve. Then, with a yardstick, continue a slanted side edge up to the Caftan outer edge at the shoulderline. Cut out along the drawn side and bottom edges through both layers. Refold the fabric on the lengthwise crease, pinning the two layers together on the shoulderline. Cut the uncut layer to match the cut edges. Cut out Back and Front Facings, piecing Front Facing at center front if necessary. Pin Back Facing to Front Facing at shoulders, right sides together. Stitch ⅝" seams. Press seams open. Trim outside facing edges with pinking shears. Open up Caftan. At center, pin facing to Caftan, right sides together, with centers and shoulderlines matching. Stitch facing to Caftan ⅝" from the inside facing edges. Trim away Caftan to make a neck opening to match facing opening. Clip seam allowances to stitching at Center Front. Turn facing to inside and press. From the outside, topstitch through both layers about ¼" away from neck edge. Bind outside edges of Caftan with foldover braid. Mark 15" long vertical stitching lines on front (*see* Fig 2), starting 15" below shoulderline and about 2" to 4" in from sides. With outer edges matching, pin front to back on the stitching lines. Try on, adjust pins (garment should be loose and roomy), then stitch.

KNITTED PILLOW

(*page 42*)

Finished pillow cover measures approximately 13" × 15".
MATERIALS: Bucilla "Fruitwood" Craft & Weaving Yarn (2 oz. skeins): 2 skeins Natural, color #1 (MC) and 1 skein Honey, color #2 (A); "Rustique" (50 gram balls): 1 ball each of Terra Cotta, color #9 (B), and Blue, color #10 (C); Tapestry yarn (40 yds): 1 skein Rose, color #079 (D) or a few yards 4-ply knitting worsted in Dusty Rose #338; knitting needles, one pair No. 5 OR ANY SIZE NEEDLE WHICH WILL OBTAIN THE STITCH GAUGE BELOW; crochet hooks sizes F and H; ½ yd. fabric for pillow lining and 1 lb. bag "Fiberloft" (Stearns & Foster) for stuffing.

GAUGE: 11 sts = 2" in MC st st; 13 rows = 2".
DIRECTIONS: (**Note:** Wind 8 bob-

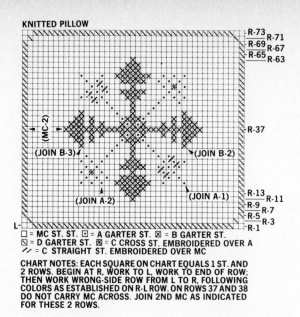

KNITTED PILLOW

□ = MC ST. ST. ⊡ = A GARTER ST. ⊠ = B GARTER ST.
◨ = D GARTER ST. ▨ = C CROSS ST. EMBROIDERED OVER A
〃 = C STRAIGHT ST. EMBROIDERED OVER MC

CHART NOTES: EACH SQUARE ON CHART EQUALS 1 ST. AND 2 ROWS. BEGIN AT R, WORK TO L, WORK TO END OF ROW; THEN WORK WRONG-SIDE ROW FROM L TO R, FOLLOWING COLORS AS ESTABLISHED ON R-L ROW. ON ROWS 37 AND 38 DO NOT CARRY MC ACROSS. JOIN 2ND MC AS INDICATED FOR THESE 2 ROWS.

bins as follows: 1 MC, 2 A [double strands] 3 B, 2 D. Color C is embroidered with darning needle after Front is completed. Color A is worked with 2 strands of yarn throughout. When changing colors, always bring new color under old, to avoid holes.)

FRONT: With MC cast on 49 sts. K1 row. P 1 row. **Inc. row:** K 1, *pick up horizontal thread bet sts and knit through back loop (inc made),* k to last st, rpt bet *, k 1. P 1 row. Continue in st st, inc at beg and end of every other row as established 6 more times (63 sts). End with p row. **Begin Inside Border:** K 1 MC, inc 1, k 11, drop MC; join D and k 39 D, drop D; join MC bobbin (MC-2) and k 11 MC, inc 1 st, k1. (Row 1 of chart completed.) **Row 2:** P 13 MC, k 39 D, p 13 MC; break off MC-2. **Row 3:** K1 MC, inc 1, k 11 MC, k 1 D, drop D, k 39 MC, join D-2 and k 1 D, drop D, k 11MC, inc 1, k 1. **Row 4:** P 13 MC, k 1 D, p 39 MC, k 1 D, p 13 MC. **Row 5:** K 1 MC, inc 1, k 11 MC, k 1 D, k 41 MC, k 1 D, k 11 MC, inc 1, k 1 (69 sts). **Row 6:** P 13 MC, k 1 D, p 41 MC, k 1 D, p MC to end. **Row 7:** K 13 MC, k 1 D, k 41 MC, k 1 D, k 13 MC. **Row 8:** P 13 MC, k 1 D, p 41 MC, k 1 D, p 13 MC. **Rows 9 & 10:** Rpt Rows 7 and 8. (Inside border established.) Continuing border D in garter st as established, and keeping 13 MC st sts at right and left edges, work center design following chart Rows 11-70. See chart notes and join additional bobbins as indicated. **Row 71 (dec row):** K 1, k 2 tog, k 11 MC, k 1 D, k 39 MC, k 1 D, k 11 MC, k 2 tog, k 1 (67 sts). **Row 72:** P 13 MC, k 1 D, p 39 MC, k 1 D, p 13 MC. **Row 73:** K 1 MC, k 2 tog, k 11 MC, k 39 D, k 11 MC, k 2 tog, k 1 (65 sts). **Row 74:** P 13 MC, k 39 D, p 13 MC. Break off D. Continue with MC in st st, decreasing 1 st at beg and end of every other row as established, until 49 sts remain, ending with k row. Bind off from wrong side

as to knit. Embroider C as shown on chart.

Border trim (worked on front only): Join C at any corner, and using H hook, crochet 1 row sl st evenly around edge; join with sl st. Turn and, working through back loops only, sl st in each sl st around. Fasten off C. Dampen front, pin out on padded board and let dry. **Do not press.**

BACK: With MC, cast on 49 sts. K 1 row. P 1 row. Continue in st st, increasing 1 st at beg and end of every other row as for Front, 10 times (69 sts). Work even until Back measures same as Front from cast-on edge to beg of dec (about 64 more rows). Dec 1 st at beg and end of every k row until 49 sts remain. Bind off from wrong side as to knit.

FINISHING: With right sides of cover tog, and front border trim turned to inside (bet front and back), sl st 3 sides of cover tog with MC and size F crochet hook, inserting hook through MC sts at outside edge of cover. Fasten MC but do not break yarn. Turn cover to right side, insert pillow (see below, to make pillow), and sl st 4th side of cover tog, inserting hook just below border trim. Fasten off, leaving short end.*(**Note:***To remove cover for hand-washing, pull out this row of sl st and re-crochet after washing.)

To make pillow: Cut 2 pieces of fabric for pillow lining, 1" larger than finished cover (slightly stretched). Seam tog, leaving ½" allowance, on 3 sides; turn and stuff. Stitch 4th side.

QUILTED PILLOW

(page 42)

MATERIALS: ½ yd. cotton fabric in a large floral print; thread to match for quilting; ½ yd. soft fabric for quilt

backing; ½ yd. velvet in a complementary color for pillow backing, if desired; 1½ yds. ⅝" velvet ribbon in a complementary color; 3 yds. 2" velvet ribbon in same color; thread to match; 3 yds. cord for gathering wide ribbon; 1½ yds. 1½" gathered crochet-type lace edging; 1 yd. polyester quilt batting; 14" pillow form (Stearns & Foster).

DIRECTIONS: Cut two 18" squares from floral fabric (or cut one from floral fabric and one from velvet.) Cut one 18" square from fabric for quilt backing and from polyester batting. Place batting between wrong sides of pillow fabric and quilt backing fabric; machine baste around all four sides. Following directions on page 128 , outline quilt around flowers in print and, if desired, quilt along some lines inside flowers. Pin ecru edging under one long edge of narrow ribbon; machine stitch on ribbon, close to edge. Pin ribbon with edging to quilted pillow front, placing inside edge of ribbon 1½" from outer raw edge and folding ribbon back to miter corners. Stitch close to inside edge of ribbon. With right sides together, pin square for pillow back to quilted pillow front, making sure ribbon and edging are not caught in seam. Sew ½" seams around 3 sides; turn; press. Gather one long edge of wide ribbon to 1⅞ yds as follows: Line a thin cord up with edge of ribbon and zigzag stitch on the ribbon, over the cord, being careful not to catch it with the needle; carefully push ribbon along cord to gather. Pin gathered edge of ribbon to pillow front, ½" in from seam on three sides and ¾" in from raw edge. Sew ribbon to pillow by hand with small stitches. Cut two more 18" squares from remainder of polyester batting; place on both sides of pillow form. Insert pillow form and batting in pillow. Fold ½" under on both raw edges of pillow opening and slipstitch closed.

NEEDLEPOINT PILLOW

(page 43)

Finished size, 16" square.
MATERIALS: DMC Art. 89 (11 yd. skeins): 8 skeins #2902 Grape, 9 skeins #2354 Cinnamon, 7 skeins #2797 True Blue, 8 skeins #2932 Blue Gray, 8 skeins #2310 Black, 15 skeins #2299 Wood Brown, 6 skeins #2233 Lavender Gray, 7 skeins #2947 Orange, 5 skeins #2741 Lt. Orange, 5 skeins #2499 Dk. Green, 5 skeins #2912 Lt. Green, 6 skeins #2302 Soft Brown, 8 skeins #2613 Sand; ½ yd. #10 needlepoint canvas; tapestry needle; ½ yd. fabric for pillow back; 14" zipper; 16" square pillow form (Stearns & Foster).

DIRECTIONS: See needlepoint tips on page 5. Draw a 16″ square in center of canvas. Tape edges to prevent raveling. Center and work motifs in cross stitch as shown in diagram. (**Note:** One square on diagram = 4 cross stitches. Diagram represents only small portion of pillow — repeat motifs until 16″ square is filled.)

FINISHING: Block finished pillow top. Cut fabric 17″ square for backing. Seam to pillow top just *inside* first row of cross stitches, inserting zipper on side according to zipper instructions. Insert pillow form.

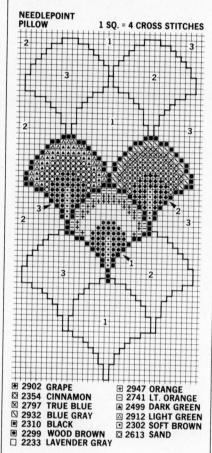

NEEDLEPOINT PILLOW   1 SQ. = 4 CROSS STITCHES

⊡ 2902 GRAPE	⊞ 2947 ORANGE
⊠ 2354 CINNAMON	⊡ 2741 LT. ORANGE
⊠ 2797 TRUE BLUE	▲ 2499 DARK GREEN
◩ 2932 BLUE GRAY	⊡ 2912 LIGHT GREEN
⊡ 2310 BLACK	⊡ 2302 SOFT BROWN
⊡ 2299 WOOD BROWN	⊞ 2613 SAND
☐ 2233 LAVENDER GRAY	

WOVEN PILLOW

(page 43)

Pillow measures 11″ x 13½″.
MATERIALS: M E Enterprises "Warp and Woof Weaving Board" Kit. (Kit includes: Weaving board measuring 13½″ x 18″; one 15″ shuttle; one 6″ shuttle; one large weaving needle.) (**Note:** It would be advisable to purchase an additional large weaving needle.) Bucilla yarns: 1 ball "Rustique," color #10 Blue (A); 1 skein "Fruitwood," color #2 Honey (B); 1 skein "Birchwood," color #100 White (C); 1 skein "Willow," color #2 Grey (D); 1 skein "Pinetree," color #2 Rust (E); 1 skein "Colossal," color #5 Chocolate (F); 1 skein "Mimosa," color #6 Orange (G); 1 skein "Rustique," color #9 Terra Cotta (H);

3 packages "Glossilla," color #24 Orange; ⅜ yd. each muslin and fabric for pillow back; 1 lb. package "Fiberloft."

DIRECTIONS: Use "Glossilla" to warp, following the directions in weaving kit. To weave, follow general directions included in the kit. Note that your woof should be loosely woven to avoid pulling the warp lines. Use small shuttle unless needle is indicated. **Step 1:** Begin by winding enough A on your small shuttle to be able to work through the warp comfortably. Begin at bottom and weave (*under and over* each warp line). Repeat for three rows. **Step 2:** With B, weave one row, pulling up a small loop at each warp with your fingers. **Step 3:** With C, weave one row pulling up a small loop at each warp with your fingers. **Step 4:** With D, using yarn *doubled* on needle, weave 2 rows *over two warps and under two warps.* **Step 5:** See diagram. Now weave a row of H and a row of D, alternating color H & D for a total of 11 rows, picking up every two warps. **Step 6:** With C, repeat step 3. **Step 7:** With B, repeat step 4. **Step 8:** With A, weave two rows. **Step 9:** With E, weave one row. **Step 10:** With A, weave two rows. **Step 11:** With B, repeat step 2. **Step 12:** With C, repeat step 3. **Step 13:** With F, weave one row. **Step 14:** With G, weave one row. **Step 15:** With D, using yarn *doubled* on needle, weave 7 rows. **Step 16:** With G, weave one row. Rpt Step 5. Rpt Step 16. Rpt Step 15. **Step 17:** With F, weave one row. **Step 18:** With C, repeat step 3. **Step 19:** With A, using yarn *doubled* on needle, weave 2 rows. **Step 20:** With H, weave 1 row. You have now reached the halfway mark of your pillow. Now, start with **Step 19** and working in reverse, repeat the first half to complete pillow top.

FINISHING: To remove weaving from frame, lift off one end at a time and knot adjoining loops together until all loops are tied, then do same for the other side. Cut piece of muslin same size as the weaving. Pin weaving to muslin and stay stitch in place. *Do not cut off any loose ends of the weaving, or it will start to ravel.* Cut pillow back same size as weaving. Place weaving and backing face to face and stitch around rectangle *twice,* leave 5″ opening at one end. Reverse pillow. Make 12 tassels, each

4″ long, from remaining yarn scraps. Attach three together to make one large tassel for each corner. Thread needle with same yarn as the tassel and attach a tassel to each corner. Tie off ends on inside. Stuff pillow with fiberfill. Slipstitch opening.

TWEEDY V-NECK SWEATER

(page 44)

Directions are given for size Small (6-8). Changes for sizes Medium (10-12) and Large (14-16) are in parentheses.

MATERIALS: Bucilla "Horizon": 5 (6,6) 2 oz. balls; knitting needles, Nos. 8 and 6 OR ANY SIZE NEEDLES WHICH WILL OBTAIN THE STITCH GAUGE BELOW.

GAUGE: On No. 8 needles, 9 sts = 2″; 13 rows = 2″.

MEASUREMENTS:

	Small	Medium	Large
Sizes:	(6-8)	(10-12)	(14-16)
Bust:	32″	35″	38½″
Width across back at underarm	16″	17½″	19¼″

DIRECTIONS—BACK: With No. 6 needles, cast on 71 (79, 87) sts. **Ribbing—Row 1** (wrong side): P 1, * k 1, p 1; rpt from * across. **Row 2:** K 1, * p 1, k 1; rpt from * across. Rpt last 2 rows until 2″ from beg, end with Row 2. Change to No. 8 needles and work in st st — k 1 row, p 1 row until 10½″ from beg, end with p row.

SLEEVES: Cast 22 sts on end of needle for left sleeve, transfer back to needle; cast on 22 sts for right sleeve; 115 (123, 131) sts. Continue to work even in st st until sleeve measures 7½ (8, 8)″ from cast on edge, end with p row. **Shape Shoulders:** Bind off 12 (13, 14) sts at beg of next 2 rows; 13 (14, 15) sts at beg of next 2 row; 14 (15, 16) sts at beg of next 2 rows, bind off rem 37 (39, 41) sts.

FRONT: Work same as Back to Underarm.

SLEEVE AND DIVIDE FOR LEFT FRONT: Cast 22 sts on end of needle for left sleeve, k across next 35 (39, 43) sts for Left Front, sl next st to safety pin for neck ribbing, sl rem 35 (39, 43) sts to holder for right front; 57 (61, 65) sts on Left Front. Working on Left Front only, dec 1 st at neck edge every 2nd row 18 (19, 20) times; 39 (42, 45) sts. Work even until same length as back from cast on edge, end with p row. **Shape Shoulder:** From arm edge, bind off 12 (13, 14) sts once, 13 (14, 15) sts once, bind off rem sts.

RIGHT FRONT: From right side, sl sts from holder to needle, k across 35 (39, 43) sts, cast 22 sts on end of needle for right sleeve; 57 (61, 65) sts. Complete to correspond to Left Front, reversing shaping. Sew left shoulder seam.

WOVEN PILLOW

▬▬ **RUSTIQUE TERRA COTTA, COLOR #9**
≡≡ **WILLOW GREY, COLOR #2**

NECK RIBBING: From right side, with No. 6 needles, pick up and k 36 (38, 40) sts on back neck, 49 (52, 53) sts along left neck edge, place a marker on needle, k seam st from safety pin, place a marker on needle, pick up and k 49 (52, 53) sts on right neck edge—134 (143, 147) sts. (**Note:** sl markers.) **Row 1 (wrong side):** P 1, * k 1, p 1; rpt from * to end. **Row 2:** *K 1, p 1; rpt from * to within 2 sts of marker, sl 1, k 1, psso, sl marker, k seam st, sl marker, k 2 tog, p 1, k 1 to end. **Row 3:** P 1, k 1, to within 2 sts of marker, sl 1, k 1, psso, sl marker, p seam st, sl marker, k 2 tog, p 1, k 1 to end. Rpt Rows 2 and 3 until 1″ from beg, bind off in ribbing. Sew right shoulder seam.

SLEEVE RIBBING: From right side, beg at underarm, pick up and k 51 (55, 59) sts. Work ribbing same as Back for 1″. Bind off in ribbing. Sew side and sleeve seams. Steam lightly.

LACY ECRU BLOUSE

(page 44)

Directions are given for size Small (6-8). Changes for sizes Medium (10-12) and Large (14) are in parentheses.
MATERIALS: J. & P. Coats "Knit-Cro-Sheen" mercerized cotton: 6 (6, 7) 250 yd balls of color #61; knitting needles, 1 pair #4 OR ANY SIZE NEEDLES WHICH WILL OBTAIN THE STITCH GAUGE BELOW.
GAUGE: 6 sts = 1″; 10 rows = 1″.
MEASUREMENTS:

Size:	Small (6-8)	Medium (10-12)	Large (14)
Body bust size:	30½-31½″	32½-34″	36″
Sweater bust size:	33″	35″	37″
Width across back or front at underarm:	16½″	17½″	18½″
Length from shoulder to lower edge:	20½″	22″	23″
Length of side seam:	14″	14½″	15″
Length of sleeve seam (excluding ruffle):	14″	14½″	15″
Width across sleeve at upper arm:	11½″	12½″	13½″

DIRECTIONS—BACK: Starting at lower edge, cast on 98 (104, 110) sts. Work in garter stitch (k each row) for 1½″. Now work in pattern as follows—**Row 1 and all odd-numbered rows:** P across. **Row 2 (right side):** * Yo, k 3, yo, sl 1, k 2 tog, psso. Rpt from * to last 2 sts, k 2. **Row 4:** * Yo, sl 1, k 1, psso, k 1, k 2 tog, yo, k 1. Rpt from *; end with yo, sl 1, k 1, psso. **Row 6:** K 1, * yo, sl 1, k 2 tog, psso, yo, k 3. Rpt from * across, end

last rpt with k 4 instead of k 3. **Row 8:** * K 2 tog, yo, k 1, yo, sl 1, k 1, psso, k 1. Rpt from * across, end last rpt with k 3 instead of k 1. **Row 10:** K 4, * yo, sl 1, k 2 tog, psso, yo, k 3. Rpt from * to last 4 sts, yo, sl 1, k 2 tog, psso, yo, k1. **Row 11:** P across. Repeating Rows 4-11 for pattern, work until total length is 14″ (14½″, 15″), end on right side.

Armhole Shaping: Continuing in pattern, bind off 6 sts at beg of next 2 rows, then 4 sts at beg of following 2 rows. **Next Row:** Decreasing one st at each end, p across. **Following Row:** Keeping in pattern, work across. Rpt last 2 rows once more—74 (80, 86) sts. Work even in pattern until length from first row of armhole shaping is 6½″ (7½″, 8″); end on right side.

Left Shoulder and Neck Shaping— Row 1: Bind off first 8 (8, 9) sts, work across until there are 21 (23, 25) sts on right-hand needle; place remaining sts on a stitch holder. Turn. **Row 2:** Bind off first 3 sts, complete row in pattern. **Row 3:** Bind off first 6 (7, 8) sts, complete in pattern. **Rows 4-5:** Rpt last 2 rows. Bind off rem sts.

Right Shoulder and Neck Shaping: Slip sts from holder onto needle, attach thread at neck edge. **Row 1:** Bind off first 16 (18, 18) sts, work in pattern across. **Row 2:** Bind off first 8 (8, 9) sts, work in pattern across. Starting with Row 2, complete as for Left Shoulder and Neck Shaping.

FRONT: Work as for Back until length is 3½″ (4½″, 5″) from first row of armhole shaping; end on right side.

Right Neck Shaping—Row 1: Work in pattern across first 28 (31, 34) sts; place remaining sts on a stitch holder. Turn. **Row 2:** Bind off first 4 (5, 5) sts, complete row. **Row 3:** Work even. **Row 4:** Bind off first 4 sts, complete row—20 (22, 25) sts. Work even until length of armhole is same as on Back, end at armhole edge.

Right Shoulder Shaping—Row 1: Bind off first 8 (8, 9) sts, complete row. **Row 2:** Work even. **Row 3:** Bind off 6 (7, 8) sts, complete row. **Row 4:** Work even. Bind off remaining sts.

Left Neck and Shoulder Shaping: Slip the sts from holder onto needle, attach thread at neck edge. **Row 1:** Bind off first 18 sts, complete row. Complete to correspond with other side, reversing shaping.

SLEEVES: Starting at lower edge, cast on 68 (74, 80) sts. Work in pattern same as for Back until piece measures 14″ (14½″, 15″); end on right side.

Top Shaping: Keeping in pattern, bind off 6 sts at beg of next 2 rows; then dec one st at each end on next row and every 4th row 3 times; then dec one st every other row until 20 sts remain. Keeping in pattern, bind off

2 sts at beg of next 4 rows. Bind off remaining sts.
FINISHING: Block to measurements. Sew side, shoulder and sleeve seams. Sew in sleeves. With a crochet hook and keeping work flat, work one rnd of sc around neck edge and around each sleeve edge. **Neck Ruffle:** Cast on 9 sts. **Foundation Row:** K 9. * **Next Row:** P 6, turn, k 6, turn. **Following Row:** P 6, k 3. **Next Row:** K 3, p 6. **Following Row:** K 6, turn, p 6, turn. **Next Row:** K 9. * Rpt directions from * to * until length of garter stitch edge is same as neck opening. Bind off. Sew narrow edges together. Sew garter stitch edge to neck edge. **Sleeve Ruffle:** Work as for Neck Ruffle until piece measures 1″ less than lower edge of sleeve. Sew narrow edges together. Sew in place, holding sleeve edge in to fit.

SHAWL-COLLAR JACKET

(page 45)

Directions are given for size Small (8-10). Changes for sizes Medium (12-14) and Large (16-18) are given in parentheses.
MATERIALS: Scott's "Linnay" 11(12,13) oz. or Coats & Clark Knit Cro Sheen, 12(14,16) 1 oz. balls (approx. 175 yds.), used 2 strands as 1; 1 button, ⅝″ or ¾″; crochet hook, size I, OR ANY SIZE HOOK WHICH WILL OBTAIN THE STITCH GAUGE BELOW.
GAUGE: 22 sts = 6″.
MEASUREMENTS:

Size:	Small	Medium	Large
Bust:	32″	34″	38″
Width across back at underarms:	17½″	18½″	20½″
Length to underarms:	15″	15½″	16″
Width across sleeve:	7½″	8″	8½″

DIRECTIONS—BACK: Start at hem, ch 60(64,72). **Row 1:** Sc in 2nd ch from hook, dc, dc in same ch. *Skip 1 ch, sc and dc in next, repeat from * across. Turn. **Row 2:** Sc and dc in 1st sc (skipping 1st dc), *sc and dc in next sc, repeat from * across, turn. **Rows 3-43 (3-44,3-45):** Repeat Row 2 for pattern. At end of Row 43(44,45), break off, turn.

SLEEVES—Row 44(45,46): Ch 22(24,26), work across Row 43(44,45) in pattern, ch 22(24,26), turn. **Row 45(46,47):** Sc in 2nd ch from hook, work across chs and Row 44(45,46) in pattern. Turn. **Rows 46-60 (47-62,48-64):** Work in pattern. At end of Row 60(62,64), sc in last sc, ch 2, turn. **Row 61(63,65):** Skip 1st st, dc in each remaining st, ch 1, turn. **Row 62(64,66):** Skip 1st st, *dc around post of next st, right to left at front of work, dc around next st at back, repeat from * across, end with dc in ch-2 space, ch 1, turn. **Row 63(65,67):** Skip 1st st, *dc around next st at back, dc around next st at front, repeat from * across, end with dc in ch-1, ch 1, turn. **Row 64(66,68):** Skip 1st st, *dc around next st at front, dc around next st at back, repeat from * across, dc in ch-1, turn. **Row 65(67,69):** Repeat Row 63(65,67), fasten off.

FRONT: Ch 36(38,42). **Rows 1-43 (1-44, 1-45):** Same as for Back, on 35(37,41) sts.

Sleeve — Row 44(45,46): Ch 22(24, 26), work across Row 43(44,45) in pattern, turn. **Rows 45-60 (46-62, 47-64):** Same as Back.

Collar Strip — Row 61(63,65): Work first 16(16,18) sts in pattern, turn. **Rows 62-78 (64-80, 66-82):** Continue without shaping on 16(16,18) sts. Fasten off.

Shoulder Ribbing — Row 61 (63,65): Going in opposite direction from Row 60(62,64) and starting in first st after collar strip, work dc in each st to end of row — 43(47,53) dcs. Turn. **Rows 62-65 (64-67, 66-69):** Continue without shaping on 43 (47,53) sts. Fasten off. Work other side to match, reversing all shaping. Block pieces, being careful not to flatten ribbing. Sl st shoulder seams on right side. Sew small back collar seam, then sew collar around neck edge. Press. Sl st or sew underarm and sleeve seam, sc across lower edge. Press.

POCKETS (Make 2): Ch 22. Work 15 rows in pattern. Sc across last row. Fasten off. Block. Sew in place. To make buttonhole at waist, sl st around edges of sts to form opening. Sew button across from buttonhole.

BEIGE V-NECK CARDIGAN

(page 45)

Directions are given for size. Small. Changes for sizes Medium and Large are in parentheses.
MATERIALS: Plymouth "Indiecita" 50 gram balls: 6 (7, 8) balls; No. 5 circular needle; knitting needles, one pair No. 8 OR ANY SIZE WHICH WILL OBTAIN GAUGE; stitch holder.
GAUGE: On No. 8 needles, 5 sts = 1".
DIRECTIONS-PATTERNSTITCH: Row 1: K 1, *p 1, k 1 TBL (through back loop); repeat from *across, ending k last st through front loop. **Row 2:** *P 1, k 1 TBL; rpt from *across ending p 1. Rpt these 2 rows for pat.
BACK: With No. 8 needles, cast on 91(97,103) sts and work in pat for 1". Decrease 1 st each side now; then every inch 4 times more 81(87,93) sts. When piece measures 7½" in all, increase 1 st each side and repeat this inc every 1½", 4 times more 91(97,103)sts. When work measures

14" in all, bind off 2 sts at beg of next 4(6,8) rows; then 1 st at beg of next 8(6,4) rows 75(79,83) sts. Work even until piece measures 20" in all. **Next Row:** Work across 31(33, 35) sts, bind off next 13 sts, work across rem sts. Working each side separately, bind off at neck edge, every other row, 4 then 3, then 2 sts 22(24,26) sts rem. Work even until piece measures 21½(21¾,22)". At shoulder edge, bind off 10(12,12) sts once, then 12(12,14) sts once.
RIGHT FRONT: With No. 8 needle, cast on 42(46,50) sts and work in pattern, increasing 1 st at right side every other row 5 times. AT THE SAME TIME, when piece measures 1", dec 1 st at left side and rpt this dec every inch 4 times more 42(46,50) sts. When work measures 7½" in all, inc 1 st at left side and rpt this inc every 1½", 4 times more. When work measures 12" in all, start V-neck shaping. Dec 1 st at right side (neck edge) on next; then every 4th row 16(17,18) times more. AT THE SAME TIME, when piece measures 14" in all, bind off 2 sts at arm edge every other row 2(3,4) times; then 1 st at arm edge every other row 4(3,2) times. When front measures same as back to shoulders, bind off, at shoulder edge same as on back.
LEFT FRONT: Work same as Right Front reversing all shaping.
SLEEVES: With No. 5 needles, cast on 50 sts and work back and forth for 10 rows in garter st (k every row). Change to No. 8 needles and work in pat for 2(1½,1½)". Inc 1 st each side on next row; then every 1½" 8(9,10) times more 68(70,72) sts. Work even in pat until piece measures 18" in all or desired length. Bind off 3 sts at beg of next 8 rows; then 1 st at beg of next 24 rows; 2 sts at beg of next 2 rows; 2(2,3) sts at beg of next 2 rows; 2(3,3) sts at beg of next 2 rows; 3 sts at beg of next 2 rows. Bind off rem sts.
FINISHING: Sew side, shoulder and sleeve seams. Set in sleeves
Frontband: With No. 5 needle and right side facing, pick up 1 st for each st along front, back and front; then 10 sts along curve on lower front, then 1 st every other row along front to neck edge, 11 sts around neck edge, 13 sts along back neck, then pick up sts on other side to match, picking up 10 sts on curve at lower left front. Join and work in garter st (K 1 row, p 1 row), inc 4 sts along lower front curves in first row. Work 4 more rows in garter st. **Next Row:** Make 4 buttonholes evenly spaced on right front, starting first buttonhole 5 sts above top of curve on right front, as follows: Bind off 3 sts; on next row cast on 3 sts over bound off sts. Continue in garter st until there 10 rows in all. Bind off on Row 11.

QUILTED TABLECLOTH

(page 47)

Finished size: Approximately 52" square, including ruffle.
MATERIALS: 2½ yds. of 1" checked gingham; 1¼ yds. lightweight 45"-wide fabric for backing; polyester quilt batting; thread.
DIRECTIONS: Cut gingham into two 1¼ yd. lengths. Quilt one piece, following general directions for diamond quilting on page 128. From remaining gingham, cut 4"-wide bias strips to total 360". Seam pieces together on the bias to form a large circle. Narrowly hem one edge of bias circle; run machine gathering line along other edge. Pin ruffle to quilted cloth, pulling up gathers to fit. Stitch ¼" seam; press seam toward cloth. Topstitch just above ruffle, through all layers.

PAINTED HURRICANE SHADE

(page 46)

MATERIALS: Purchased hurricane shade; ballpoint paint tubes; items for design inspiration.
DIRECTIONS: Shade must be clean and dry. Avoid getting fingerprints on area to be painted. Hold or tape design on inside of shade and paint on outside, following directions on paint tubes. (Be sure to practice on cardboard if you've never worked with ballpoint paints.)

QUILTED CASSEROLE COVER

(page 47)

Fits any medium-sized square or rectangular baking dish.
MATERIALS: ⅜ yd. each of green and pink 1" checked gingham, or other fabrics of your choice; polyester quilt batting; 1 pkg. double-fold bias tape; thread.

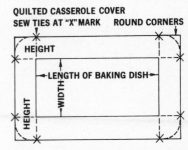

QUILTED CASSEROLE COVER
SEW TIES AT "X" MARK   ROUND CORNERS

HEIGHT

←LENGTH OF BAKING DISH→

WIDTH

HEIGHT

DIRECTIONS: Quilt as much gingham as you will need (see measurements below). To quilt, follow general directions for diamond quilting on page 128, using one color as top, other color as backing. From quilted fabric, cut a rectangle to measure as follows: Length — length of casserole plus twice its height. Width — width of casserole plus twice its height. (Round corners slightly.) Inside this rectangle, stitch a smaller rectangle the length and width of baking dish. Bind outside edge with bias tape. Stitch remaining tape along open edge to form ties; cut eight 6″ strips. Place one tie at each "X" mark as shown; topstitch in place with zigzag or straight stitch. Tie pairs of ties together to shape cover.

WATER LILY NAPKIN

(page 48)

MATERIALS: Square paper or cloth napkins.
DIRECTIONS: Open napkin out flat. Fold so corners (A) meet at center point (Fig. 1). Without turning napkin, fold newly-formed corners to center (Fig. 2). Repeat once more (Fig. 3). Now turn napkin over; it should look like (Fig. 4). Fold corner flaps (B) to center (Fig. 5). Your napkin should now look like (Fig. 6). Place a glass (or your fingertips) firmly over the center. Reach underneath the folded napkin and firmly but gently (to avoid tearing napkin, if paper) pull the first row of points up

WATER LILY NAPKIN

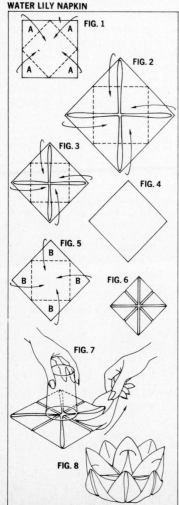

FIG. 1
FIG. 2
FIG. 3
FIG. 4
FIG. 5
FIG. 6
FIG. 7
FIG. 8

(Fig. 7). Repeat with second row of points to get completed water lily (Fig. 8).

HOT PLATE MAT

(page 49)

MATERIALS: Lily Jute-Tone (75 yd ball): 1 ball #17 Spun Gold (A), 1 ball #129 Burnt Orange (B), 1 ball #11 Canary Yellow (C); crochet hook, size G.
GAUGE: 3 sc = 1″.
DIRECTIONS: Starting at center with color B, ch 2. **Rnd 1:** Work 6 sc into 2nd ch from hook. Do not join rnds but mark beg of each rnd. **Rnd 2:** Work 2 sc into each sc around (12 sc), fasten off color B. **Rnd 3:** Attach color C, work * 1 sc in first sc, 2 sc into next sc. Repeat from * around (18 sc). **Rnd 4:** Work * 1 sc into each of first 2 sc, 2 sc in next sc. Repeat from * around (24 sc). Fasten off color C. **Rnds 5 and 6:** Attach color A and work 2 rnds, increasing 6 sts evenly spaced around (36 sc). Fasten off. **Rnds 7 and 8:** Attach color B and repeat rnds 5 and 6 (48 sc). Fasten off. **Rnds 9 and 10:** Attach color A and repeat rnds 5 and 6 (60 sc). Fasten off. **Rnd 11:** Attach color C and work 1 row sc, increasing 6 sts evenly spaced around (66 sc). Fasten off. Sew in ends.

APPLIQUÉD TEA COZY & NAPKIN

(page 49)

MATERIALS: ½ yd. 45″ off-white linen-like fabric (or three purchased napkins, approximately 18″ square); ⅓ yd. quilted fabric for tea cozy lining; scraps of small-printed cotton fabrics in black, red and green; matching thread.
DIRECTIONS: Enlarge diagrams, following directions on page 18. From linen or two napkins, cut front and back of tea cozy ("house"), adding ½″ seam allowance on all sides. Cut one 18″ square and narrowly hem, for napkin. Cut duplicate front and back quilted fabric. From prints, cut appliqué pieces—door, windows, roof, flower, etc. Cut two of each if you wish to appliqué back of tea

APPLIQUÉD TEA COZY   1 SQ. = 1″

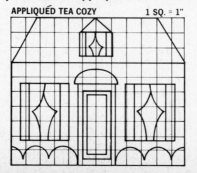

APPLIQUÉD NAPKIN   1 SQ. = 1″

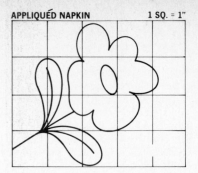

cozy. Place pieces as shown on front (and back, if desired) piece of linen; zig-zag around all edges to hold pieces in place. Zig-zag additional details—"panel" on door, stem and veins of flower—as shown. Right sides together, stitch linen front to back at top & sides along seam line. Repeat for quilted front and back. Pin lining inside cozy, right sides together, and stitch around bottom, leaving an opening for turning. Turn right side out; slipstitch opening. Tack lining to tea cozy along seam line at top and sides.

LARGE BASKET

(page 49)

MATERIALS: Lily Jute-Tone (75 yd ball): 1 ball #17 Spun Gold (A), 1 ball #129 Burnt Orange (B); crochet hook, size G.
GAUGE: 3 sc = 1″.
DIRECTIONS: Starting at center with Color A, ch 2. **Rnd 1:** Work 6 sc into 2nd ch from hook. Do not join rnds but mark beg of each rnd. **Rnd 2:** Work 2 sc into each sc around (12 sc). **Rnd 3:** Work * 1 sc into first sc, 2 sc into next sc. Repeat from * around (18 sc). **Rnd 4:** Work * 1 sc into each of first 2 sc, 2 sc into next sc. Repeat from * around (24 sc). **Rnds 5-9:** Continue to work in sc, increasing 6 sts evenly spaced around (54 sc). **Rnds 10-13:** Work evenly in sc. Drop color A and attach color B. **Rnd 14:** Work * 1 sc into first st, long dc into next st. (To work a long dc: yoh, insert hook in the *bottom* of the stitch on Row 13, draw up a loop, yoh, take off 2 loops, yoh, take off 2 loops—one long dc complete.) Repeat from * around. Fasten off color B. **Rnds 15-18:** Repeat Rnds 10-13. **Rnd 19:** Repeat Rnd 14. **Rnd 20:** With color A, work in sc and dec 6 sts evenly spaced around (48 sc). **Rnd 21:** Repeat Rnd 20 (42 sc). Fasten off and sew in ends.

PATCHWORK TABLECLOTH

(page 49)

MATERIALS: Calico fabrics (44-45″ wide) in the following colors: ⅝ yd.

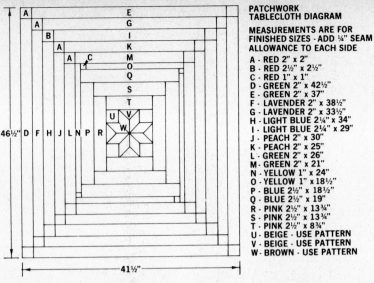

**MEASUREMENTS ARE FOR
FINISHED SIZES - ADD ¼" SEAM
ALLOWANCE TO EACH SIDE**

A - RED 2" x 2"
B - RED 2½" x 2½"
C - RED 1" x 1"
D - GREEN 2" x 42½"
E - GREEN 2" x 37"
F - LAVENDER 2" x 38½"
G - LAVENDER 2" x 33½"
H - LIGHT BLUE 2¼" x 34"
I - LIGHT BLUE 2¼" x 29"
J - PEACH 2" x 30"
K - PEACH 2" x 25"
L - GREEN 2" x 26"
M - GREEN 2" x 21"
N - YELLOW 1" x 24"
O - YELLOW 1" x 18½"
P - BLUE 2½" x 18½"
Q - BLUE 2½" x 19"
R - PINK 2½" x 13¾"
S - PINK 2½" x 13¾"
T - PINK 2½" x 8¾"
U - BEIGE - USE PATTERN
V - BEIGE - USE PATTERN
W - BROWN - USE PATTERN

of green; ⅜ yd. each of lavender, light blue, peach, blue and pink; ¼ yd. of yellow; scraps of red, beige and brown, or substitute colors of your choice; bias tape or, for optional lining, 1⅜ yds. of a soft fabric (44-45" wide) in a complementary color.

DIRECTIONS: Cut fabric as follows: From green, cut two strips each 2½" x 43" (D), 2½" x 37½" (E), 2½" x 26½" (L), 2½" x 21½" (M); from lavender, cut two strips each 2½" x 39" (F), 2½" x 34" (G); from light blue, cut two strips each 2¾" x 34½" (H), 2¾" x 29½" (I); from peach, cut two strips each 2½" x 30½" (J), 2½" x 25½" (K); from yellow, cut two strips each 1½" x 24½" (N), 1½" x 19" (O); from blue, cut two strips each 3" x 19" (P), 3" x 19½" (Q); from pink, cut two strips each 3" x 14¼" (R), 3" x 14¼" (S), 3" x 9¼" (T); from red scraps, cut 16 squares 2½" x 2½" (A), four squares 3" x 3" (B) and four squares 1½" x 1½" (C). (**Note:** These measurements include ¼" seam allowance.) Following directions on page 18, enlarge pattern diagram onto white paper, adding ¼" all around each piece for seam allowance. Cut beige and brown scraps using patterns as follows: From beige, cut four squares (U) and four triangles (V); from brown, cut eight diamonds (W).

To Assemble: Sew pieces together beginning with the center star pattern, sewing inside edges of diamond pieces (W) to each other with ¼" seams, matching points in center and using pattern diagram as a guide. Follow pattern and illustration of finished tablecloth to attach beige squares (U) and triangles (V) to outer edges of diamond pieces with ¼" seams. Press all seams flat toward center of finished square. Sew strips (T) to top and bottom of square with ¼" seams; press seams flat toward center. Sew strips (R) along each side to strips (T) and square, as shown in diagram; press seams toward center.

Repeat this procedure for attaching strips (S), (P) and (Q). Sew one small red square (C) to one end of each yellow strip (O) and (N) with ¼" seams. Sew strips (O), then strips (N) to strips (Q) and (P) respectively, lining up red squares (C) as shown in diagram. For remaining strips, sew corner squares (A) to each end of strips (L), (J), (F) and (D) and square (B) to each end of strips (H). Sew top and bottom strips (M) to strips (O), then follow with matching side strips (L). Repeat, alternating with strips (K) and (J), (I) and (H), (G) and (F), and (E) and (D). Press all seams flat.

FINISHING: Sew bias tape on right side to raw edge of completed rectangle; blind or machine stitch hem in place or use optional lining. For lining, cut a rectangle of lining fabric 42" x 47"; sew around all sides to tablecloth, right sides together, with a ¼" seam, leaving opening for turning. Turn, press, slipstitch closed.

**PATCHWORK TABLECLOTH
HALF PATTERN**

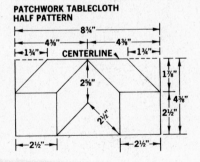

CROCHETED PLACEMAT

(page 49)

Measures approximately 9" × 14".
MATERIALS: DMC Brilliant Crochet Cotton, one 218-yd. ball; steel crochet hook, size 8 OR ANY SIZE CROCHET HOOK WHICH WILL OBTAIN THE STITCH GAUGE BELOW.
GAUGE: 7 dc = 1"; 4 rows = 1".
DIRECTIONS: Ch 84. **Row 1:** Dc in

6th ch from hook, *ch 1, skip 1 ch, dc in next ch. Repeat from * ending row with dc in last ch. Ch 4, turn. **Row 2:** Skip 1st dc, * dc in next dc, ch 1. Repeat from * ending row with dc in last dc, ch 1, dc in 2nd ch of ch-6. **Row 3:** Skip 1st dc, * dc in next dc, ch 1. Repeat from * ending row with dc in last dc, ch 1, dc in 2nd ch of ch-4. Repeat Row 3 until 25 rows are completed. Fasten off.

Border: With right side facing, attach yarn to bottom right corner. **Row 1:** Ch 2, 4 dc in corner space, * 2 dc in next dc and in each dc to next corner space, 6 dc in corner space, 2 dc in each ch-1 space to next corner, 6 dc in corner space. Repeat from * ending row with 2 dc in 1st corner space; join with sl st to top of ch-2. **Row 2:** Ch 2, dc in next dc, 3 dc in next dc, * dc in next dc and in each dc to next corner space, 3 dc in corner. Repeat from * to end of row; join with sl st to top of ch-2. **Row 3:** Ch 4, skip 1 dc, 3 dc in next dc, * ch 1, skip 1 dc, dc in next dc. Repeat from * working 3 dc in each corner dc and ending row with sl st in 2nd ch of ch-4. **Row 4:** Ch 2, dc in next dc, * 3 dc in corner dc, dc in next dc and in each dc to next corner. Repeat from * ending row with sl st in top of ch-2. **Row 5:** Repeat Row 4. **Row 6:** Ch 2, 2 dc in 1st dc, * skip 3 dc, sc in next dc, skip 3 dc, 3 dc in next dc, ch 4, sl st in 2nd ch, (picot formed) ch 1, 3 dc in same dc. Repeat from * ending row with 3 dc in same dc as 1st dc-2, ch 4, sl st in 2nd ch (picot), ch 1, sl st in top of ch-2. Fasten off.

CROCHETED WHITE TABLECLOTH

(page 49)

Finished size approximately 48" square.
MATERIALS: DMC Cordonnet Special Thread No. 20: 27 balls; steel crochet hook, No. 9 OR ANY SIZE HOOK WHICH WILL OBTAIN THE MOTIF SIZE GIVEN BELOW.

DIRECTIONS—MOTIFS (4½" diameter): (**Note:** All motifs are worked from right side.) Ch 4, join with sl st to form ring. **Rnd 1:** Ch 8 (counts as first tr and 4 ch), * tr in ring, ch 4; rpt from * around 6 times, join with sl st in 4th ch of ch-8—8 spokes. **Rnd 2:** Ch 4 (counts as first tr), 4 tr in next ch-4 space, * ch 2, 5 tr in next ch-4 sp; rpt from * around, end ch 2, join to top of ch-4 at beg of rnd—8 groups of 5 tr. **Rnd 3:** Ch 4, tr in each of next 4 tr of first group, * (tr, ch 4, tr) in next ch-2 sp, tr in each of 5 tr of next tr-group; rpt from * around, end (tr, ch 4, tr) in last ch-2 sp, join to top of ch-4 at beg of rnd—8 groups of 7 tr. **Rnd 4:** Ch 4, (yo twice, pull up a lp in next tr, yo and through 2 lps twice) 4 times, yo and through 5 lps on hook (cl [cluster] made over 5 center tr), * ch 4, 5 tr in next ch-4 sp, ch 4, sk next tr, cl of 5 tr over center 5 tr of next group (yo and through 6 lps on hook); rpt from * around, end with ch 4, 5 tr in last ch-4 sp, ch 4, sl st in top of first cl. **Rnd 5:** Ch 8, * tr (close to tr group) in next ch-4 sp, tr in each of next 5 tr, tr (close to tr group) in next ch-4 sp, ch 4 †, tr in top of cl, ch 4; rpt from * around, end at † symbol, join in 4th ch of ch-8. **Rnd 6:** Ch 11, * sk first tr of next group, cl of 5 tr over next 5 tr, ch 11, sk next 4 ch of sp, sc in next tr, ch 11, sk next ch 4 sp; rpt from * around, ending with cl, ch 11, sk 4 ch of next sp. sl st in next tr—8 cls. Fasten off.

TABLECLOTH: Consists of 144 motifs and 121 center joining motifs. All motifs are joined right side up.

First Strip—First Motif: Rnds 1-6: Work as for motif. Fasten off. Mark this motif. **Second Motif—Rnds 1-5:** Work as for motif. **Rnd 6 (joining rnd):** Ch 5, drop lp off hook, insert hook in 6th ch of ch-11 to right of a cl on first motif, pick up dropped lp and work a sl st (always join this way, keeping work from twisting), ch 5, work cl over 5 center tr of next group of 2nd motif, ch 5, join to 6th ch of ch-11 to left of same cl on first motif, ch 5, * sk next 4 ch of next sp on 2nd motif, sc in top of next tr, ch 11, cl of 5 tr over center 5 tr of next group, ch 11; rpt from * to end of rnd, sk ch 4 of last sp, sl st in next tr. Fasten off. Repeat 2nd motif until 12 motifs are joined. **Second Strip—First Motif—Rnds 1-6:** Work as for motif. Fasten off. **Second Motif—Rnds 1-5:** Work as for motif. **Rnd 6:** This rnd joins motif to top of first motif on first joined strip. Ch 5, join to 6th ch of ch-11 to right of 2nd cl from joining on first motif of first joined strip, ch 5, work cl over center tr of next group of first motif on 2nd strip, ch 5, join to 6th ch of ch-11 to left of same cl on first motif of first strip (1 cl is free between joining on first strip), ch 5, * sk next 4 ch of next sp on first motif of 2nd strip, sc in top of next tr, ch 11, cl of 5 tr over center 5 tr of next group, ch 11; rpt from * to end of rnd, sk ch-4 of last sp, sl st in next tr. Fasten off.

Third Motif: (Note: This motif will be joined to side of first motif of 2nd strip and to top of 2nd motif on first strip, having 1 cl free between joining.) Work **Rnds 1-5** of motif. **Rnd 6:** * Ch 5, join in 6th ch of ch-11 to right of 2nd cl from top edge of joining of first motif on first strip, ch 5, cl over center 5 tr of next group of 2nd motif on 2nd strip, ch 5, join in 6th ch of ch-11 to left of same cl of first motif on 2nd strip, ch 5, sc in next tr after sp on 2nd motif on 2nd strip, ch 11, cl over cen-

ter 5 tr of next group of 2nd motif on 2nd strip, ch 11, sc in tr after sp; rpt from * once (joining bottom of 2nd motif of first strip in same way). * * Then ch 11, cl over center 5 tr of next group, ch 11, sc in tr after sp; rpt from * * to end of rnd, sl st in next tr. Fasten off. Repeat 2nd motif until 12 motifs are joined. Continue to work as for second strip until 12 strips of 12 motifs are joined.

CENTER JOINING MOTIFS (1¾″ diameter): (Note: This motif will join 4 free inside edges of 4 motifs [2 motifs on 1 strip and 2 on next strip].) Ch 4, join with sl st to form ring. **Rnd 1:** Ch 7, (dc in ring, ch 4) 3 times, join to 3rd ch of ch-7—4 spokes. **Rnd 2:** Ch 4, 6 tr in first ch-4 sp, * ch 3, 7 tr in next ch-4 sp; rpt from * twice, ch 3, join with sl st in ch 4 at beg of rnd—4 groups of 7 tr. **Rnd 3 (joining rnd):** Ch 4, sk next tr, cl of 4 tr over next 4 tr, ch 5, join in 6th ch of ch-11 to right of free cl of first motif on first strip, ch 5, join to ch-3 sp of jm (joining motif), ch 5, join in 6th ch of next ch-11 to left of same cl of same motif, ch 5, work 5 tr cl over center 5 tr of next group on jm, ch 5, join in 6th ch of ch-11 to right of cl of 2nd motif on first strip, ch 5, join in ch-3 sp of jm, ch 5, join in ch-6 of ch-11 to left of same cl of 2nd motif, ch 5, cl of 5 tr over center of tr group of jm, ch 5, join in 6th ch of ch-11 to right of cl of 3rd motif, ch 5, join to ch-3 sp of jm, ch 5, join to 6th ch of ch-11 to left of same cl on 3rd motif, ch 5, cl over center 5 tr of group on jm, ch 5, join in 6th ch of ch-11 to right of cl of 4th motif, ch 5, sl st in ch-3 sp of jm, ch 5, join in 6th ch of ch 11 to left of cl on 4th motif, ch 5, join with sl st in top of first cl of jm. Fasten off. Continue to make and join motifs in same way until 121 motifs are completed. Run in all ends on wrong side.

FINISHING—Edging: Make lp on hook, work 16 dc in every ch-11 sp, 8 dc in every ch-5 sp around entire edge of tablecloth, keeping edge from pulling, join in first dc. Fasten off.

BRAIDED PLACE MAT

(page 49)

Finished size approx 12″ × 15″.
MATERIALS: 1 yd. each of three 45″-wide cotton fabrics; heavy-duty thread for lacing; braid folders (optional; see Note for HOOKED RUG WITH BRAIDED BORDER on page 104); braid clamp (optional); lacing needle or

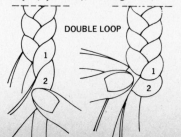

DOUBLE LOOP

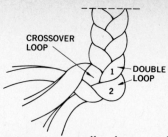

CROSSOVER LOOP

DOUBLE LOOP

large tapestry needle; large-eyed chenille (sharp) needle.
DIRECTIONS: Please refer to instructions for braiding on page 104. Cut fabrics crosswise into 2″ widths. Make T-start and begin to braid as instructed on page 104. Braid for 4″. then braid a double loop (see diagram) to form center of mat. Continue braiding. Lace two center rows together securely with a backstitch, then braid and lace successive rounds, increasing lacing on curves (see page 104) until placemat is desired size (ours has 12 rounds). Taper ends and finish as on page 104.

HEART DRESS

(page 56)

Directions are given for Size 2. Changes for Sizes 4, 6 and 8 are in parentheses.
MATERIALS: Lion Brand Knitting Worsted, 4 Ply (4 oz. skeins): 1 (2, 2, 3) skeins Red (A), 1 oz. each of Emerald Green (B) and Olive Green (C); ½ oz. each of Yellow, Orange, Lavender, Cardinal, White, Geranium (or any desired colors) for embroidery; crochet hook, Size G OR ANY SIZE CROCHET HOOK WHICH WILL OBTAIN THE STITCH GAUGE BELOW; tapestry needle; 2 buttons, ¾″ in diameter.
GAUGE: 7 sts=2″; 2 dc rows=1″.
MEASUREMENTS:

Sizes:	2	4	6	8
Width across heart motif:	7″	7″	8″	8″
Waist:	20″	21½″	23″	24½″
Width around lower edge of skirt:	27½″	30″	32″	34″

DIRECTIONS—SKIRT: Starting at waist with A, ch 70 (75, 80, 85) to measure 21 (22½, 24, 25½)″. Being careful not to twist chain, join with sl st to first ch to form a circle. **Rnd 1:** Ch 1, sc in same ch as joining, sc in each ch around. Join with sl st to first sc—70 (75, 80, 85) sc. Do not turn. **Rnd 2:** Ch 3, sk joining, dc in each of next 12, (13, 14, 15) sc, * 2 dc in next dc, dc in each of next 12 (13, 14, 15) sc, * 2 dc in next dc, dc in each of next 13 (14, 15, 16) sc; rpt from * around, ending with 2 dc in last dc. Join with sl st to top of ch-3—75 (80, 85, 90) dc, counting ch-3 as 1 dc. Always count ch-3 as 1 dc. (**Note:** Joining of rnds is

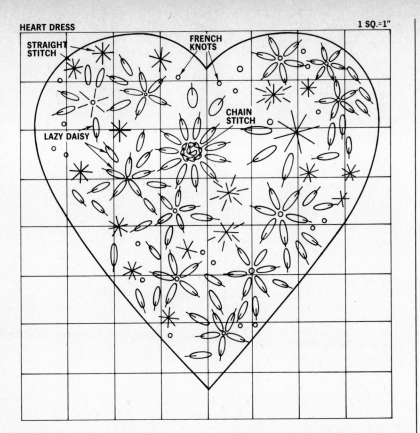

HEART DRESS 1 SQ.=1"

STRAIGHT STITCH

FRENCH KNOTS

CHAIN STITCH

LAZY DAISY

center back seam.) **Rnd 3:** Ch 3, sk joining, dc in each dc around. Join with sl st to top of ch-3. **Rnd 4:** Ch 3, sk joining, increasing 5 dc evenly spaced around, dc in each dc around. Join to top of ch-3 — 80 (85, 90, 95) dc. Rpt last 2 rows (Rows 3 and 4) alternately until there are 95 (105, 110, 120) dc. Rpt Rnd 3 only until total length is 7 (8½, 11, 14)" from beg or ½" shorter than desired length. At end of last row, break off and fasten. **Next Row:** Attach B to sam ch used for joining, ch 1, sc in same st and in each st around. Join with sl st to first sc. Break off and fasten. **Next Rnd:** Using C, work same as last rnd. Break off and fasten. **HEART MOTIF—Circle (Make 2):** Starting at center with A, ch 4. Join with sl st to form ring. **Rnd 1:** 8 sc in ring. Do not join; mark beg of each rnd. **Rnd 2:** 2 sc in each of 8 sc. **Rnd 3:** (sc in next sc, 2 sc in next sc) 8 times — 24 sc. **Rnd 4:** Increasing 8 sc evenly spaced, sc in each sc around. Rpt last rnd 0 (0, 1, 1) time — 32 (32, 40, 40) sc. At end of last rnd, sl st in next sc. Break off and fasten. Working through back lps of sts, sew circles together across 5 sts. **Next Rnd:** Attach A to the 8th (8th, 9th, 9th) sc before joining of circles on first circle, ch 1, sc in same sc, * sc in each sc to within one sc before next joining, *draw up a lp in next sc, sk joining, draw up a lp in next free sc on next circle, yarn over hook, draw through all 3 lps on hook* — dec made; rpt from * once more; sc in each rem sc around. Join with sl st to first sc. Do

not break off. **Triangle For Lower Section—Row 1:** Ch 1, sc in same sc as joining, sc in each of next 6 (6, 7, 7) sc, dc in dec between circles, sc in each of next 7 (7, 8, 8) sc; do not work over rem sts — 15 (15, 17, 17) sts. Ch 1, turn. **Row 2:** Sc in each st across last row. Ch 1, turn. **Row 3:** Sk first sc, sc in each sc across. Rpt last row until 7 sc rem. Ch 1, turn. **Next Row:** Sk first sc, sc in each sc to within last 2 sc, sk next sc, sc in last sc. Ch 1, turn. **Next Row:** Rpt last Row. Ch 1, turn. **Next Row:** Draw up a lp in each of 3 sc, yarn over hook, draw through all 4 lps on hook. Break off and fasten. **Heart Border:** With right side of circles facing, attach A to first free sc on right-hand side circle. **Rnd 1:** Sc in same sc; increasing 2 sc evenly spaced across top edge, sc in each sc along same circle, sl st in st between circles, sc in each sc along next circle, increasing 2 sc evenly spaced across top edge; making 3 sc in tip at lower end of heart, sc evenly along the 2 free edges of triangle, being careful to keep work flat. Join with sl st to first sc. Break off and fasten. **Rnd 2:** Attach B to same sc as joining; work along circles same as for Rnd 1, then, making 3 sc in center sc of 3-sc group at lower tip, sc in each sc around. Join to first sc. Break off and fasten. **Rnd 3:** With C, work same as Rnd 2. Break off and fasten. **Shoulder Strap (Make 2):** Starting at front end, ch 6. **Row 1:** Sc in 2nd ch from hook, sc in each sc across — 5 sc. Ch 1, turn. **Row 2:** Dc in each sc across. Ch 1, turn. Rpt last row until

strap measures approximately 12 (13½, 14½, 16)" from beg. Ch 1, turn. **Buttonhole Row:** Sc in each of first 2 sc, ch 1, sk next sc, sc in each of end 2 sc. Ch 1, turn. **Next Row:** Sc in each sc and in ch st. Ch 1, turn. **Next Row:** Sc in each of 5 sc. Ch 1, turn. Rpt last 3 rows. Break off and fasten.

FINISHING: Pin each section to measurements on a padded surface; cover with a damp cloth; allow to dry; **do not press.** With joining of rnds of skirt at center back, sew lower end of heart over first 3 rnds at center front of skirt. Sew front end of strap in back of each top curved edge of heart. Sew 2 buttons on top edge of center back of skirt, about 2 (2½, 2½, 3)" apart.

EMBROIDERY: Following diagram, with pins, mark center of each flower on crocheted heart (inside border). Using colors as desired, embroider flowers as indicated, in Lazy Daisy sts with contrasting French Knot at center, or (for large flower) with a spiral of contrasting Lazy Daisy sts at center; embroider small flowers in Straight sts of different lengths. With B and C colors, embroider single Lazy Daisy sts for leaves around and in between flowers throughout heart.

TYROLEAN SHORTS

(page 57)

Directions are given for Size 2. Changes for Size 4 are in parentheses.

MATERIALS: Lion Brand Knitting Worsted, 5 Ply (4 oz. skeins): 1 (2) skein of Forest Green (A), 1 oz. Red (B), several yards each of Lt. Green, Orange and White for embroidery; crochet hook, Size G OR ANY SIZE CROCHET HOOK WHICH WILL OBTAIN THE STITCH GAUGE BELOW; 2 buttons, ¾" in diameter; tapestry needle; 1 yd. round elastic.

GAUGE: 7 sts = 2"; 4 sc rows = 1"; 2 dc rows = 1".

MEASUREMENTS:

Sizes:	2	4
Width across bib (excluding edging):	4½"	5½"
Width around hips:	22"	24"

DIRECTIONS—BIB: Starting at top edge with A, ch 16, (20). **Row 1:** Sc in 2nd ch from hook, sc in each ch across — 15 (19) sc. Ch 1; turn. **Row 2:** Sc in each sc across. Ch 1, turn. Rpt last row until bib measures 4½ (5½)" from beg. Ch 1, turn. **Edging — Rnd 1:** 3 sc in first sc, sc in each of next 13 (17) sc, 3 sc in end sc. Working over ends of rows along next side edge, make 13 (17) sc evenly spaced across to within next corner st, 3 sc in corner st; working along opposite side of starting chain, sc in each of next 13 (17) ch, 3 sc in corner st; make 13 (17) sc along next side edge. Join with sl st to first sc. Break off and fasten. **Rnd 2:** With right side of last rnd facing, attach B to first sc of first 3-sc group on last rnd, ch 1, sc in same sc, sc in each of next 2 sc, *working over last rnd, insert hook in st directly below next sc, yarn over hook, draw up a lp, pull up this lp to measure ½", complete sc* —long sc made; sk next sc on last rnd (covered by long sc), sc in each of next 3 sc; rpt from * around, ending with long sc over last sc. Join with sl st to first sc. Break off and fasten.

SHORTS: With right side of edging facing, attach A to corner st at beg of lower edge of bib. **Rnd 1:** Ch 3, dc in each of next 16 (20) sts across bib; ch 61 (65); being careful not to twist chain, join with sl st to top of ch-3 at beg of this rnd. Break off and fasten. Do not turn. Shorts are worked entirely from right side. **Rnd 2:** Attach A to center ch of long chain just made, ch 3 for center back of seam; be sure to have 30 (32) ch sts at each side of this ch-3; dc in each ch and in each dc around. Join with sl st to top of ch-3 — 78 (86) dc, counting ch-3 as 1 dc. **Rnd 3:** Ch 3, sk joining, dc in each dc around. Join to top of ch-3. Rpt last rnd 10 (12) more times (or for desired length to crotch).

First Leg: Sl st in next dc. **Rnd 1:** ch 3, dc in each of next 37 (41) dc; do not work over rem sts, ch 10 for crotch. Join with sl st to top of ch-3 at beg of this rnd. **Rnd 2:** Ch 3, sk joining, dc in each dc and in each ch around. Join to top of ch-3 — 48 (52) dc, always counting ch-3 as 1 dc. **Rnd 3:** Ch 3, dc in each dc around. Join to top of ch-3. Rpt last rnd, 1 (3) more time.
Edging — Rnd 1: Ch 1, sc in joining, sc in each st around. Join with sl st to first sc. **Rnd 2:** Rpt last rnd. Break off and fasten. **Rnd 3:** Turn, attach B to same sc as joining, sc in same st, sc in next st, rpt from * on rnd 2 of Bib Edging around, ending with sc in last sc. Join to first sc. Break off and fasten.
Second Leg: With right side facing, sk next free dc on last rnd made before First Leg; attach A to next dc. Starting with Rnd 1, work same as First Leg.
Crotch Section: With right side facing, attach A to joining of last rnd made before Legs. **Row 1:** Ch 3, 3 dc in same st. Ch 3, turn. **Row 2:** Sk first dc, dc in each of next 2 dc, dc in top of ch-3. Ch 3, turn. Rpt last row, 4 more times. Ch 3, turn. **Last Row:** Sk first dc, holding back on hook last lp of each dc, dc in each of next 3 sts, yarn over, draw through all 4 lps on hook. Break off and fasten. Sew crotch section in place, in between legs.
Shoulder Strap (Make 2): With A, ch 5. **Row 1:** Sc in 2nd ch from hook and

in each of next 3 ch. Ch 1, turn. **Row 2:** Sc in each of 4 sc. Ch 1, turn. Rpt last row until total length is 11 (13)". Ch 1, turn. **Buttonhole Row:** Sc in final sc, ch 2, sk 2 sc, sc in next sc. Ch 1, turn. **Next Row:** Sc in each sc and in each ch across. Ch 1, turn. Rpt Row 2 once; then rpt Buttonhole Row and following row. Ch 1, turn. **Last Row:** Sk first sc, sc in next sc, sk next sc, sc in end sc. Break off and fasten.
Edging — Row 1: With A, starting at one end of Row 1, work 1 row of sc evenly along long edge of strap, across top and down other side edge, being careful to keep work flat. Break off and fasten. **Next Row:** Do not turn; attach B to first sc at beg of last row made, sc in same sc, sc in next sc; rpt from * on Row 2 of Bib Edging across row, ending with sc in end sc. Break off and fasten.
FINISHING: Pin shorts to measurements on a padded surface, cover with a damp cloth, allow to dry; **do not press.** Sew straight ends of shoulder straps to center back of top edge of shorts. Sew button to each top corner of bib. From wrong side, run elastic through sts worked along chain at top edge of shorts; gather to desired fit and allowing 1" length at each end, cut elastic. Sew ends to wrong side at each side of bib.
EMBROIDERY: Following diagram, embroider mushroom motif on bib in Chain stitches, using Red and Orange; embroider dots in White French Knots and grass in Lt. and Dk. Green Straight sts.

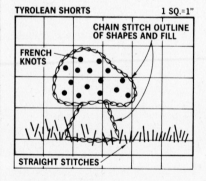

TYROLEAN SHORTS   1 SQ.=1"

CHAIN STITCH OUTLINE OF SHAPES AND FILL

FRENCH KNOTS

STRAIGHT STITCHES

PEASANT JACKET

(page 58)

Directions are given for Size 2. Changes for Sizes 4 and 6 are in parentheses.
MATERIALS: Lion Brand Knitting Worsted, 4 Ply (4 oz. skeins): 1 (2, 2) skeins of Black (A); several yards each of Red, Yellow, Orange, Lavender, Lt. and Dark Green for embroidery; crochet hook Size G OR ANY SIZE CROCHET HOOK WHICH WILL OBTAIN THE STITCH GAUGE BELOW; 2 yards of narrow lace; 6 (6, 8) buttons, ½" in diameter; tapestry needle.

GAUGE: 7 sts =2"; 4 sc rows =1"; 2 dc rows =1".
MEASUREMENTS:

Sizes:	Small	Medium	Large
	2	4	6
Chest:	19"	21"	24"
Width across sleeve at upper arm:	8½"	9½"	10½"

(**Note:** Body of jacket is worked all in one piece.)
DIRECTIONS — RIGHT FRONT: Starting at center front edge with A, ch 25 (29, 33) to measure 7½ (8½, 9½)". **Row 1 (right side):** Sc in 2nd ch from hook, sc in each ch across —24 (28, 32) sc. Ch 1, turn. **Row 2:** Sc in each sc across. Ch 1, turn. Rpt last row 4 (6, 6) more times. At end of last row, ch 11 (13, 15), for side edge of neck, turn. **Shoulder Section — Row 1:** Dc in 4th ch from hook, dc in each of next 7 (9, 11) ch, dc in each sc across last row —33 (39, 45) dc, counting chain at beg of row as 1 dc. Work this row for right side. Ch 3, turn. **Row 2.** Sk first dc, dc in each dc, dc in top of turning chain. Ch 3, turn. Always count turning ch-3 as 1 dc. Rpt last row 3 (3, 5) more times. Ch 3, turn.
Armhole Shaping — Row 1: Sk first dc, dc in each of next 19 (23, 27) dc; do not work over rem sts — armhole edge. Ch 3, turn. **Row 2:** Sk first dc, dc in each dc, dc in top of ch-3 —20 (24, 28) dc. Ch 3, turn. **Row 3:** Rpt last row. At end of row, ch 15 (17, 19) for other edge of armhole, turn.
BACK — Row 1: Dc in 4th ch from hook, dc in each ch and in each dc across last row, dc in top of ch-3 —33 (39, 45) dc. Ch 3, turn. Rpt Row 2 of Shoulder Section 4 (4, 6) times, ending at lower edge. Ch 3, turn. **Next Row:** Sk first dc, dc in each of next 26 (32, 38) dc; do not work over rem sts — neck edge. Ch 3, turn. Rpt Row 2 of Shoulder Section over these 27 (33, 39) sts, 4 (4, 6) times, ending at next edge. At end of last row, ch 8 for all sizes, turn. **Next Row:** Dc in 4th ch from hook, dc in each of next 4 ch sts, dc in each dc and in top of ch-3 —33 (39, 45) dc, ch 3, turn. Work 4 (4, 6) more dc rows over these sts, ending at lower edge. **For other Armhole Shaping and Left Front:** Rpt directions for Armhole Shaping and for Row 1 of Back. Complete Left Front to correspond with Right Front, reversing shaping. Fold fronts over back. Sew shoulder seams.
SLEEVES: With right side facing; attach A to center of underarm edge. **Rnd 1:** Ch 3, 2 dc along end of next row at underarm, dc in each ch and in each dc along entire armhole edge, ending with 2 dc over end of next row at underarm. Join with sl st to top of ch-3 —31 (35, 39) dc, counting ch-3 as 1 dc. Do not turn. Entire sleeve is worked from right side. **Rnd 2:** Ch 3,

sk joining, *holding back on hook last lp of each dc, make dc in each of next 2 dc, yarn over hook, draw through all 3 lps on hook*—dec made; dc in each dc to within last 2 dc, dec over last 2 dc. Join with sl st to top of ch-3. **Rnd 3:** Ch 3, sk joining, dc in each st around. Join to top of ch-3—29 (33, 37) dc. Rpt last rnd until sleeve measures 6 (7½, 9)" from underarm. **Edging—Rnds 1 through 4:** Ch 1, sc in same st as joining, sc in each st around. Join to first sc. **Rnd 5:** Ch 1, sc in same st as joining, * in next st make sc, dc and sc; sc in each of next 2 sts; rpt from * around, ending with sc in each rem st (if any). Join to first sc. Break off and fasten.

Jacket Edging—Rnd 1: With right side facing, attach A to lower right front corner st, 3 sc in same sc; with pins, mark the position of 3 (3, 4) buttonholes evenly spaced along each front edge, placing first pin on each front 1¼" above lower edge and last pin ½" below neck edge. Working along right front edge (sc in each ch st to within next pin, ch 2, sk next 2 sts for buttonhole, sc in next st) 3 (3, 4) times; sc in each st to next corner, 3 sc in corner st; sc evenly along next edge to next corner, easing in edge to desired fit, 3 sc in next corner st, work along left front edge to correspond with opposite edge, ending with 3 sc in lower corner st; sc evenly along entire lower edge, being careful to keep work flat. Join with sl st to first sc. **Rnd 2:** Work same as Rnd 5 of Sleeve Edging, counting each ch of previous rnd as one st. Break off and fasten.

FINISHING: Pin jacket to measurements on a padded surface, cover with a damp cloth, allow to dry; **do not press.** Sew lace along front and neck edges in back of last rnd of edging. Sew lace along each sleeve edge in same manner. Using 2 strands of yarn held together, make 3 (3, 4)

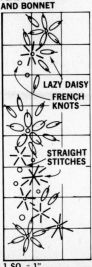

PEASANT JACKET AND BONNET

LAZY DAISY

FRENCH KNOTS

STRAIGHT STITCHES

1 SQ. = 1"

chains, each 1¼" long. Break off and fasten at end of each chain. Sew a button securely to each end of each chain. Slip buttons of each set through the 2 corresponding buttonholes on front edges.

EMBROIDERY: Following diagram, with pins, mark center of each flower along sc sections on each front end along lower edges of sleeves. Using colors as desired, embroider flowers in Lazy Daisy sts, with contrasting French Knot at center of each flower and in Straight sts, as indicated. With Lt. and Dark Green, embroider single Lazy Daisy sts for leaves.

CHILD'S CHALLIS SKIRT

(page 58)

MATERIALS: One 25"-27" square challis print scarf with border; 1" bias tape to match; ¾" elastic.
DIRECTIONS: Cut scarf in half. With right sides together, sew side seams along inside of side borders, matching bottom borders on right side. Trim and press seams open; invisibly stitch seam flat at hem. Measure bias tape to go around top of skirt for facing; with right sides together, sew to scarf along fold line on tape, matching raw edges and tucking under end. Turn facing to inside and stitch close to both edges, leaving an opening at bottom to insert elastic. Cut elastic to waist measurement plus 2"; insert and sew ends together. Stitch over opening.

PEASANT BONNET

(page 59)

Directions are given for bonnet to fit 1- to 4-year-olds.
MATERIALS: Lion Brand Knitting Worsted, 4 Ply (4 oz. skeins); 2 oz. each of Black (A) and Red (B); several yards each of Yellow, Orange and Green for embroidery; crochet hook Size G OR ANY SIZE HOOK WHICH WILL OBTAIN THE STITCH GAUGE BELOW; tapestry needle.
GAUGE: 7 sts=2"; 2 dc rows=1".
DIRECTIONS—BACK SECTION: Starting at Center with B, ch 4. Join with sl st to form ring. **Rnd 1 (right side):** Ch 3, 10 dc in ring. Join with sl st to top of ch-3—11 dc, counting ch-3 as 1 dc. **Rnd 2:** Ch 3, dc in same st as joining, 2 dc in each of next 4 dc, 3 dc in next dc, 2 dc in each of next 5 dc. Join with sl st to top of ch-3—23 dc. Always count ch-3 as 1 dc. Ch 3, turn. **Next Row:** Dc in first dc, (dc in next dc, 2 dc in next dc) 5 times; 3 dc in next dc, 2 dc in next dc, (dc in next dc, 2 dc in next dc) 5 times, (working last 2 dc in top of ch-3); do not join—

37 dc. Ch 3, turn. **Next Row:** Dc in first dc, (dc in each of next 2 dc, 2 dc in next dc) 5 times; dc in each of next 2 dc, 3 dc in next dc, (dc in each of next 2 dc, 2 dc in next dc) 6 times (working last 2 dc in top of ch-3)—51 dc. Ch 1, turn. **Short Rows:** Sc in each of first 15 dc, sl st in next dc. Break off and fasten. Sk next 19 dc, attach B with sl st to next dc, sc in each of rem 15 sts. Break off and fasten.
FRONT SECTION—Row 1: Do not turn. Work center 9 sts on last long row (lower point of back section), sk these marked 9 sts, attach A to next st, ch 3, dc in each of next 2 sts, hdc in each of next 2 sts, sc in each of next 16 sts across short rows, ch 5 across top opening, sc in each of next 16 sts on next short row, hdc in each of next 2 sts, dc in each of next 3 sts. Ch 3, turn. **Row 2:** Sk first st, dc in each st and in each ch across last row, dc in top of ch-3—47 dc, counting ch-3 as 1 dc. Ch 3, turn. **Row 3:** Sk first dc, dc in each dc across, dc in top of ch-3. Ch-3, turn. **Rows 4, 5 and 6:** Rpt last row. At end of last row, ch 1, turn. **Row 7:** Sc in each dc across, sc in top of ch-3. Ch 1, turn. **Row 8:** Sc in each sc across. Ch 1, turn. Rpt last row once, or for desired depth of bonnet. Break off and fasten.
Edging—Row 1: With right side facing, attach A over end of Row 1 on Front Section. Working along ends of rows, make 2 sc over end of each dc row, 1 sc over end of each sc row, 3 sc in corner st, sc in each sc across last row to within end st, 3 sc in end st, work along next side edge of front section to correspond with opposite edge. Break off and fasten. Do not turn. **Row 2:** Attach A to first sc at beg of last row, sl st in same st, *in next sc make sc, dc and sc; sc in each of next 2 sc; rpt from * across to center sc; make a chain 12" long for tie, sc in 2nd ch from hook and in each ch, sc in same corner sc as last sc made before tie (sc in next 2 sc, in next sc make sc, dc and sc) 15 times; sc in each sc to center sc of 3-sc group at corner, sc in center sc, make other tie in corner st; then continue edging as before along next side edge, ending with sl st in end sc. Break off and fasten.
EMBROIDERY: Following diagram, embroider leaves and flowers.

GREEN VESTED DRESS

(page 59)

Directions are given for Size 2. Changes for Sizes 4, 6 and 8 are in parentheses.
MATERIALS: Lion Brand Knitting Worsted, 4 Ply (4 oz. skeins): 1 (2, 2, 3) skein each of Green (A) and Black

(B); several yards each of White, Red, Lavender, Orange and Yellow for embroidery; crochet hook Size G OR ANY SIZE CROCHET HOOK WHICH WILL OBTAIN THE STITCH GAUGE BELOW; 2 buttons, ½" in diameter; tapestry needle.

GAUGE: 7 sts=2"; 4 sc rows=1".

MEASUREMENTS:

Sizes:	2	4	6	8
Chest:	18"	20"	21"	23"
Width across lower edge of skirt:	30"	32"	34"	36"

DIRECTIONS — VEST: Starting at center front edge with A, ch 19 (21, 23, 25) to measure 5½ (6, 6½, 7)".
Row 1: Sc in 2nd ch from hook, sc in each ch across — 18 (20, 22, 24) sc. Ch 1, turn. **Row 2:** Sc in each sc across. Ch 1, turn. Rpt last row until piece measures 17½ (19½, 20½, 22½)". Ch 1, turn.

Border: 3 sc in first sc, sc in each sc to within end sc, 3 sc in end sc, working along ends of rows, make 62 (68, 72, 78) sc evenly spaced along next long edge to next corner, 3 sc in corner st, working along opposite side of starting chain, sc in each ch to within next corner st, 3 sc in corner st, sc evenly along next long edge to correspond with opposite edge (be sure to have same number of sts). Join with sl st to first sc. Break off and fasten. Do not turn. Mark this side for right side and mark one long edge for top edge. Short edges are center front edges of vest.

Shoulder Straps — Row 1: With right side facing, sk 5 (5, 6, 7) sts after corner group on top edge, attach A to next sc, sc in same sc and in each of next 4 sc. Ch 1, turn. **Row 2:** Sc in each of 5 sc. Ch 1, turn. Rpt last row for 7½ (8, 8½, 9)". Ch 1, turn. **Buttonhole:** Sc in each of first 2 sc, ch 1, sk next sc, sc in each of next 2 sc. Ch 1, turn. **Next Row:** Sc in each sc and in ch st — 5 sc. Ch 1, turn. **Next Row:** Sk first sc, sc in each of next 2 sc, sk next sc, sc in end sc. Break off and fasten. work other strap at opposite end of same long edge to correspond with first strap. **Edging:** With pins, mark the position of 5 loops evenly spaced along each front (short) edge, placing first and last pin 1 sc in from corner group and being very careful to have pins on each edge in line with pins on opposite edge. With right side of border rnd facing (right side of vest), attach A to center st of 3-sc group at upper left front corner, ch 1, 3 sc in same st, working along left front edge, (sc in each sc to next pin, ch 3 for loop, sc in next sc) 5 times; sc in each sc to center sc of next corner group, 3 sc in front lp of center sc; working in front lp only of each sc along lower edge, make * sc in each of next 2 sc, in next sc make sc, dc and sc; rpt from * across to center st of

next corner group, 3 sc in front lp of center sc; working through both lps of each st for remainder of rnd, work along right front edge to correspond with opposite edge, ending with 3 sc in center sc of corner group; work edging as before along top and strap edges (along straps, place sts over end sts of rows, skipping every 4th row to keep work flat). At end of rnd, join with sl st to first sc. Break off and fasten.

SKIRT — Rnd 1: With right side facing, working in back of edging, along lower edge of vest, attach B to center sc, of left front corner group on border rnd (worked before edging), working in back lp only of each sc along border rnd, sc in same sc, sc in each sc across entire lower edge, ending with sc in center sc of next corner group, ch 6 for center front of skirt. Join with sl st to first sc — 66 (72, 76, 82) sc, plus ch 6. **Rnd 2:** Ch 1, dc in same sc as joining, * 2 dc in next sc, 1 dc in next sc; rpt from *around, ending with 2 dc in last sc, dc in each of next 6 ch; do not join this or any other rnd, but mark beg of each rnd. There are 105 (114, 120, 129) dc. **Rnd 3:** Dc in each dc around. Rpt last rnd until length of skirt is 7 (8½, 11, 14)" (or ½" shorter than desired length), at end of last rnd, work hdc in each of next 2 dc, sc in each of next 2 dc, sl st in next 2 dc. **Edging:** Ch 1, sc in same st as last sl st, * in next st make sc, dc and sc, sc in each of next 2 sts; rpt from * around, ending with sc in last st. Join with sl st to first sc. Break off and fasten.

FINISHING: Pin dress to measurements on a padded surface; cover with a damp cloth; allow to dry. **Do not press.** With B, make a chain 1 (1, 1¼, 1½) yd long. Break off and fasten. Slip chain between center 2 dc at center front top edge of skirt, fold in

half; lace chain through loops up front edges of vest; tie into a bow. Sew 2 buttons at center back of top edge of vest, about 1" apart. Cross straps at back and slip buttons through buttonholes.

EMBROIDERY: Using diagram as a guide, with pins, mark center of each flower along each front edge of vest. Using colors as desired, embroider flowers in Lazy Daisy sts with contrasting French Knot at center, and in Straight sts as indicated. With A, work stems in Chain st.

BIB DRESS

(page 59)

Directions are given for Size 2. Changes for Sizes 4, 6 and 8 are in parentheses.

MATERIALS: Lion Brand Knitting Worsted, 4 Ply (4 oz. skeins): 1 (2, 2, 3) skeins of Black (A); several yards each of Red, Orange, Yellow, Lavender, Lt. and Dk. Green for embroidery; crochet hook, Size G OR ANY SIZE CROCHET HOOK WHICH WILL OBTAIN THE STITCH GAUGE BELOW; 1 yd., 2"-wide lace; 1 yd.⅜"-wide black elastic; 2 buttons, ¾" in diameter; tapestry needle.

GAUGE: 7 dc=2"; 2 dc rows=1".

MEASUREMENTS:

Sizes:	2	4	6	8
Width across bib (excluding edging):	5"	5½"	6"	6½"
Width across skirt at lower edge:	30"	32"	34"	36"

DIRECTIONS — BIB: Starting at side edge with A, ch 19 (21, 22, 24).
Row 1: Sc in 2nd ch from hook, sc in each ch across — 18 (20, 21, 23) sc. Ch 1, turn. **Row 2:** Sc in each sc across. Ch 1, turn. Rpt last row until bib mea-

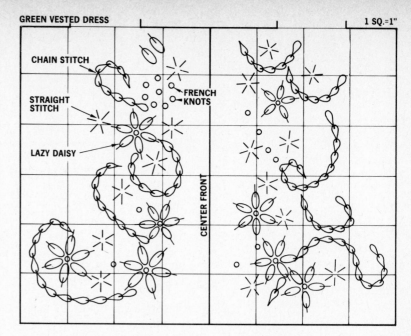

GREEN VESTED DRESS — 1 SQ.=1"

CHAIN STITCH

STRAIGHT STITCH

FRENCH KNOTS

LAZY DAISY

CENTER FRONT

sures 5 (5½, 6, 6½)". Ch 1, turn. **Border Row:** Sc in each sc to within end sc, 3 sc in end sc, working along ends of rows (top edge), make 17 (19, 20, 22) sc across to next corner, 3 sc in corner st; working along opposite side of starting chain, sc in each ch across to corner; do not work along next edge (lower edge) of bib. Break off and fasten.

Shoulder Straps: With right side facing, attach A to right-hand side corner st on top edge of bib. **Row 1:** sc in same st, sc in each of next 3 sc; do not work over rem sts. Ch 1, turn. **Row 2:** Sc in each of 4 sc. Ch 1, turn. Rpt last row for 12 (13½, 14½, 16)". Ch 1, turn. **Buttonhole Row:** Sc in first sc, ch 2, sk next 2 sc, sc in end sc. Ch 1, turn. **Next Row:** Sc in each sc and in each ch across. Ch 1, turn. **Next 2 Rows:** Sc in each sc across. Ch 1; turn. Rpt Buttonhole and following row once. Break off and fasten. Work other strap at opposite end of top edge to correspond with first strap.

Edging: With right side of border row of bib facing, attach A to first sc on right-hand side edge of bib, sc in same st, *in next sc make sc, dc and sc, sc in each of next 2 sc, rpt from * across side edge to shoulder strap; continue same edging along shoulder strap edges, across top, along other strap and next side edge (along straps, place sts over end sts of rows, skipping every 4th row to keep work flat), end with sc in last sc at end of left side edge of bib; do not work across lower edge. Do not fasten off.

SKIRT—Rnd 1: Ch 1, working along lower edge of bib, make 20 (22, 24, 26) sc evenly spaced across bib to next corner; ch 61 (63, 69, 71). Being careful not to twist chain, join with sl st to first sc of skirt. Break off and fasten. **Rnd 2:** Do not turn (entire skirt is worked from right side), attach A to center ch st of long chain, ch 3, dc in each ch and in each sc around. Join with sl st to top of ch-3—81 (85, 93, 97) dc, counting ch-3 as 1 dc. Joining is at center back seam. **Rnd 3:** Ch 3, dc in next 19 (20, 22, 23) dc, *2 dc in next dc —inc made; rpt from * 3 more times. Join with sl st to top of ch-3—4 incs made. **Rnd 4:** Ch 3, dc in each dc around. Join—85 (89, 97, 101) dc. Working in dc rnds, inc 4 dc evenly spaced in next rnd, then every other rnd until there are 105 (113, 121, 125) dc in rnd. Work even (same as Rnd 4) until skirt measures 7 (8½, 11, 14)" from beg.

Edging: Ch 1, sc in same st as joining, * in next dc make sc, dc and sc, sc in each of next 2 dc, rpt from * around, ending with sc in last 1 or 2 sts. Join with sl st to first sc. Break off and fasten.

FINISHING: Pin dress to measurements on a padded surface, cover

with a damp cloth, allow to dry; **do not press.** Sew lace under edging at lower edge of skirt. Sew 2 buttons at center back edge of skirt, about 1½" apart. Starting at beg of foundation chain for skirt, run elastic through sts of first dc rnd of skirt up to face of bib. Pull to desired fit, and allowing 1" at each end for sewing, cut elastic. Sew ends securely on wrong side.

EMBROIDERY: Following diagram, with pins, mark center of each flower throughout bib (inside border row). Using colors as desired, embroider flowers in Lazy Daisy sts with contrasting centers in Single or Satin sts and small flowers in Straight sts, as indicated. With Lt. and Dk. Green, embroider single Lazy Daisy sts for leaves around and in between flowers throughout bib.

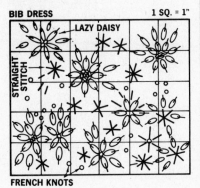

BIB DRESS — LAZY DAISY — STRAIGHT STITCH — FRENCH KNOTS — 1 SQ. = 1"

WHITE JACKET

(page 59)

Directions are given for Size 2. Changes for Sizes 4 and 6 are in parentheses.

MATERIALS: Lion Brand Knitting Worsted, 4 Ply (4 oz. skeins): 1 (2, 2) skeins of Eggshell; scraps of as many different colors as desired for embroidery; crochet hook, Size G OR ANY SIZE CROCHET HOOK WHICH WILL OBTAIN THE STITCH GAUGE BELOW; 4 buttons.

GAUGE: 7 sts = 2"; 7 rows of pattern = 3".

MEASUREMENTS:

Sizes:	Small (2)	Medium (4)	Large (6)
Chest:	21"	23½"	26"
Width across back at underarms:	10"	11"	12"
Width across each front at underarm:	5½"	6¼"	7"
Width across sleeve at upper arm:	8"	9"	10"

DIRECTIONS—BACK: Starting at lower edge, ch 37 (40, 43) to measure 11 (12, 13)". **Row 1: (wrong side):** Dc in 4th ch from hook, dc in each ch across—35 (38, 41) dc, counting chain at beg of row as 1 dc. Ch 3, turn. **Row**

2: Sk first dc, dc in next dc, *yarn over hook, from front of work, insert hook from right to left, under post of next dc, yarn over hook, draw up lp, complete a dc —front raised dc made; dc in top of each of next 2 dc; rpt from * across, ending last rpt with dc in last dc, dc in top of turning chain. Ch 3, turn. **Row 3:** Sk first dc, dc in next dc, *yarn over hook, from back of work, insert hook over for next dc, yarn over hook, draw up lp; complete a dc — back raised dc made; dc in top of each of next 2 dc; rpt from * across, ending last rpt with dc in last dc, dc in top of ch-3. Ch 3, turn. Rpt last 2 rows (Rows 2 and 3) alternately for pattern until total length is 9 (10½, 12)" from beg. Ch 3, turn.

Neck and Shoulder Shaping—Row 1: Work in pattern over first 13 (14, 15) sts; do not work over rem sts. Ch 2, turn. **Row 2:** Sk first st, work in pattern to end of row. Break off and fasten. Turn. Sk next free 9 (10, 11) sts on last row made before neck and shoulder shaping, attach yarn to next st, ch 3; work to correspond with opposite side. Break off and fasten.

LEFT FRONT: Starting at lower edge, ch 22 (25, 28) to measure 6½ (7½, 8)". **Row 1:** Dc in 4th ch from hook, dc in each ch across—20 (23, 25) dc, counting chain at beg of row as 1 dc. Work in pattern as for Back until length is about 7 (8½, 9)" from beg, ending with a wrong-side row. Ch 3, turn.

Neck Shaping—Row 1: Work in pattern across to within last 2 dc and turning chain, *holding back on hook last lp of each dc, make dc in each of next 2 sts, yarn over hook, draw through all 3 lps on hook —dec made at neck edge; do not work in turning chain. Ch 2, turn. **Row 2:** Sk first st, dc over next 2 sts; keeping continuity of pattern, work to end of row. Ch 3, turn. **Row 3:** Work in pattern to within last 2 sts and ch-2, dec over next 2 sts; do not work in ch-2—15 (18, 21) sts. Ch 2, turn. Rpt last 2 rows (Rows 2 and 3) 1 (1, 2) more time—12 (15, 15) sts. Ch 3, turn. **Next Row:** Sk first 0 (2, 1) st, work in pattern to end of row. Break off and fasten.

RIGHT FRONT: Work to correspond with Left Front, reversing shaping.

SLEEVES: Starting at top edge, ch 31 (34, 37). Having 29 (32, 35) sts in each row, work same for Back until length is 7½ (9, 10)" from beg or desired length of sleeve. Break off and fasten.

FINISHING: Pin each section to measurements on a padded surface; cover with a damp cloth and allow to dry; do not press. Tearing upper 4 (4½, 5)" of side edges open for armholes, sew side seams, sew shoulder and sleeve seams. Sew in sleeves.

EDGING: With right side facing, attach yarn to lower right front corner,

1 SQ.=¾"

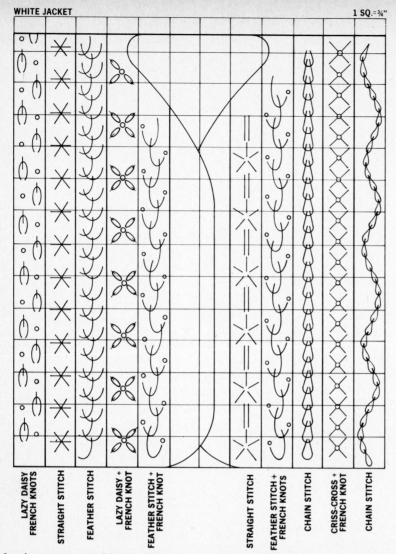

LAZY DAISY + FRENCH KNOTS | STRAIGHT STITCH | FEATHER STITCH | LAZY DAISY + FRENCH KNOT | FEATHER STITCH + FRENCH KNOTS | | STRAIGHT STITCH | FEATHER STITCH + FRENCH KNOTS | CHAIN STITCH | CRISS-CROSS + FRENCH KNOT | CHAIN STITCH

3 sc in corner st, making 3 sc in lower left front corner, sc evenly along entire outer edge of jacket, being careful to keep work flat. Join with sl st to first sc. Do not break off.

BUTTONLOOPS: With pins, mark the position of 4 buttonloops evenly spaced along right front edge, placing first pin 1½" above lower edge and last pin directly below beg of neck shaping. Sl st in next sc, *sc in each sc to within next pin, ch 3, sk next sc, sc in next sc; rpt from * 3 more times; sl st in each of next 2 sc. Break off and fasten. Sew buttons opposite buttonholes.

EMBROIDERY: Using as many different colors as desired, embroider a row in any appropriate stitch or combination of stitches (as Lazy Daisy, Chain, Zig-Zag Chain, Feather, Cross, Straight, French Knot) in each ridge between raised dc lines throughout jacket and sleeves (see diagram).

RICKRACK-TRIMMED SKIRT

(page 59)

MATERIALS: ⅜ yd. of (44-45" wide)

stiff cotton print fabric; 1" bias tape to match; 1¼ yds. each of rickrack in three complementary colors and narrow crochet-type edging in ecru color; thread to match; ¾" elastic.

DIRECTIONS: Lay fabric out flat. Measure in from one long side and mark a line 3¼" over from edge. Mark four more lines, each ½" over from previous line. Sew rickrack and trim over lines, alternating colors as shown in photo on page 59. Fold fabric in half crosswise with right sides together; sew seam ⅜" from selvages. Press seam open. Measure bias tape to go around top of skirt for facing; with right sides together, sew to skirt along fold line on tape, matching raw edges and tucking under end. Turn facing to inside; stitch close to both edges, leaving an opening in bottom to insert elastic. Cut elastic to waist measurement plus 2"; insert and sew ends together securely. Stitch over opening. Press up 1" hem on bottom of skirt; finish raw edge and pin hem in place. On right side of fabric, machine stitch ¾" in from bottom folded edge to hem.

(Note: Press rickrack flat before sewing for easy manageability.)

TASSEL VEST

(page 62)

(FOR EXPERIENCED KNITTERS ONLY)
Directions are given for "One Size Fits All," to fit over big shirt or coat.

MATERIALS: Bernat "Blarney Spun" (2 oz. balls): 2 balls Oatmeal #7916 (A); Bernat "Mohair Plus" (1.4 oz. balls): 3 balls Mink #5316 (B), 1 ball Brown #5318 (C); Bernat "Sesame" (4 oz. balls): 1 ball Terra Cotta #7538N (D); Bernat "Tapestria" (12 ½ yd. skeins): 3 skeins each of Mauve #R14-504 (E), Terra Cotta #R17-362 (F), 29" circular knitting needle No. 10½ OR ANY SIZE NEEDLE WHICH WILL OBTAIN THE STITCH GAUGE BELOW; crochet hook size H.

GAUGE: 3 sts = 1" in st st (double strands); 11 sts = 4" in seed st (double strands).

MEASUREMENTS:

Bust:	39"
Armhole to shoulder:	8½"
Length to underarm:	10"

(Note: Vest is worked in one piece beg at lower edge and using varying combinations of yarns in seed st, garter and st st. Carry yarns not in use loosely along side, being sure to twist working yarn under carried yarns at beg of every other row to avoid long loops.)

DIRECTIONS—Seed Stitch (Sd st)—Row 1: * K 1, p 1, rpt from *. **Row 2:** K the purl sts and p the knit sts *as they face you*. Rpt Row 2 for pat.
RTB: Return to beg of last row worked without turning, and work across from same side. Be sure to keep sd st pat correct when working RTB rows.

BODY: With No. 10½ circular needle and 2 strands of color C, cast on 115 sts. K 1 row C (right side). Drop 1 strand C, join 1 strand B, and work 1 row sd st with B and C tog (BC). Join 1 strand D and p 1 row D. RTB, pick up B, join 1 strand E and work 1 row sd st BE. Join 2nd strand E and work 1 row sd double E. RTB and work 1 row sd st BC. K 1 row double C. Join 2nd strand D and k 1 row double D. K 1 row BE. Break off colors C, D and E.

Next row (wrong side): With 1 strand each A and B (AB) worked tog, p across. Continue in st st and AB until 7" from beg, end with p row.

Dec row: K 27, k 2 tog twice, k 53, k 2 tog twice, k to end (111 sts). Work even until 9" from beg, ending with p row.

Dec row: K 27, k 2 tog, k 53, k 2 tog, k to end (109 sts). Work even until 10" from beg (or desired length to underarm), ending with a p row. Drop AB.

Begin Yoke Pat (right side): With double strand of D, p 1 row. Drop D.

Divide for Fronts and Back (right

side): RTB, pick up AB, join 1 strand E and with these 3 strands tog, p 22 sts and place on holder for Right Yoke; bind off next 10 sts, p 44 and place 45 sts just worked on holder for Back; bind off next 10 sts, p to end (22 sts on needle).

LEFT YOKE: Following pat st and color sequence and arm and neck shaping directions for each row, work on these 22 sts as follows (where 2 colors are indicated, e.g. AB, use one strand of each worked tog)—**Row 1 (wrong side):** P double D, dec 1 st at neck and at arm edge. **Row 2:** P double D, dec 1 st at arm edge. **Row 3:** P AB, dec 1 st at arm edge. **Rows 4 and 5:** Join E and work 2 rows sd st BE. **Rows 6 and 7:** Work 2 rows sd st AB. **Row 8:** RTB, k single D, dec 1 st at neck. **Row 9:** P BE. Break off BE. **Row 10:** RTB, k AB. **Row 11:** Sd st AB. **Row 12:** Sd st AB, dec 1 st at neck edge. **Rows 13 and 14:** Sd st AB. **Row 15:** K single D. **Row 16:** RTB, k BE, dec 1 st at neck and inc 1 st at arm edge. **Row 17:** K BC. **Row 18:** Sd st AB, inc 1 st at arm edge. **Row 19:** Sd st BE. **Row 20:** Sd st BE, dec 1 st at neck edge. **Row 21:** K double D. **Row 22:** K double C, dec 1 st at neck and inc 1 st at arm edge. **Row 23:** Sd st BE. **Row 24:** Sd st BE, dec 1 st at neck. Break off E. **Rows 25 and 26:** Sd st AB, dec 1 st at neck each row (13 sts). **Rows 27 and 28:** Sd st AB. **Rows 29 and 30:** Sd st BC. **Row 31:** RTB, p double D. **Row 32:** P AB. **Row 33:** Sd st AB. Break off A. **Rows 34 and 35:** Sd st BC. **Rows 36 and 37:** K double D. Break off D.

Bind off for shoulders: Working remainder of shoulder in BC and st st, when arm measures 8½" from dividing row, bind off 4 sts at beg of arm edge, work to end. Keeping st correct, work 1 row even. Continue to bind off at beg of arm edge 4 sts, then 5 sts, working 1 row even in between.

RIGHT YOKE: Place 22 sts for right yoke on needle and work as for Left Yoke, joining 2 strands D on wrong side at arm edge, and working shaping to correspond.

BACK: Place 45 sts for back on needle. Join 2 strands D on wrong side and, dec 1 st at beg and end of each row, p 2 rows (41 sts). Break off D. Join AB and, dec 1 st at beg and end of row, p 1 row (39 sts). Work even with AB in st st for 7 more rows. Drop AB. Join 1 strand D and k 1 row (wrong side). RTB, pick up AB and k 2 rows. Continue in st st with AB for 12 more rows **and at same time,** when arm measures 4" from dividing row, inc 1 st at beg and end of every other row 2 times, and on following 4th row once (6 sts inc—45 sts). Arm should measure 6" from dividing row. Drop AB. Join 2 strands D and p 2 rows. Break D. Continue in AB and st st for

6 more rows. Drop AB. Join 1 strand D and k 1 row.

Shape Neck (wrong side): RTB, pick up AB and k 16 sts; join 2nd AB and bind off next 13 sts for neck; k to end. Working each side separately, k next row, dec 1 st at neck edge. Drop B and break off A. Join double D (wrong side) and, dec 1 st at neck edge each row, p next 2 rows—13 sts. Break off D. Work remainder of back in BC and st st, binding off for shoulders as for front yokes.

FINISHING: With BC and right sides tog, using size H crochet hook, ch st shoulder seams from wrong side, working through inner loops only for a flat seam. Weave in ends on wrong side.

Front and Neck Edging: Using one strand each of D and F and size H hook, join DF at right front edge just above patterned border (edging will even out gap caused by difference in gauge between border and st st sections). With right side facing, work 1 row sc evenly along right front edge, around neck and down left front edge, ending just above lower border; take care to keep work flat. Do not turn. Ch 1, and working from left to right, work rev sc in each sc, inserting hook through both loops (corded edging made).

Sleeve edging: Join B at back underarm and with size H hook, sl st from right side evenly around armhole; join with sl st and fasten off. Join DF and with right side facing, work around in rev sc from left to right as for Front. Fasten off.

Tassels (Make 2): Cut 16 strands D and 8 strands F, each 9" long. Fold in half and tie tightly through fold, leaving ends for tacking. About ¾" from tied end, wind 2 strands D tightly around tassel about 10 times. Fasten and leave end for tacking. Trim bottom ends of tassel evenly and tack to vest, placing top of tassel at top of front border, and tacking at tied end and at wound section. Steam lightly with a damp cloth; let dry. **Do not press.**

CAP SLEEVE VEST

(page 63)

Directions are given for 35" finished bust. Changes for 38" finished bust size are in parentheses.
MATERIALS: Stanley Berroco "Nature Wool" (4 oz. skeins): 4(5) skeins Brown #402 (MC); Berroco "Homespun" (2 oz. skeins): 1(2) skeins Beige #438-18 (A); 4 oz. each of any 4-ply knitting worsted in Black (B) and Dark Rose (C); a few yards each of Berroco "Homespun" Rust #438-36 (D) and Berroco "Mirabella" Dark Turquoise #1531

(E) or any worsted weight yarns at hand; 29" circular knitting needle No. 10½ OR ANY SIZE NEEDLES WHICH WILL OBTAIN THE STITCH GAUGE BELOW; crochet hook size I (or size required to keep edgings flat).
GAUGE: 3 sts = 1" in Pat Rib; 10 sts = 3" in st st and garter st pat insert.
MEASUREMENTS:

Finished bust size:	35"	38"
Length to underarm:	14"	14½"

To adjust for longer waist, work additional rows in Pat Rib #2.
DIRECTIONS: (Note: Use 2 strands of each yarn worked together throughout. Rewind yarns into double strand balls for easier working. Vest is worked in one piece to underarm starting at lower edge. Basic knowledge of crochet directions is required for special edging trim.)
PATTERN RIB #1—Row 1 (right side): K across. **Row 2:** K 1, *p 1, k 1, rpt from * to end. Rpt these two rows for pat.
PATTERN RIB No. 2 (MC and C)—Row 1 (right side): K 2 MC, *k 1 C, k 1 MC, rpt from *, ending k 2 MC. **Row 2:** K 1 MC, * p 1 MC, k 1 C, rpt from * to last 2 sts, p 1 MC, k 1 MC.
POCKET LININGS (make 2): With MC and No. 10½ needle, cast on 13 sts. Work even in st st for 5", ending with p row. Place sts on holder.
BODY: With MC, cast on 107(115) sts. Do not join. K 2 rows. Work in Pat Rib No. 1 until 5½" from beg, ending with Row 2.
Pocket Openings: K 10 sts, bind off next 13 sts, k to last 23 sts, bind off next 13 sts, k to end.
Join Linings (wrong side): Keeping Row 2 of pat correct, work 10 sts, work in pat across 13 sts of pocket lining, work to 2nd opening, work across 2nd pocket lining, work to end. Continue in pat until 7"(7½") from beg. Do not break yarn. Join B (double strand) and K 2 rows. Break off B. Join C, pick up MC and work 6 rows (about 1¾") in Pat Rib No. 2. Break off MC and C. Join B and k 2 rows. Break off B.
Begin Pat Insert: Join A and work 2 rows st st, *inc 1 st at end of 1st row*—108(116) sts. (**Note:** Wind 2 strands C and 1 strand D tog in small ball for color M. Motif is worked with M in garter st [K every row]. Color A is always worked in st st using 2 strands throughout. When changing colors, bring new color under color just worked to avoid holes. Carry colors not in use loosely along back, twisting under working yarn every 2 sts to avoid long loops.) **Row 1:** K 5 A, *k 2 M, k 6 A, rpt from * ending k 5 A. **Row 2:** P 5 A, *k 2 M, p 6 A, rpt from * ending p 5 A. **Row 3:** *K 4 A, k 4 M, rpt from *, ending k 4 A. **Row 4:** *P 4 A, k 4 M, rpt from *, ending p 4 A. Drop A. **Row 5:** K 5 M, join E (dou-

ble) and *k 2 E, k 6 M, rpt from *, ending k 5 M. **Row 6:** K 5 M, *p 2 E, k 6 M, rpt from *, end k 5 M. Break off E. **Rows 7 and 8:** Rpt Rows 3 and 4. **Rows 9 and 10:** Rpt Rows 1 and 2. Break off M. With A, work 2 rows st st. Break off A. Join B and k 2 rows, *dec 1 st at beg of 2nd row* —107 (115) sts. Break off B. With MC and C, work even in Pat Rib No. 2 until 14″(14½″) from beg or desired length to underarm, ending with pat row 2.

Divide for Fronts and Back (right side): Keeping pat correct, work 26(28) sts and place on holder for Right Front; bind off next 2 sts for underarm, work in pat until 51(55) sts are on needle, place on holder for back; bind off next 2 sts for left underarm, work to end —26(28) sts on needle.

LEFT FRONT: Working on these 26(28) sts in Pat Rib No. 2, dec 1 st at arm edge every other row 5 times, then on following 8th row once— 20(22) sts after decs completed, **and at same time** when 6 rows of Pat Rib No. 2 have been completed, break off C, k 2 rows B, break off B and work rem of front in MC and Pat Rib No. 1. Continue working on 20(22) sts until 7″(7½″) from dividing row, ending at front edge.

Shape Neck: Keeping pat correct, bind off 2 sts at neck edge every other row 3 times **and at same time** inc 1 st at arm edge every other row twice— 16 (18) sts. Continue in pat, dec 1 st at neck edge only, every row, 3(4) times—13(14) sts. Work even until 9¼″(9½″) from dividing row, ending at arm edge. Bind off 6(7) sts in pat st, work to end of row. Work 1 row even. Bind off rem 7 sts.

RIGHT FRONT: Place 26(28) sts for Right Front on needle. With wrong side facing, join MC and C and beg with Row 2 of Pat Rib No. 2, work as for Left Front, keeping all pat sts correct and working arm and neck shapings as directed.

BACK: Place 51(55) sts for Back on needle. Join MC and C on wrong side and work Row 2 of Pat Rib No. 2. Working balance of 6 rows total in Pat Rib No. 2, 2 rows in garter st, and remainder in MC and Pat Rib No. 1 to match Front, **at same time** dec 1 st at beg and end of next row and every other row 5 times —41(45) sts. Work even in pat as established until 7″(7½″) from dividing row. Inc 1 st at beg and end of next row —43(47) sts. Work even in pat until 9¼″(9½″) from dividing row, ending with Row 2 of pat.

Shape Shoulders and Neck: Keeping pat rows correct, work as follows: **Row 1:** Bind off first 6(7) sts for right shoulder, work to end. **Row 2:** Bind off first 6 (7) sts for left shoulder, work 9 more sts (10 sts on needle);

attach 2nd MC and bind off next 11(13) sts for neck, work to end (10 sts each side). Working each side separately, bind off 7 sts at beg of arm edge once **and at same time**, dec 1 st at neck edge, every row, 3 times.

FINISHING: With right sides tog and crochet hook, ch st shoulder seams from wrong side, inserting hook through 2 inside loops only for a flat seam. Sew pocket linings in place. Weave in ends on wrong side.

Flat Braid Pocket Trim: With double strand B and crochet hook, work 1 row sl st evenly across pocket top from right side, taking care to keep work flat and elastic. Turn and work 1 more row of sl st, inserting hook through back loop only.

Front and Neck Edging and Button Loops: Mark center of each of the 3 pattern bands at right front edge for button loops. Beg at bottom of right front edge with double B, sl st evenly along right front edge, around neck and down left front edge, taking care to keep work flat. Turn, and from wrong side, work 2nd row of sl st through back lps only as for pocket trim —**and at same time**, work 3 button loops on right edge as follows: *sl st to marker, ch 8, join with sl st in next st, rpt from * twice more; sl st to end. Break off yarn. Go back to beg of 2nd row (bottom left front), join double B and, working from left to right with right side facing, work 1 row rev sc along left edge, around neck and down right edge. Fasten off. Sew buttons inside edging on wrong side of left front, opposite loops.

Armhole Edging: Starting at underarm with right side facing, join double B and sl st evenly around armhole; ch 1, and without turning, work from left to right in rev sc back to start. Join with sl st and fasten off.

SLEEVE CAP (Make 2): With double MC and No. 10½ needle, loosely cast on 25(27) sts. Working back and forth in Pat Rib No. 1, bind off 3 sts at beg of next 2 rows. Continue in pat, binding off 2 sts at beg of every row until 5 sts rem. Bind off. With right sides tog and center of cap at shoulder seam, pin bound-off edge of cap to inside MC edge of armhole (armhole trim will be on right side bet the 2 pieces). With MC and wrong side facing, ch st seam through inner loops only. With double B and crochet hook, work flat braid along outside edge of cap as for pocket, being careful to keep work elastic. With damp cloth, steam lightly and let dry.

SHORT BROWN VEST

(page 63)

Directions are given for size Small (8-10). Changes for size Medium (12-

14) are in parentheses.

MATERIALS: Coats & Clark Sport Yarn, 2 oz. skeins: 3 (4) skeins Cocoa Brown, color #355 (MC); "Bulky Loop", 50 gram balls: 2 balls Off-White, color #35 (A); "Fabulend", 4 oz. skeins: 1 skein Black, color #12 (B); Persian-type Needlepoint Yarn, 12 yd. skeins: 2 skeins Red, color #500 (C); circular knitting needle #9 OR ANY SIZE NEEDLES WHICH WILL OBTAIN THE STITCH GAUGE BELOW; crochet hook size H; 16 (18) bobbins. **GAUGE:** 4 sts = 1″ in MC st st; 5 rows = 1″.

(**Note:** MC is worked with 2 strands held together throughout. Wind 8 (9) bobbins each of colors A and B for charts 1 and 2. *When changing colors, always bring new color under color just used to avoid holes.*)

	Small (8-10)	Medium (12-14)
Bust (including binding):	36″	40″
Length to Underarm:	11½″	11½″
Armhole depth:	8¼″	8½″

DIRECTIONS—BODY (worked in one piece to underarm): With MC and

SHORT BROWN VEST - CHART #1

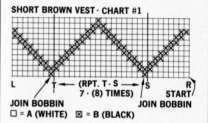

L T (RPT. T - S → 7 - (8) TIMES) S R
START
JOIN BOBBIN   JOIN BOBBIN
□ = A (WHITE)   ⊠ = B (BLACK)

VEST CHART #2

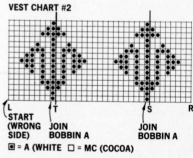

L T S R
START
(WRONG SIDE) JOIN BOBBIN A   JOIN BOBBIN A
⊡ = A (WHITE) □ = MC (COCOA)

#9 needle, cast on 142 (160) sts. Do not join. K 10 rows (5 garter ridges). Break off MC. Join B and k 2 rows. Break off B. Join A and work 2 rows st st. **Next row (Row 1 of Chart #1):** K 8 A; *join B bobbin and k 1 B, k 17 A, * rpt bet * 6 (7) more times; join B bobbin and k 1 B, k 7 A. Continue following Chart #1 in st st, working p rows from L to R, and k rows from R to L as established (11 rows). With A, work 2 rows st st. Purl 2 rows B, inc 1 st at end of 2nd row —143 (161) sts. Break off A and B. Join MC and work 2 rows st st. Begin Chart #2 on wrong side at left (L) of chart: P 8 MC, join A bobbin and p 1 A; *p 17 MC, join A bobbin and p 1 A; * rpt bet * 6 (7) more times; p 8 MC. Work remainder Chart #2 (15 rows). Work 2 rows MC st st. Break off MC and A. Join B and k 2 rows. Join A and work Chart #3 (6 rows). (Note on Chart #3 — For Medium Size only: Begin at R, work R-S 12 times, then X-Y once. Work wrong-side rows from Y-X, then from S-R, 12 times.) Break off A. K 1 row B, dec 1 st at end of row — 142 (160) sts. Divide for fronts and back (wrong side): With B, k 29 (33) sts, place on holder for Left Front; bind off next 12 (14) sts as to k, k 59 (65) sts; place 60 (66) sts just worked on holder for Back; bind off next 12 (14) sts; k to end — 29 (33) sts on needle.

RIGHT FRONT: Working on these 29 (33) sts, dec 1 st at arm edge on next and every other row 4 times, *and at same time*, work stripes as follows: Join MC and work 2 rows st st; drop MC, join 2 strands C (worked double throughout) and k 2 rows; break off C, pick up MC and work 2 rows st st; drop MC; join B and k 2 rows; break off B — 25 (29) sts. (Size medium only: Working in MC and garter st, dec 1 st at arm edge once more — 28 sts.) Work remainder of Front in MC and garter st. Work even until 6″ from beg of armhole; end at front edge. Shape neck: Bind off 4 sts at neck edge every other row twice — 17 (20)

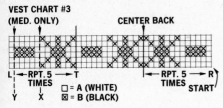

VEST CHART #3
(MED. ONLY)   CENTER BACK

L ⟵ RPT. 5 ⟶ T   ⟵ RPT. 5 ⟶ R
     TIMES   TIMES   START
Y   X   □ = A (WHITE)
                             ⊠ = B (BLACK)

sts. Dec 1 st at neck edge every row 2 (3) times, then every other row 2 (3) times — 13 (14) sts. Work even until 8¼″ (8½″) from beg of armhole (dividing row), end at arm edge. Bind off first 7 sts at arm edge. Work 1 row even. Bind off remaining 6 (7) sts.
LEFT FRONT: Place 29 (33) sts for Left Front on needle. Join MC at arm edge (right side), and work to correspond to Right Front.
BACK: Place 60 (66) sts for back on needle. Join MC on right side and work stripes as for Front, dec 1 st at beg and end of first and every other row 5 (6) times — 50 (54) sts. Work even in MC and garter st until 7½″ from dividing row. Shape neck: K 15 (17) sts; join 2nd MC and bind off next 20 sts, k to end — 15 (17) sts each side. Working each side separately, dec 1 st at neck edge every other row 2 (3) times — 13 (14) sts each shoulder. When 8¼″ (8½″) from dividing row, bind off from arm edge as for Front.
FINISHING: With right sides tog, sew shoulder seams. Weave in ends.
Front binding: Starting at bottom of right front, with MC and #9 needle (right side facing), pick up and k 1 st in each row evenly along front edge to beg of neck. K 5 rows. Bind off

loosely, being careful to keep work flat. Repeat along front edge of left side, starting at top (right side facing). Neck binding: Beg at right front edge with MC, pick up and k 1 st in each row (or st) evenly around neck edge — approx 72 (78) sts. Work same as for front edges. Fold edgings to wrong side along 2nd garter ridge to form binding; pin in place, mitering corners at neck fronts, and sew to wrong side with single strand MC.
Front and Neck Border Trim: Starting at bottom of right front edge, join B, and with size H crochet hook, sl st evenly around right front, neck and left front edges, inserting hook into loop made by turning ridge of binding; ch 1, turn, and working through back loop only, sl st in each sl st around. Fasten off B. Armhole Trim (left side): Join B at front of underarm, and with H hook (right side facing), sl st evenly around arm opening to beg of back underarm (trim is not worked on bound off edge of underarm). Ch 1, *do not turn*. Working from left to right (right side facing), make 1 rev sc in every other sl st, adjusting length of sts to keep work flat. Right side: Join B at back of underarm (right side facing), and work as for Left Side. Block. Do not press.

THREE SWEATERS/ONE PATTERN

(pages 66-67)

Instructions provide for three styles, three sizes, three yarns and one pattern (Green-Gray-Cranberry Sweaters). Directions are given for size Small (8-10). Changes for sizes Medium (12-14) and Large (16-18) are in parentheses.
MATERIALS — STYLE "A" — Green Long Sleeves with Cuff and 16″ cowl neck: Spinnerin "Pippin" color #4815, 50 gram skeins: 10 (11, 12) skeins; knitting needles, No. 7 OR ANY SIZE NEEDLES WHICH WILL OBTAIN THE STITCH GAUGE BELOW. STYLE "B" — Grey Short Sleeve with abbreviated cowl neck: Unger "Naturwool" color #5000, 1⅝ oz. balls: 10 (11, 12) balls; knitting needles, No. 6 OR ANY SIZE NEEDLES WHICH WILL OBTAIN THE STITCH GAUGE BELOW. STYLE "C" — Cranberry Long Sleeve with round neck: Melrose "Sherwood Mohair" color Cranberry, 40 gram balls: 15 (16, 17) balls; knitting needles, No. 6 OR ANY SIZE NEEDLES WHICH WILL OBTAIN THE STITCH GAUGE BELOW; crochet hook, size G.
GAUGE: 6 sts = 1″; 8 rows = 1″.
MEASUREMENTS:

	Small	Medium	Large
Size:	(8-10)	(12-14)	(16-18)
Bust:	34″	36″	38″

DIRECTIONS — PATTERN STITCH

(Multiple of 4 + 3) — Row 1: K 3, * p 1, k 3, rpt from * to end of row. Row 2: K 1, * p 1, k 3, rpt from * ending p 1, k 1. Rpt these 2 rows for pattern.
BACK: Cast on 111 (115, 119) stitches. Work in pattern until piece measures 19″ (all sizes) for "A"; 12″ (12½″, 13″) for "B"; 16″ (all sizes) for "C".
Armhole: Keeping to pattern st, bind off 10 sts at beg of next 2 rows (all sizes, all styles). Work on 91 (95, 99) sts even, until armhole measures 7″ (7½″, 8″) from bound-off stitches.
Shoulder: Bind off 7 sts at beg of next 4 rows; bind off 7 (9, 9) sts at beg of next 2 rows. Bind off remaining 49 (49, 53) sts.
Neck: When front measures 4″ above armhole, with right sides facing, work in pattern across 31(33, 33) sts. Bind off next 29(29, 33) sts. Work across rem 31(33, 33) sts.
RIGHT FRONT (Shoulder Edge): In pat, work across 31(33,33) sts. You are now at neck edge. At neck edge, bind off 3 sts once, 2 sts once, 1 st 5 times. Work even on rem 21(23,23) sts until piece measures same as back from beg of armhole shaping.
SHOULDER: At armhole edge, bind off 7(7,7) sts every 2nd row twice. At armhole edge, bind off rem 7(9,9) sts.
LEFT FRONT: Same as Right Front.
SLEEVES: At armhole edge, with right side facing, pick up 43 (45, 49) sts from back armhole, 1 st from shoulder, 43 (45, 49) sts from front armhole. Work in pattern on 87 (91, 95) sts until sleeve measures 23″ for "A", 8″ for "B", and 19″ for "C". Bind off loosely in pattern.
COWL NECK (for "A" and "B" only): With right side facing, pick up 135 (135, 139) sts around neck. Work in pattern until piece measures 14″ for "A" and 7″ for "B".
POCKET (make 2, all sizes, all styles): Cast on 37 sts. Work in pattern for 7½″. Bind off loosely.
FINISHING: Seam sides, sleeves. Sew cowl neck seam.
For "A" and "C" — Attach pockets to front of sweater 1½″ in from side seam, matching bottom of pocket to bottom of sweater front, matching pattern sts. Sew across top of pocket, along side towards center front, across bottom, and up 3″ from bottom along side next to side seam. Do other pocket in same way.
For "B" — Place pocket 1½″ in from side seam, matching bottom of pocket at a point ½″ above bottom of sweater front, matching pattern sts. Sew across top, down side towards center of front, across bottom, and up 3″ along side next to side seam. Do other pocket in same way.
Neck (for "C" only): With right side facing and size G crochet hook, work 3 rows of single crochet around neck. Join neatly with sl st.

RECYCLED SWEATERS

(pages 70 and 71)

With a little imagination, almost any worn sweater can be recycled as long as the worn or torn part can be eliminated. Or, you may want to redesign a perfectly good sweater that does not fit. Men's long sleeved sweaters can be cut down into women's pullovers or cardigans. They can also be turned into sleeveless vests if only the elbows are worn out. Women's sweaters cut down best into vests and tank tops or into children's sweaters with sleeves.

GENERAL DIRECTIONS:

1. Make sure the sweater is clean before you start the alteration.
2. Almost all machine-knit sweaters can be taken apart at the seams. Find the joining thread and open, being very careful not to cut into the knit.
3. Ribbing from the neckline, wrists and waistline can be removed and used as finished edges on the new sweater. Also, you can stretch and shape the ribbing to make it fit if you need to.
4. It is *imperative* to machine stitch a double row of stitching ½" apart wherever you plan to cut and reuse both pieces. This prevents the knit from unraveling.
5. Often the body of the sweater need not be changed when only the neckline and sleeves are to be altered.
6. Use a commercial pattern if you are doing a major recut of armholes, shoulders and sleeves. Mark with tailor's chalk for hold line for stitching.
7. No two sweaters are alike and you will always have different amounts of usable knit. For that reason, no pattern will fit exactly, but you can depend on the stretch of the sweater to "give" if you block it carefully.
8. Often the wrong side of the sweater is in better condition. If so, use it for the right side of your new sweater.

SWEATER INTO BOLERO

(Page 71)

Made from a man's old shetland pullover with holes at the elbows. Run a double row of stitching down the center front and just above the ribbing as shown. Cut between the rows. By removing the ribbing the sweater will lie flat at the bottom. Place your pattern on the sweater as shown. Mark with tailor's chalk. Machine stitch on marks and cut. Seam shoulders and sides. Use ½" of the waistband folded in half to bind each armhole with the finished edge to the outside. Bind all other edges with fabric to match a skirt or with novelty foldover braid, if you wish.

SWEATER INTO BOLERO

TURTLENECK INTO BLOUSON

(page 70)

Made from a man's lambswool turtleneck with a large burn hole. Machine stitch as shown in diagram and cut. Use ribbing from waistline to bind neckline by folding in half with the finished edge on the outside. Bind sleeves with the ribbing from the wrists (stretching if necessary) the same as you did the neckline. Make two pockets from the full height of the turtleneck and stitch in place from the bottom. Turn under a ½" casing at the bottom of the sweater and insert ¼" elastic and adjust to fit.

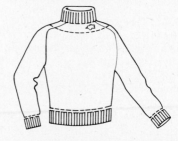

TURTLENECK INTO BLOUSON

DRAWSTRING PULLOVER

(page 71)

Made from a loosely knit stretched-out sweater (man's or woman's will work) and fabric drawstrings at waist and cuffs; plus fabric bow at neckline. Remove sleeves. Use a dress pattern to mark neckline, armholes and sleeves. Do not alter the width of the sweater because of the ease for drawstring. Stitch hold lines on markings and cut. Seam shoulders and stitch in sleeves. Join ribbings from both sleeves and use to bind the neckline by folding in half with the finished edge to the outside. Run a drawstring through the knit (we made ours of a cording to match the skirt) and tie in front. Fold back sleeves and run drawstrings through both layers as shown. Add a matching fabric bow at the neckline.

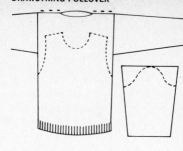

DRAWSTRING PULLOVER

TANK TOP

(page 71)

Made from a woman's worn out shetland pullover with holes in elbows. Open side seams and remove sleeves. Place a pattern on the front and back and mark for U neckline and armholes. Stitch hold lines. Stitch side seams using the wrong side for the outside. Baste back all raw edges ⅜" and steam flat. Use a double row of machine stitching for a neat, flat finish.

TANK TOP

MAN'S NOVELTY SWEATER INTO A JACKET

(page 71)

You will need 1 yd. 60" Sherpa fabric in addition to a man's worn out shetland crew neck pullover. Open all seams on sweater and cut off all ribbing after doing a hold stitch as shown. Find center front and put two rows of hold stitches ½" apart and cut. Reverse sweater and join side seams. Place sweater on one width of 60" Sherpa fabric with wrong sides facing, allowing 4" extensions on fronts and bottom (as shown in sketch). Baste and stitch sweater to Sherpa before cutting. (Be sure to allow 4" extensions on front and bottom). Stitch sleeve seams and join to body of sweater (sleeves remain unlined). Fold Sherpa fabric in half on fronts and bottom and fold to right side and zig-zag stitch in place *without* turning edge under. From extra fur fabric cut a strip 4" x neck measurement plus seam allowance on ends to bind neckline. Cut two 6" strips in the right length to bind the sleeves. Be sure to check sleeve length before stitching on cuffs.

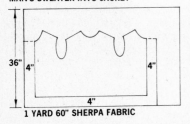

MAN'S SWEATER INTO JACKET

36" · 4" · 4" · 4"

1 YARD 60" SHERPA FABRIC

MOHAIR TUNIC

(page 74)

One size fits all.
MATERIALS: Bernat "Mohair Plus" (Natural, color #5359) 12 (1½ oz.) balls; aluminum crochet hook, size I, OR ANY SIZE HOOK WHICH WILL OBTAIN THE STITCH GAUGE BELOW.
GAUGE: 5 dc = 2"; 5 rows = 4".
MEASUREMENTS:
Width across back
  at underarms: 28½"
Length (shoulder
  to hem):   34"
(**Note:** Tunic is worked in one piece without shoulder seams.)
DIRECTIONS—BODY: Starting at right side, ch 142. **Row 1:** Dc in 4th ch from hook and in each ch to end of row—140 dc. Ch 3, turn. **Row 2:** Dc in each dc of previous row. Ch 3, turn. Continue without shaping until 17 rows are completed.
Divide for neck opening—Row 18: Dc in 1st 56 dc, ch 28, skip 28 dc, dc in next 56 dc. Ch 3, turn. **Row 19:** Dc in 1st 56 dc, dc in 28 ch, dc in next 56 dc—140 dc. Ch 3, turn. Continue without shaping for 16 more rows—35 rows completed. (Or work less rows here if shorter tunic is desired.) Fasten off.
Pockets (Make 2): Ch 16. **Row 1:** Dc in 4th ch from hook and in each ch to end of row—14 dc. Ch 3, turn. Continue without shaping until 12 rows are completed. Fasten off.
FINISHING: Stitch pockets to wrong side of tunic, leaving pockets open along side edge. (Line up bottom edge of pocket about 12" from bottom of tunic.) Sew side seams; at pockets, join back edge to pocket edge to form pocket opening. Slip stitch around neck edge.
Bottom edge: Join wool (worked double) at center back. Work 94 sc evenly around bottom edge. Work 2 more rows—3 sc rows. Fasten off.

OVERSIZED WRAP SWEATER

(page 74)

Directions are for Short (5'-5"4"). Changes for Medium (5'5"-5'8") and Tall (5'9" plus) in parentheses.
MATERIALS: Plymouth "Mohair Delight," 1 oz. balls: 11 (12, 14) balls color #508 Lt. Blue (A); 7 (8, 9) balls color #506 Beige (B); 1 ball (for all sizes) color #509 Mink (C); knitting needles, 1 pair each No. 6 and No. 15 OR ANY SIZE NEEDLES WHICH WILL OBTAIN THE STITCH GAUGE BELOW; 4 yds. elastic cord; yarn needle.
GAUGE: On No. 15 needles, 5 sts = 2"; 2 ridges = 1".
DIRECTIONS: On No. 6 needles with A, cast on 28 (32, 36) sts. Rib in k 1 and p 1 for 6½". **Next Row:** Inc 1 st in every st—58 (64, 72) sts. **Next Row:** Inc 1 st in every other st—84 (96, 108) sts on needle. K 1 row. Change to No. 15 needles and B, work throughout in garter st (k always). Work even for 8 (9, 10)" Change to A, work even until desired length of overarm from wrist to shoulder **plus** shoulder **plus** 1½" for back of neck. Change to C for Right Front, k 1". On next row for Right Front Opening, bind off 48 (55, 61) sts. K across rem 36 (41, 47) sts. for back. On next row k 36 (41, 47) sts, then cast on 48 (55, 61) sts for Left Front Opening. K for 1". Change to A and work even until same length as Right Front. Change to B and work even for 8 (9, 10)". Change to No. 6 needles and B, k 1 row. Then k 1 and k 2 tog across row—56 (64, 72) sts. Next row k 2 tog across row—28 (32, 36) sts on needle. Rib in k 1 and p 1 for 6½". Bind off loosely.
FINISHING: Seam sleeves for wrist to 1" above start of A stripe. Block. Slipstitch sweater front overlap together at bottom edge and (if desired) at front edge. Run elastic cord through k sts on wrong side of cuff: begin at bottom and rpt for 4 rows 1¼" apart. Run elastic through k sts on wrong side at bottom edge of sweater and 1" above edge. (Alternate finish: Chain a drawstring 60" long and thread through bottom.)

BIG PONCHO SWEATER

(page 75)

One size fits all.
MATERIALS: Bernat Mohair Plus, 1.4 oz balls: 14 balls: Bernat-Aero straight knitting needles, 1 pair each Nos. 11 and 13 (Canadian needle nos. 1 and 00) OR ANY SIZE FOR GAUGE.
GAUGE: 5 sts = 2"; 3 rows = 1".
DIRECTIONS—PATTERN ST:
Row 1 (**wrong side**): K 3, *(k2 tog)4 times, (k 1, yo) 8 times, (k 2 tog) 4 times; rpt from * across row; ending k 3. **Rows 2, 4 and 6 (right side):** Knit.

Rows 3 and 5: K 3, p to last 3 sts, k 3. Rpt. these 6 rows for pat st.
BACK: Using larger needles, cast on 102 sts and knit 4 rows. Then work in pat st until there are 17 pats. Work 5 more rows of pat. **Next Row:** Bind off very loosely as if to knit.
FRONT: Work same as Back.
CUFFS: Using smaller needles, cast on 30 sts and work in k 1, p 1 ribbing for 7". Bind off.
COLLAR: Using larger needles, cast on 64 sts. and work in k 1, p 1 ribbing for 15½". Bind off loosely.
FINISHING: Mark center of top and count 12 sts over on each side of center. Pin front and back together at these points, right sides facing. Place the 2 pieces on a flat surface and pat each side out so that it measures 16" on each side of pins. Pin and sew these shoulder seams. Count down 4 patterns from top at side edge and pin the 2 pieces together. Count down 9 patterns from top and again pin the 2 pieces together. Sew side seams between these 2 pins. Seam collar and sew to neck opening. Seam cuffs, and sew to top openings on each side.

GREEN BLOUSON WITH TIES

(page 76)

One size fits all.
MATERIALS: Stanley Berrocco "DJI-DJI" Mohair (2 oz. skeins): 8 skeins of #8440; knitting needles. No. 13 OR ANY SIZE FOR GAUGE.
GAUGE: In Garter St, 3½ sts = 1"; 7 sts = 2".
DIRECTIONS—BODICE: With No. 13 needles, cast on 66 sts. **Rows 1 through 6:** Work in garter st (k every row). **Row 7 (Chevron):** *K2 tog through front loops, k2, (k in front and back of next st [inc.]) twice, k3, k 2 tog through back loop, repeat from * 5 more times. **Row 8:** P. **Row 9:** Same as Row 7. **Row 10:** P. **Row 11:** Same as Row 7. **Rows 12 thru 17:** Garter st. On 17th row of garter st, bo 22 st at each end (22 sts remaining). Break yarn and attach to remaining 22 sts. **Row 18:** *K 1, yo, repeat from * to end of row (44 sts). **Row 19:** K. **Row 20:** *K 1, yo, repeat from * to end of row (88 sts). Continue even in garter st for 50 more rows (25 ridges). **Next row:** In garter st, work across 25 sts, bo next 38 sts, work across remaining 25 sts. **Next row:** In garter st, k 23 sts, k 2 tog (neck edge). **Next row:** In garter st, k 2 tog, k remaining 22 sts. Continue to decrease at neck edge every row until 12 sts remain. Bind off. Work other side of neck to correspond.
SLEEVES: Cast on 22 sts. **Rows 1 thru 6:** Work in garter st. **Row 7:** *K2 tog through front loops, k 2 (k in front and back of next st) twice, k 3, k2 tog

thru back loop, repeat from * to end. **Row 8:** P. **Row 9:** Same as Row 7. **Row 10:** P. **Row 11:** Same as Row 7. **Rows 12 thru 17:** Garter st. On 17th row of garter st, *k1, yo, repeat from * to end (44 sts). **Row 18:** K. **Row 19:** *K1, yo, repeat from * to end (88 sts). Continue even in garter st for 48 rows (24 ridges). Bind off after 24 ridges.

COLLAR: Cast on 110 sts. **Rows 1 thru 6:** Garter st. **Row 7:** *K2 tog thru front loops, k 2, (k in front and back of next st) twice, k 3, k 2 tog through back loops, repeat from * 9 times more. **Row 8:** P. **Row 9:** Same as Row 7. **Row 10:** P. **Row 11:** *K 2 tog thru front loops, k 7, k 2 tog thru back loops, repeat from * (increases have been eliminated), decreasing 22 sts (90 sts). **Row 12:** K. decreasing 1 st at each end (88 sts). **Rows 13 thru 17:** Garter st. **Row 18:** *K 2 tog thru front loops, k 2, (k in front and back of next st) twice, k 3, k 2 tog thru back loops, repeat from * 7 times more. **Row 19:** P. **Row 20:** Same as Row 18. **Row 21:** P. **Row: 22** *K 2 tog thru front loops, k 7, k 2 tog thru back loops *(72 sts.) **Row 23:** K, dec 1 st at beg and end of row. **Row 24:** K. **Row 25:** Same as Row 23. **Row 26:** K. **Row 27:** Same as Row 23. **Row 28:** K. **Row 29:** *K 2 tog thru front loops, k 2, (k in front and back of next st) twice, k 3, k 2 tog thru back loops, repeat from * 5 more times. **Row 30:** P. **Row 31:** Same as Row 29. **Row 32:** P. **Row 33:** *K 2 tog thru front loops, k 7, k 2 tog thru back loops, repeat from *5 more times (54 sts). **Rows 34 thru 38:** Garter st. **Row 39:** Bind off 54 sts in garter st.

FINISHING: Sew shoulder and sleeve seams. On right side, crochet sleeve to bodice, starting at the 28th row of bodice, counting chevron and lower part of bodice. Sew collar together. Placing seam of collar on center of bodice back, on right side, crochet collar to bodice. Bodice is not seamed below armholes.

GREEN SLEEVELESS V-NECK

(page 76)

One size fits all.
MATERIALS: Tahki "Donegal Tweed" 3.6 oz. skeins: 2 skeins of color #852; "Manos" 3½ oz. skeins: 4 skeins of #803 Lt. Green (see Note below); aluminum crochet hook, size J OR ANY SIZE HOOK WHICH WILL OBTAIN THE STITCH GAUGE BELOW.
(Note: "Manos" [thick & thin] yarn is available by mail from Coulter Studio, 118 East 59th St., New York, N.Y. 10022. Yarn is $3.70 per skein. Send exact amount payable to the above. [N.Y. residents add 8% Sales Tax.] It will arrive postage COD.)

GAUGE: 11 dc = 4"; 6 rows = 4".
MEASUREMENTS:

Width across back
at underarms: 26"
Length (shoulder
to hem): 23½"
(Note: Pullover is worked in one piece without shoulder seams.)

DIRECTIONS — BODY: With "Manos," starting at back, ch 70.
Row 1: Dc in 4th ch from hook and in each ch to end of row — 68 dc. Ch 3, turn. **Row 2:** Dc in each dc of previous row. Ch 3, turn. Continue without shaping until 32 rows are completed. Divide for front and back as follows.

Right Front — Row 33: Dc in 1st 25 dc of previous row, ch 3, turn. Continue without shaping on 25 dc until 31 more rows are completed — 64 rows. Fasten off.

Left Front — Row 33: Rejoin wool at neck edge (skip 18 dc from Right Front), ch 3, dc in last 25 dc of previous row. Continue without shaping to match Left Front — 64 rows. Fasten off.

BUYER'S GUIDE

American Thread
High Ridge Park
Stamford, Connecticut 06905
Belding Lily Co.
P.O. Box 88
Shelby, North Carolina 28150
Emile Bernat & Sons Co.
Depot & Mendon Sts.
Uxbridge, Mass. 01569
Stanley Berroco, Inc.
140 Mendon St.
Oxbridge, Mass. 01569
Brunswick
230 Fifth Avenue
New York, N.Y. 10001
Bucilla
30-20 Thomson Avenue
Long Island City, N.Y. 11101
Coats & Clark
75 Rockefeller Plaza
New York, N.Y. 10022
Columbia-Minerva Corp.
295 Fifth Avenue
New York, N.Y. 10016
Coulter Studio
118 East 59th Street
New York, N.Y. 10022
D. M. C.
107 Trumbull Street
Elizabeth, New Jersey 07206
Lion Brand Yarn Co.
1270 Broadway
New York, N.Y. 10001
Melrose Yarn Co.
1305 Utica Avenue
Brooklyn, N.Y. 11203
Paternayan Bros., Inc.
312 East 95th Street
New York, N.Y. 10028

Border: Attach "Manos" at bottom edge of back and sc across bottom row; place right front next to back and continue in sc across bottom row of Right Front. Join Left Front to Right Front and Back in same way by working row of sc across bottom row. Fasten off. Starting at center back attach "Donegal Tweed" (2 strands worked as one). **Row 1:** Ch 1, sc in each sc of previous row, ch 1, turn. Repeat Row 1 until 6 rows are completed. Fasten off. Sew back seam.
Armhole Edgings: Row 1: Starting at lower edge, attach "Manos" and work 95 sc evenly around armhole edge, join with sl st. **Row 2:** Ch 3, dc in next sc and in each sc of previous row, join with sl st. **Row 3:** Repeat Row 2. Fasten off.
FINISHING: With "Manos", work 1 row sc evenly around neck edge — 95 sc. Fasten off. Attach single strand of "Donegal Tweed" and work 1 more sc row. Fasten off. Tack bottom of "V" neck together. Tack each side together at one point 12" from top of shoulder. ∎

Pinecroft
Dunbarton,
New Hampshire 03301
Plymouth Yarn Co.
Bristol,
Pa. 19007
Reynolds Yarn Co.
15 Oser Avenue
Hauppague, L.I., N.Y. 11787
Scotts Woolen Mill
Hecla Street & Elmdale Road
Uxbridge, Mass. 01569
Shillcraft
500 N. Calvert Street
Baltimore, Md. 21202
Spinnerin Yarn
230 Fifth Avenue
New York, N.Y. 10001
Tahki Imports Ltd.
62 Madison Street
Hackensack, New Jersey 07601
William Unger Yarns
230 Fifth Avenue
New York, N.Y. 10001

FABRIC COMPANIES:

American Silk Mills through
Logantex
1450 Broadway
New York, N.Y. 10018
Ameritex
1407 Broadway
New York, N.Y. 10018
Apsco
1412 Broadway
New York, N.Y. 10018
Cannon Mills
1271 Avenue of the Americas
New York, N.Y. 10020
Collins & Aikman (Sherpa®)
200 Madison Avenue
New York, N.Y. 10016
Hamilton Adams
104 West 40th Street
New York, N.Y. 10018

International Printworks
110 Gould Street
Needham, Mass. 02194
Liberty of London
108 West 39th Street
New York, N.Y. 10018
A. E. Nathan (White Rose)
P.O. Box 401
3530 Oceanside
Oceanside, N.Y. 11572
Peter Pan
1071 Avenue of the Americas
New York, N.Y. 10018
Roth Imports
13 West 38th Street
New York, N.Y. 10018
Stylecrest Fabrics, Ltd.
214 West 39th Street
New York, N.Y. 10018
Wamsutta
1430 Broadway
New York, N.Y. 10018
White Rose (see A. E. Nathan)
Arthur Zeiler
215 West 39th Street
New York, N.Y. 10018

NOTIONS AND OTHER SOURCES:

Baldwin Pottery (Unglazed Bisque
Tiles)
540 La Guardia Place
New York, N.Y. 10012
C. J. Bates (Knitting Nobby)
P.O. Box E
Route 9A
Chester, Conn. 06412
Binney & Smith (Crayola®)
1100 Church Lane
Easton, Pa. 18042

Braid-Aid
466 Washington Street
Pembroke, Mass. 02359
Caldwell Alexander (Table Settings)
135 Main Street
Westhampton Beach, N.Y. 11978
Conso Products Co. (Fringe)
261 5th Avenue
New York, N.Y. 10016
Fairfield Processing Corp.
(Quilt Batting/Pillow Forms)
88 Rose Hill Avenue
Danbury, Conn. 06810
Liquitex Gloss Medium (available at
Art Supply Stores)
(Acrylic Polymer Emulsion)
Permanent Pigment Inc.
Cincinnati, Ohio 45212
M E Enterprises (Weaving Board)
P.O. Box 344
Temple City, Calif. 91780
Nelco Sewing Machine Co., Inc.
164 West 25th Street
New York, N.Y. 10001
C. M. Offray (Ribbons)
261 Madison Avenue
New York, N.Y. 10016
Rit Dye
Best Foods
A Div. of C. P. C. Int'l., Inc.
Indianapolis, Ind. 46206
The Stearns & Foster Co. (Quilt
Batting/Pillow Forms)
Williams St. & Wyoming Avenue
Lockland, Cincinnati, Ohio 45215
Talon
Div. of Textron Inc.
41 East 51st Street
New York, N.Y. 10022
Vogart Crafts Corp.

230 5th Avenue
New York, N.Y. 10001
Wrights (Trim)
West Warren,
Mass. 01092

**TURNING THE TABLES
— Pages 46-49**
Accessory Information
Gingham Checks—Gingham fabric
by White Rose; polyester quilt batting by Fairfield Processing; checked
china from Caldwell Alexander;
ballpoint paints (for hurricane shade)
by Vogart (available in hobby/craft
stores). **Sign In Please**—Glass table-
ware from Sears catalog; cutlery
from Caldwell Alexander. **Orient
Express**—"Imari" paper plates by
Pam Marker from Paper House, 741
Madison Ave., N.Y., N.Y. 10021;
"Imari" cups from Caldwell Alexander. **Classic Crochet**—Wedgewood
"Drabware" plates and beehive
dome from Tiffany & Co., 727 Fifth
Avenue, N.Y., N.Y. 10022; "Gold
Bamboo" flatware from Caldwell
Alexander. **Patchwork**—Armetale
plates and accessories from Batterie
de Cuisine, 104 Main St., Westhampton Beach, N.Y. 11978. **Wake
Up**—White bed tray from Ham-
macher Schlemmer, 147 East 57th
St., N.Y., N.Y. 10022; "Bon Jour"
plate and mug from Caldwell Alexander. ∎

(Continued from page 25.)

McCALL'S 5829—page 40. Misses' Cape. Misses' sizes 8-16. $2.25.
Size 16 requires 3 yds. of 54"-wide fabric.

SIMPLICITY 8547—page 40. Women's Jumper. Women's sizes 40-52.
$2. Size 40 requires 2¾ yds. of 54"-wide fabric.

SIMPLICITY 8162—page 40. Misses' Top. Misses' sizes Petite. Small,
Medium and Large. $1.75. Requires 2 yds. of 44/45"-wide fabric.

McCALL'S 5762—page 41. Misses' Dress Misses' sizes Petite, Small,
Medium, Large and X-Large. $2.25. Requires 3⅜ yds. of 44/45"-wide
fabric.
•**To order McCall's 5762,** send check or money order, size and pattern
number to: McCall's, Box 9119, Manhattan, Kans. 66502.

McCALL'S 5917—page 41. Misses' Top & Pants. Misses' sizes Petite,
Small, Medium, Large and X-Large. $2. Top requires 1¾ yds. and pants
2⅜ yds., both of 58/60"-wide fabric.

SIMPLICITY 8571—page 52. Misses' 2-piece Dress. Misses' sizes

10-16. $2.00 Requires 4 yds. of 45" fabric.

SIMPLICITY 8588—page 65. Misses' Pullover Dress Misses' sizes
10-16. $2.00 Requires 3⅛ yds. 54" fabric.

SIMPLICITY 8651—page 64. Misses' Top and Skirt. Misses' sizes 6-16.
$2.50. Top requires 1¾ yds. and skirt 1⅜ yds. both of 54" fabric.

SIMPLICITY 8673—page 53. AVAILABLE AUG. 1, 1978. Misses'
Pullover Dress. Misses' sizes 8-14. $2.00. Requires 3⅛ yds of 54" fabric.

SIMPLICITY 8676—page 64. AVAILABLE AUG. 1, 1978. Misses'
Pullover Dress. Misses' sizes 6-18. 99¢. Requires 3⅛ yds. of 54" fabric.

SIMPLICITY 8723—AVAILABLE AUG. 1, 1978. Tie Pattern (View 2).
$1.75. Requires approximately ¾ yd. of 33" fabric.

For further information on the above patterns, please write to: Simplicity Pattern Co., Inc., 200 Madison Ave., New York, N.Y. 10016; McCall's,
230 Park Ave., New York, N.Y. 10017; for Vogue & Butterick, write: Butterick Fashion Marketing, 161 6th Ave., New York, N.Y. 10013.

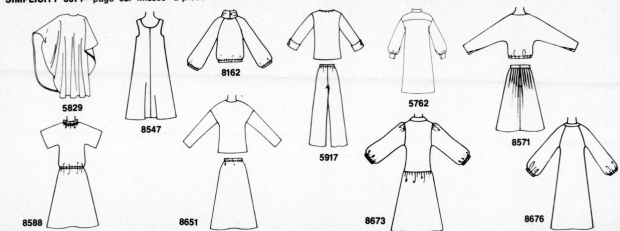

5829

8547

8162

5917

5762

8571

8588

8651

5917

8673

8676

HOW TO QUILT

This technique, known and used for centuries, produces padded fabrics held together by stitching. The resulting fabric sandwich is warm, durable and decorative all at the same time. It is often the final step in making patchwork or appliqué, whether it's for a large project or small. Quilting can also be used to transform a plain fashion fabric into an interesting, dimensional material with great design potential.

MATERIALS: The fabrics you use should be compatible in weight and texture and should have the same care qualities. If you use cotton or cotton blends for the top, then use the same type of fabric for the backing. Consider using ready-made sheets for top and backing; their size is ideal. Cotton or polyester batting comes in several standard sheet or bedspread sizes. You can easily cut down or add to batting to get the exact size needed. Either type of batting will wash or dry-clean. If you'd like a very thick, puffy filling, like a comforter, you can stack two or three layers.

Figuring Yardage: For a garment made of quilted fabric, use the yardage chart on the pattern envelope as a guide. Quilting tends to draw up the fabric slightly, thereby reducing the size; it's best to quilt fabric for garment sections first, then cut them out. Or, for a large item like a coverlet, allow an extra inch (2.5 cm) around all edges when planning and cutting. If only part of your project will be quilted, complete the quilted portions before joining them to the other parts. If you are making a fairly large item like a quilt, cut the backing 2″ (5 cm) longer and wider than the top to allow for finishing edges.

Thread: Use any all-purpose thread, or try quilting thread, which is especially firm and lustrous. Whether you match or contrast the color depends on the effect you'd like to achieve. To make a really strong impact, try polyester buttonhole twist or metallic thread for quilting. Always make a sample first to determine the most pleasing quilting design and thread color, the best tension, pressure and stitch length. To start, loosen tension slightly, lighten pressure and sew 8 stitches per inch (2.5 cm). Then make

any necessary adjustments.

SECURING LAYERS: Place the backing fabric wrong side up on a flat surface. Spread the batting, cut or pieced to the same size, over the backing, smoothing it from the center out. Now place the top fabric right side up over the batting, smoothing it in the same way. Pin the layers together. To secure the layers, baste from the center out to each side, diagonally to corners and around edge (A).

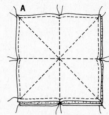

QUILTING DESIGNS: Your design choice will depend to some extent on the top fabric. Geometric fabrics lend themselves to square (B) or diamond (C) quilting; free-form motifs suggest outline quilting. Cartridge (channel) quilting is also attractive (D). The simplest kind of quilting is done in squares or diamonds with the aid of a

B SQUARE

C DIAMOND

D CARTRIDGE

quilting foot attachment on the machine. Set the guide bar on the quilting foot for the desired spacing between rows, mark the first row of stitching on the fabric, and then stitch. The remaining rows need not be marked since you use the bar to space parallel rows of stitching (E).

Square Quilting: Mark the center of each edge. With a yardstick and chalk, draw a line connecting the marks at the top and bottom edge and another line connecting the marks at the two side edges to mark the first two rows of quilting. Set the guide bar for the desired spacing between rows — usually 2″ to 3″ (5 to 7.6 cm) — and quilt from the center out. Do all the rows in one direction before working in another direction (F).

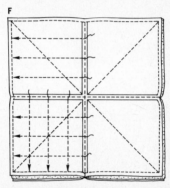

Diamond Quilting: Mark the first two rows by drawing diagonal lines connecting opposite corners, forming an X. Proceed as above.

Cartridge Quilting: Use the quilting foot guide bar as an aid in cartridge quilting, too. Just mark your first row and let the bar space the succeeding rows.

Outline Quilting: To do outline quilting around a simple motif, first hand-baste along the lines that you intend to quilt. Try to keep most stitching lines 2″ to 3″ (5 to 7.6 cm) apart in order to preserve the puffiness of the quilting. Use the quilting foot without guide bar (G).

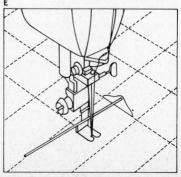

Courtesy of Simplicity "Sew Something Special" Publication.